Cross-Cultural Reentry:
A Book of Readings

Contributors

Sidney Werkman, M.D., Professor of Psychiatry, University of Colorado
School of Medicine, Denver, CO

Arthur M. Freedman, Ph.D., Director, Stress Management Institute, Chicago,
IL

Nessa P. Loewenthal, Director, Trans/Cultural Services, Orinda, CA

Nancy L. Snedden, Senior Human Resources Development Consultant with
PMI Mortgage Insurance Co., San Francisco, CA

Coralyn M. Fontaine, Ph.D., President, Fontaine and Associates, Pittsburgh,
PA

Diane P. Jansson, R.N., M.S., Director of Visiting Nurses Association, Inc.,
Providence, RI

Jean Boley--When her article was submitted to the *American Foreign
Service Journal,* she resided in Buenos Aires.

Jack Perry, Ph.D., Director of The Dean Rusk Program in International
Studies, Davidson College, Davidson, NC

92851

Contributors

Hugh Sidey, Washington Contributing Editor, *Time*

Sam Longsworth, Former Peace Corps Volunteer and subsequently a staff member in Togo and Dahomey. Current address unknown.

Nancy Koehler, Free-lance writer, Poway, CA

Jane Hipkins Sobie, Free-lance journalist, Virginia Beach, VA

Robert R. Faulkner, Ph.D., Professor of Sociology, University of Massachusetts, Amherst, MA

Douglas B. McGaw, Ph.D., professor for seven years, now a self-employed businessman in Emporia, KS

Clyde N. Austin, Ph.D., Professor of Psychology, Abilene Christian University, Abilene, TX

D. W. Kendall, Manager, Employee Benefits, Rohm and Haas Company, Philadelphia, PA

iv Cecil G. Howard, Ph.D., Professor of Management, Department of Management, School of Business and Public Administration, Howard University, Washington, DC

Judy L. Markey, Free-lance writer, Wilmette, IL

James R. Corey, Ph.D., Associate Professor of Humanities, New Mexico Institute of Mining and Technology, Socorro, NM

Ruth Hill Useem, Ph.D., Professor Emeritus of Education and Sociology, Institute for International Studies in Education, Michigan State University, East Lansing, MI

Richard D. Downie, Ph.D., Assistant Dean and Director, International Student Services, University of Florida, Gainesville, FL

Leila Merritt, Student, Abilene Christian University, Abilene, TX

Victor L. Hunter, M.Div., Minister and author, Conifer, CO

Betty Jane Harrell, Author, PSC Box 1850, APO Miami 34004 (Panama)

Harold D. Guither, Ph.D., Professor of Agricultural Policy, University of Illinois, Champaign, IL

Contributors

William N. Thompson, Ph.D., Former Associate Dean and Director of International Agricultural Programs, University of Illinois, Champaign, IL

Richard W. Brislin, Ph.D., Research Associate, Culture Learning Institute, East-West Center, Honolulu, HI

H. Van Buren IV, Business Consultant, Tokyo, Japan

Dick Irish, Vice President, TransCentury Corporation, Washington, DC

Campus Crusade for Christ, Training Department of International Resources, San Bernardino, CA

Printed in the United States of America.

Manuscript reader: David Williams, Ed.D.
Book Design: Mel Ristau, M.F.A.
Research Assistant: Debbie Gordon, B.S.

Library of Congress Cataloging in Publication Data
Library of Congress Card Number 85-73568
Austin, Clyde Neal, 1931–
    Cross-cultural reentry.

    Includes index.
    1.

ACU Press 1986   4   5
ISBN 0-915547-74-0
Third Printing 1989

Dedication

To my father and mother, Clyde and Jessie Lee Austin, who sacrificed to provide me with a legacy of formal and informal cross-cultural experiences.

To my sister and brother-in-law, Amy Jane and Preston Parsons, two of the most magnanimous individuals to grace my life and the life of our family.

Contents

ix

Unit A: An Introduction and Overview to Reentry

Contents

Chapter 1

Chapter 2

Chapter 3

Chapter 4

x

Chapter 5

Unit B: Reentry of Federally Employed Citizens

Chapter 6

Contents

Unit C: Reentry of Business and Missionary Families and International Students

Contents

Chapter 13

Chapter 14

Chapter 15

Chapter 16

Chapter 17

Unit D: Reentry of Third-Culture Children and Their Parents

Chapter 18

Contents

Chapter 19

Chapter 20

Chapter 21

Unit E: How to Make Reentry Work: Guidelines for Reentry

Chapter 22

Chapter 23

Chapter 24

Contents

Chapter 25

Topical Contents

Topical Contents

Topical Contents

Topical Contents

xviii

Foreword

As a practitioner in the intercultural field, I have always been particularly pleased and proud that I experienced and caught a near fatal dose of both culture shock and reverse culture shock before we even knew what to call them. When I first went through culture shock, we were still calling it "homesickness," although even at the time I knew I was going through something far more serious than longing for my loved ones. Then in the early 1950s "culture shock" was identified, diagnosed, and given a catchy new name. With that simple act, a phenomenon that had likely been around since prehistoric humans first moved across this planet suddenly became something that sounded almost "scientific"--as scientific, at least, as the social sciences could ever aspire to being.

Now, in retrospect, it seems absolutely amazing that it took the field another twenty years after noticing culture shock to discover the phenomenon of "reverse culture shock." Yet that is the case. Of course after something has once been observed and named, it then seems so very obvious. But before that first discovering and naming, it was anything but obvious. I would say that the uncovering of culture shock, and then of reverse culture shock, have been two of the most monumental milestones in the development of the intercultural field, achievements which, once in place, have allowed us to move on to still higher achievements in the delineation of the field.

This volume and the previous volume which Clyde Austin has so carefully put together represent a milestone of a different kind, yet one of equal enormity in intercultural communication. In the former volume, *Cross-Cultural Reentry*, much that had been written on the topic was lovingly and painstakingly drawn together, analyzed, evaluated, and annotated to produce the best bibliography of books and articles on re-entry phenomena. Now, with this second volume, Dr. Austin increases his contribution by making accessible a collection of the best articles on reverse culture shock, many of which are fugitive and difficult to track down.

I have told him personally that the only way he can possibly contribute more to the field than he already has with these two books is to do the same, in two companion volumes, with the subject of culture shock itself. Professor Austin is an intelligent man, so he gave me no assurance that he would take on such an enormous undertaking. There must be at least two or three times as much written on culture shock as there has been on reverse culture shock; the task would be even larger than he has already achieved to date. Yet if anyone is qualified to take on the job, and to do it with the highest level of dedication and professionalism, it would surely be Clyde Austin. I want to go on record with this public challenge to him to carry his work to this next logical step. If he does, I can promise him the gratitude of all intercultural professionals and of countless intercultural students and sojourners in other countries. Dr. Austin's background in psychology, combined with his overseas living experience and his counseling of many returning missionaries, more than qualifies him to make such major contributions.

Another phenomenon relating to reverse culture shock worth pointing out is that this subject has, especially in the past half-dozen years, elicited a great deal of enthusiasm and missionary zeal among cross-cultural trainers. Many of them have campaigned to encourage buyers of pre-departure training for Americans going overseas to look farther into the future and also to plan, from the very beginning, a later workshop to prepare these same people to return home successfully after their tour of overseas duty. Yet up to now, they have been largely unsuccessful in convincing those organizations sensitive enough to see the need for initial cross-cultural training to become sensitive enough to provide them re-entry training.

The reason for this apparent lack of success, it seems to me, is that it is beyond the scope of American logic to believe that people could possibly need more training before returning to their own country of birth and enculturation. Yet such is the undisputed case.

In fact many intercultural specialists confirm, almost like an "old wives' tale," that those who most successfully adjust to the foreign country are the very ones who can expect to have the hardest time in readjusting to their own country upon returning home.

Everyone who gives the matter a second thought can see that one might require some help in fitting into a foreign country because of its obvious differences from our own. But it seems patently unreasonable that any of us should have difficulty fitting back into a country with whose values and customs we are so intimately familiar.

Those who have learned the lesson of culture shock, however, are no longer the same innocent people they were when they first left home. The message of culture shock is that what we were raised to believe were absolutes are, in reality, just another set of possibilities no inherently better or worse than hundreds of other possible sets of values and assumptions. Having received this "mind blowing" revelation, one then faces the return to a whole nation of people--your own--who haven't the slightest inkling of this new truth, not to mention the further insult that they don't really want to hear about all the unbelievable adventures you have just experienced and are dying to share.

Professor Austin cannot eliminate this pain completely for us, but the most helpful aspect of his book is that many of his selections do not merely describe the pathological characteristics of reverse culture shock, but actually suggest what works in bringing about its cure. Cross-cultural sojourners might avoid or alleviate substantially many psychological and social problems associated with returning home if they follow some of the practical suggestions provided by these authors.

Stateside officials of multi-national organizations who read these articles will have a much greater appreciation of the problems faced by their returning expatriates. Lay members of religious groups should receive their returning missionaries with more compassion and understanding of what they are going through.

All of us owe a tremendous debt to Dr. Austin for his careful job in selecting and sharing the best articles currently available on this timely topic and for providing us such a pleasurable reading experience.

L. Robert Kohls, Ph.D.
Executive Director,
Washington International Center
and Vice President,
Meridian House International
Washington, DC 20009

Preface

My brother-in-law, Vic Hunter, writes movingly in his chapter, "Closure and Commencement: The Stress of Finding Home:"

> *Today I must say goodbye. Goodbyes are important. Without a meaningful goodbye, an effective closure, there cannot be a creative hello, a new beginning and hopeful commencement. I have always found it important to mark the times and seasons, the significant events in my life and my family's life, with ritual and symbol. Such marking somehow reaches beyond the commonplace and ordinary and has the power to reach those recesses of one's being which, though not easily accessible to conscious thought, nonetheless exercise a remarkable power in one's life.*

Goodbyes are rarely easy. Much of one's heart is invested in the people, institutions, and experiences of the land of sojourn. As you depart, perhaps with loved ones, you realize that your lives will be "forever changed." A constructive "commencement" in your homeland is a spiritual, psychological, and financial necessity.

The new location is not always your native homeland. Your new "journey" may take you to a "commencement" in yet a third country. In this book, however, I have endeavored to limit my selection of articles to those about the stresses experienced upon return to one's homeland--particularly reentry or reverse culture shock. My reviews of the literature reveal that for most journeys the pain of reentry is often much greater than the initial culture shock.

My first book on reentry, *Cross-Cultural Reentry: An Annotated*

Bibliography, was a quest to discover what had been spoken or published on reentry in the USA and Canada. More than 300 resources on reentry were identified and 291 items chosen for inclusion in the annotated bibliography.

My search for additional materials on reentry led to a thirty-day labor of love in England and Scotland in the summer of 1984. Using computer database facilities of the British Library and the University of London, I found a number of stimulating documents published by United Kingdom scholars. My wife, Sheila, and I also visited with scores of industrial, governmental, religious, and educational leaders.

The number of doctoral dissertations, master's theses, journal articles, book chapters, research reports, unpublished manuscripts, videotapes, magazine and newspaper articles, speeches, newsletters, and class syllabi in my files on reentry now exceeds 400. For the present book, after reviewing these materials, I selected a preliminary group of 50 articles. An editorial committee composed of Dr. Carley Dodd, Dr. David Williams, Mr. Merlin Mann, my wife, Mrs. Sheila Austin, and I, designated the present representative collection. I am deeply grateful for their investment of scores of hours in the book.

On countless occasions individuals have written or called me requesting materials on reentry. With the publication of this book, I have the opportunity to serve a wide audience of caring people. The primary purpose of the book is to educate "senders" and "receivers," as well as sojourners, about the nature and continuing demands of reentry. Reentry is no respector of persons. It applies equally to young and old, male and female, and persons in all types of overseas affiliation--corporate, governmental, educational, or religious. This volume does not attempt to cover all kinds of reentry situations, foreign or domestic. As a licensed psychologist, for example, I have a host of feelings I would like to express about the manner in which society receives reentering mental patients. A local probation officer might wish the same privilege in reference to the positive treatment of parolees. In many ways, however, their readjustment process is comparable to those situations highlighted in this book. I yearn for the time when we will *prevent* or *modify* the intensity of reentry through intelligent personnel planning. We must envision expatriation ("leaving") and repatriation ("returning") as parts of an integrated whole (Clague and Krupp, 1980). As in my initial book, this book is offered "with immense hope that we will be concerned with the wholeness of man throughout the international cycle."

The volume is organized into five sections.

Unit A, *An Introduction and Overview to Reentry:* The first chapter describes the psychological stresses of each step of the international cycle. Chapter Two emphasizes the successful management of stateside cultural transitions, to include reentry. The major theme of Chapters Three and Four is the necessity of a holistic approach in planning overseas moves. Concrete reentry issues are explored in Chapter Five.

Unit B, *Reentry of Federally Employed Citizens:* In this unit representatives of the Departments of State and Defense, a distinguished journalist, and university professors impressively describe reentry shock for diplomats, the military, and personnel in a presidential party. The woman's viewpoint is aptly represented by Boley, Koehler, and Sobie.

Unit C, *Reentry of Business and Missionary Families, and International Students:* "Reentry Stress: The Pain of Coming Home" is selected for its concise overview of missions reentry issues, as well as a lengthy reference list. For business repatriates, Kendall develops an intriguing case history. Howard's ideas, if carefully followed, will enhance the repatriation retention ratio. The challenge of "choice" dumbfounds Markey. Corey's article expertly and succinctly sets forth some of the dilemmas facing returning international students.

Unit D, *Reentry of Third Culture Children and Their Parents:* Useem and Downie's work is based on personal foreign experience and a brilliant series of dissertations written at Michigan State University. Their article was chosen to give the reader a well-balanced perspective of TCKs. Merritt speaks convincingly for young ladies of the Third Culture. In a beautiful and moving statement, Hunter describes a "split-family" decision; two of their children remained in England. Working at the University of Oklahoma, Harrell develops a masterpiece of guideline statements for rearing missionary children. She covers the entire spectrum of teenage development on the mission field.

Unit E, *How to Make Reentry Work: Guidelines for Reentry:* In Chapter 21 the authors provide a comprehensive view of reentry from a positive perspective. No statement on reentry programs for international students would be complete without the inclusion of Brislin and Van Buren's early success. Since a considerable number of reentrants do change employment, the observations of Irish are invaluable. The final chapter offers an unusually extensive list of practical suggestions about how to cope with unexpected reentry situations.

Reference

Clague, L., & Krupp, N. B. (1980, Spring) International personnel: The repatriation problem. *The Bridge*, pp. 11–13. (Reprinted from *The Personnel Administrator*, April 1978.)

Acknowledgments

Remarkably, *no* authors or publishers denied my request to include their materials. Even though permission statements are printed with each chapter, I reiterate here my gratitude for their generosity. Dr. Gaston Welborn, Vice President for Legal Service and General Counsel, Abilene Christian University (ACU), diligently reviewed the permission statements.

Dr. William J. Teague, President, ACU, has been unwavering in his commitment to my research on the international cycle. The chairman of the Research Council, Dr. Paul Schulze, is a valued colleague and trusted resource person. I deeply appreciate the sustaining support of members of the ACU Research Council. Dr. Bruce Evans, Dean of the Graduate School, has given me invaluable assistance in seeking financial resources for the book's publication. My department chairman, Dr. Ed Headrick, has placed complete confidence in my teaching, counseling, and research.

Dr. David Williams of the ACU Department of English was the epitome of resourcefulness and excellence as manuscript editor. Dr. Carley Dodd adroitly assisted me in making numerous critical judgments about the style and organization of the units and chapters. Mel Ristau creatively used his remarkable talent to make the book visually appealing. His art work richly conveys the dilemmas confronting the homecomer.

Dr. Tom Olbricht, Director of ACU Press, has been the unifying force in the ultimate production of the book. He has orchestrated the efforts of

Acknowledgments

Mr. James Fulbright, Mr. Neil Fry, and Mr. Tom Spain. I am deeply grateful to my long-time friend, Dr. Howard Norton, Editor, *The Christian Chronicle,* for serving as an outside reviewer.

Miss Debbie Gordon, Mrs. Diana Walla, and Mr. John Beyer spent countless hours working directly or indirectly on both books on reentry as research assistants. For eighteen months, Debbie has integrated many essential facets of this second book. She has been creative, patient, and thorough.

I thank many anonymous donors for believing in the book and giving me such warm and unflagging support. These generous friends will never fully realize the benefits of the extraordinary investment they have made in intercultural sojourners.

My wife, Sheila, deserves very special recognition. In addition to performing indispensable household duties, savoring her fortune as a new grandmother, and fulfilling hostess roles to scores of members of the University "family" each year, she has lovingly and unselfishly served as encourager, constructive critic, and marketing statistician. Because she has been a co-presenter in various workshops, Sheila brought to the Editorial Committee a host of incisive viewpoints.

List of Acronyms

AID	—Agency for International Development
DOD	—Department of Defense
EAP	—Employee Assistance Program
FSO	—Foreign Service Officer
MK	—Missionary Kid
MNC	—Multinational Corporation
NCO	—Noncommissioned Officer
PC	—Peace Corps
PCV	—Peace Corps Volunteer
RPCV	—Returned Peace Corps Volunteer
SIL	—Summer Institute of Linguistics
TCA	—Third Culture Adult
TCK	—Third Culture Kid
TCP	—Third Culture Person
VA	—Veterans Administration
WA	—Wycliffe Associates

Unit A

An Overview of Reentry

Overview of Reentry

2

The authors provide a number of fundamental, essential concepts about transitions, especially reentry: (1) The sojourner and sponsor must take a broad, comprehensive view of the overseas assignment from initial selection to repatriation; (2) A diagram (W–Curve Hypothesis Model) can provide the overseas candidate an overview of the necessary transitions involved in cross-cultural migration; (3) There are varied types of reentry experiences. Reentry from a foreign country has much in common with temporary migrations into and out of such institutions as prisons, mental and general medical hospitals, residential rehabilitation centers, and residential communities; and (4) Employee Assistance Programs (EAPs) can help employees at each stage of the international relocation process.

In Chapter 1, Werkman draws on his clinical experience and instructive research studies to describe psychological stresses involved in the homecoming process. Return to the United States involves separation and loss, tactful elimination of international fantasies, and inability to communicate adequately what one has experienced. Adjustment reactions which may be seen in returnees are nostalgia for a lost way of life, a different self-concept, and rootlessness. Werkman's illustrations are "classic." Recommendations for successful reentry are noted.

In Chapter 2, Freedman discusses the general applicability of the elements of the "migration" process to many types of "cultural" transitions at home and abroad. An employee who attends a workshop may leave "home" and enter a new "world." When he returns "home," he may find it difficult to persuade his colleagues to accept him and the new ideas he learned. Migration from a "foreign" culture to one's "native" culture is delineated in terms of three stages: conflict, disconfirmation, and renegotiation. The W-Curve allows a "migrant" to anticipate some of the difficulties of the "journey."

In Chapter 3, Loewenthal and Snedden embrace a "holistic" approach to an overseas assignment. Every single part of the whole must be thoughtfully studied. The design of career paths, selection, training, on-the-field performance, and reentry must be properly understood by the employee, his family and management. The orientation program of the Bechtel Group is highlighted.

The article by Fontaine (Chapter 4) illustrates the role that mental health professionals in a university organization such as Corporate Services can play in helping families and companies in international relocation processes. Psychological and interpersonal factors in overseas work are given special attention. Mental health interventions developed by Corporate Services are included.

In Chapter 5, Jansson views reentry issues from her vantage point of a returned Peace Corps Volunteer (RPCV) nurse. She challenges the reader to note the reentry difficulties common to RPCVs, ex-convicts, former mental patients, and ex-nuns. She suggests that it is not uncommon for a person about to reenter a social system to be viewed as one who has deviated from that system's norms. Hence, many reentrants may have a "deviant" identity. Problems which might be difficult to resolve are euphoria/denial; anger; sense of powerlessness; fear of rejection, regression, and guilt; immobilization/recidivism; and intimacy issues.

4

1

Coming Home: Adjustment of Americans to the United States after Living Abroad

Sidney L. Werkman

The task of readapting to the United States after living overseas is, for many, the most difficult hurdle in the cycle of international life. People who have lived overseas emphatically report that it is far less stressful to leave the United States and find a place in a new country than it is to experience the unexpected jolt of coming back home. As a 20-year-old woman recalled: "People pushed and shoved you in the New York subways; they treated you as if you simply don't exist. I hated everyone and everything I saw here and had to tell myself over and over again: 'Whoa, this is your country; it is what you are part of.' "

Very little attention has been paid both in research studies and in the literature of the behavioral sciences to the issues involved in return and readjustment to the United States of people who have lived overseas (Borus, 1973a, b; Bower, 1967; Cleveland, Mangone, & Adams, 1960).

Yet clinical experience and the anecdotal reports of returnees—in the United States we do not even have a sanctioned term such as "colonials" to describe them—indicate that the problems of fitting into the United States once again can be serious and, at times, long-lasting. Both clinical and research interests have focused my professional concern in this area (Werkman, 1972,

From *Uprooting and Development: Dilemmas of Coping with Modernization* by G. V. Coelho and P. I. Ahmed (Eds.), 1980, New York: Plenum Press. Copyright 1980 by Plenum Press. Reprinted by permission.

1975) which promises to become an increasingly important one for students of transitional phenomena.

This chapter, based on my professional experience, will describe the nature of psychological stresses brought to bear upon the traveler who returns to the United States. Certain characteristic reaction patterns in these stresses will then be delineated. From a knowledge of characteristic stresses and patterns of reaction a group of methods for dealing effectively with the transition to the United States will be developed.

Subjects: The population from which these observations were made consists of four groups: (1) adolescents and adults interviewed by the author during consultation trips to international schools overseas; (2) extensive tape-recorded interviews with 30 university students (average age, 21) who had lived overseas at least one year and were attending the University of Colorado at Boulder; (3) patients from the author's clinical practice whose problems began in relationship to living overseas; and (4) a research sample of 172 adolescents living overseas compared with a control group of 163 adolescents who had never lived overseas. The research sample, matched for age, sex, and socioeconomic background, consisted of young people who had not sought psychiatric help and were overtly adapting effectively.

Approximately 1,700,000 Americans live overseas, of whom 230,000 are children attending international schools. In 1970 military personnel and their families were the largest category, 1,375,000, followed by 236,000 people in private-sector activity, and 110,000 government employees. Of the civilian adults, the major categories were, in decreasing order: religious workers, engineers, teachers, scientists, and technicians. The nonmilitary population, with whom the author has had the greatest experience, is predominately a highly selected group of professionals and college-educated administrative personnel, largely with intact families, who probably represent a more than usually stable, psychologically resilient, competent group of people.

As the prevalence and incidence of psychiatric disorders in the United States cannot be stated accurately, it is even more difficult to estimate the number of such disturbances overseas. However, as most people living overseas are of at least middle-class socioeconomic status, we would expect fewer clinical psychiatric disorders to be present than are represented in a continental United States population. Indeed, this generalization appears to be accurate (Kenny, 1967; Smith, 1966). It must be recognized, however, that the stresses of overseas living may well be important predisposing factors in the development of later depressions, character difficulties, and subtle but important aspects of a person's interpersonal relationships and thought processes. Obviously, it is impossible to generalize accurately from such a diverse group of people. However, some recurring, seemingly fundamental characteristics common to Americans who have been overseas have emerged, regardless of the range of differences in life experience that occur throughout the world with its enormous variety of cultural and work patterns.

To best understand the psychological styles and problems that develop when Americans return home, it is necessary to consider issues related to the entire cycle of leaving the United States, settling in overseas, and then being uprooted a second time in order to reenter the United States. Many of the problems that come into focus upon return to the United States are composed of elements that developed in one or another stage of the complex cycle of living overseas.

Leaving
Common to all overseas Americans is the experience of leaving the United States at least once for a prolonged period of time. At first glance this may not appear to be a significant stress. However, anyone who moves overseas must relinquish ties with relatives and friends, give up the many sociocultural supports present in the United States, and attempt to find substitutes for these crucial social-system elements in a foreign country. The act of leaving involves issues of separation, repudiation, and loss that often have important consequences for later adaptation.

Goals: Motivations for a move overseas are indeed various. An overseas assignment is a normal part of careers in international business, the foreign service, or the military, and people who pursue such careers may not even question the need for such travel. For others, moving overseas contains a large measure of uncertainty combined with a search for meaning and significance in life. Families may move to bolster an unhappy marriage, to give children a fresh start in a new culture, or to escape painful living situations. Obviously, the consequences of such diverse motivations may turn out to be adaptive or pathological. However, some element of dissatisfaction must play a part in the decision to choose the complicated, demanding peripatetic existence of living overseas.

The majority of families who go overseas for the first time are young families. For them, leaving the United States is not a particularly difficult hurdle, as they are in the process of seeking their roots in society and tend to be open to new experiences. Older families who have already made life-defining commitments may encounter more serious opposition to the need to invest in new ties. As one father whose family had lived overseas for a considerable period of time described it: "It is easier to travel when your children are small; then it gets more and more difficult. Move by move, I felt more and more resistance to change from everybody in the family, until the time came when they just refused to be bounced around anymore."

Certain characteristic styles of behavior and thought may be developed in people who live overseas; indeed, such styles may well be decisive factors in the choice of an overseas career. Many people overseas seem to thrive on novelty and short-term relationships. Conversely, they may become uncomfortable at the prospect of longer-term, intimate and dependent involvements. They like to complete a job and then start over somewhere

7

else. A Foreign Service officer put it this way: "I really thrive on getting a new pack of cards every four years; you're not stuck with anything, and when you finish a job you just close your desk on it and go off to a new one." The more disturbing side of such a view of life was described by a teenager who said: "We're pretty good at adapting to other people's manners, but part of you gets lost when you do that too much. You get to look at everything as an outsider. Nothing is good or bad anymore." This important group of character issues will be discussed in detail later in the chapter.

Settling In

Fathers of overseas families tend to be highly selected members of their business or government organizations, and often must travel, frequently on special assignments. They become highly visible representatives of the United States in the city and country in which they live.

Because of the father's heightened sense of role, a greater child-rearing burden is placed on mothers who, themselves, are undergoing a cultural transition. One overseas-reared adult remembered his life in Hong Kong this way: "I don't have any recollection of my father when we lived in Asia. He doesn't fit in. My mother was around a good deal, and I divided my time between her and the maid."

8

Settling in overseas may place unusual strains on the relationship between a husband, heavily involved in a demanding career as a representative of a company or the United States government, and a wife who is often left without the support of relatives or close friends in an alien culture in which she has little work to do and little opportunity to pursue a career outside her home. Such strains may contribute to drinking problems, depression, or other incapacitating symptoms that powerfully affect her ability to nurture her children. Because of the high visibility of American families overseas, many psychological difficulties are hidden from the view of others, only to become apparent when the family returns to the United States. The feeling of being constantly on display may prevent a family from attempting to initiate changes that would help them settle in satisfactorily. An executive described the pitfalls of his showcase existence in this way:

> Here in Afghanistan we all watch each other too closely. Call it a fishbowl syndrome. People won't admit they have problems with drinking or with their children or when they feel their jobs are on the line. Most people want to hide their problems, and in a way they are right. There is just no place to talk about the things that bother you, much less the little things that make you feel good. You always have the sense that somebody is going to judge you, somebody that doesn't know you very well. People just want to get through the year or through their tour and get out. It's a feeling that they just don't want anyone else to know what their problems are.

Many overseas families employ servants and nursemaids in their household, whereas the possibility of having such help would be rare for them in the United States. The introduction of a new and significant member to the household may enrich or destroy the nuclear family in ways that have no precedents in ordinary family life in the United States.

A major geographic change necessitates an adaptation to new culture and language, new friends, new neighborhoods and schools, as well as novel social and recreational activities. As Americans overseas tend to be on one- to four-year tours, it is difficult for them to put down deep roots in any community. Instead, they must become adept at developing short-term friendships and comfortable in fitting into differing international sports, celebrations, styles, and inconveniences. And while doing all this, they must keep in mind the necessity of eventually returning to the culture of the United States.

Too much change may result in the well-known syndrome of culture shock, as described by a young woman who finally had to be returned to the United States. She said:

> When I got to North Africa I suddenly lost all my perspectives. It was a pretty hard blow, because I had never been knocked down in my life before. Everything friends would talk about would make me really homesick. I had no concept of the dirt and filth, of people urinating in the streets or the way they treat animals here. The food was terrible, and they didn't repair the toilet I had to use for three months.

An inability to settle in overseas, even for some who do not need to be evacuated, may breed feelings of defeat and pessimism that continue to plague them on their return to the United States.

If a unique and satisfying way of life has been discovered overseas, the United States may seem pallid by comparison. A disappointed returnee put it this way:

> In London there was a touch of something different. There is one pub to every fifty hamburger joints in the United States, but that one pub is better than the fifty put together. Something about living there gives a special flavor to things. You make an occasion of even just walking down to the Green Park in London. Yet, though we have so much available in America, it just doesn't seem worth the effort to get away from the TV to see it.

Having learned a fresh and thrilling way of experiencing life, such a person finds it exceedingly difficult to settle down in the United States once again.

Special Competences
People living overseas accumulate a group of special competences that help them adapt to new situations successfully. They learn to use the Paris Metro skillfully, to interact tactfully with a wide variety of people, to converse about restaurants, museums, monuments, and political parties throughout the world. Mastery of these bits and pieces of knowledge makes life infinitely easier overseas, and contributes to an aura of distinctiveness. Many variations on the foregoing themes can be described, all of which contribute to make up a special consciousness in people who have lived abroad. Special competences are of little use when a person returns to his original home. As one returnee put it:

> You have a language, French, that is a part of you, and you cannot share it. You learn about

9

painting and architecture. In Paris you really learn to look at things, and they are worth looking at. The people back home don't care about how I have lived, who I have met, what I have done, what I am now. They ask questions, but they don't care about the answers.

Return to the United States

Separation and Loss

Returnees leave a significant part of themselves behind when they give up a foreign way of life. They must learn to live without cherished friends and family customs at the same time that they attempt to find secure places in American culture. Unfinished tasks, unfulfilled dreams must be dropped or forgotten. The need to abandon intense friendships and cultural supports frequently results in disturbing feelings characteristic of a grieving process. Though most returning Americans seem to make a good surface adjustment to this country, that adjustment may, at times, cover over a host of barely contained feelings of uncertainty, alienation, anger, and disappointment. The following reports describe some of the underlying feelings:

I felt out of everything when I came back. I didn't know about the music, what to wear, or how to get into the tight cliques that have formed from people who have been together all their lives.

I had lots of friends and played on the school soccer team overseas. When I got back to the United States nobody noticed me in school and nobody went out of his way to be nice to me. My marks slipped and I was miserable for two years.

My junior high school graduating class in Saudi Arabia had just 15 other kids. This high school has 2,000 kids and it is unbelievable. You even have to get a pass to go to the john. The school is filled with cliques, the kids who do dope, the cheerleaders, the sports kids. I just couldn't get in with any of them. I didn't like them and they didn't like me. I felt I was more mature than the other kids, and the things they thought were important seemed trivial to me. "What am I going to wear to school today?" "Who am I going to walk home with?" Those are just not big things in my life. I was afraid of these kids because, even though I felt mature, they knew a lot more about living in America than I did.

Values may be difficult to reconcile. A teenage girl put it this way:

I was miserable the first few months, and my parents never knew what I was going through. I was over-developed physically, but I never really realized it until I got into school here in the United States. That and boys expecting you to go to bed with them right away were just too much for me. It made me feel so odd. I just wasn't aware of it ahead of time, that people really do go through these kinds of problems.

For some, the return to the United States is seen as merely one move among many. A Foreign Service officer had this to say about the issue:

Once the habit of moving gets into your blood, you always itch for the next challenge. I love the contrast in work from one country to another. When I go back to New York I can see my friends doing the same thing they have always done and it depresses me.

Men who had been involved in multinational negotiations overseas may feel let down when their work no longer affects global politics. Women must make career choices that have been postponed during an overseas tour; they must take on again the roles of chauffeur, cook, handyman, and sole care-taker of the children. Children begin again in their quest for friends and a place in the social sun.

A Life of Fantasy

Living away from the United States frees a person from participation in fam-ily and community problems. He cannot visit aging parents or comfort lonely aunts, nor can he participate in church committees and local political campaigns. His lifelines to current issues in this country, *Newsweek* and the *International Herald Tribune*, are no substitute for daily participation in what is happening here. Issues that grip people in the United States lose their urgency, and the person overseas frequently develops a new group of interests based on an entirely different premise, that of being an observer and guest. As a visitor, his attention tends to be drawn to the timeless, proud expressions of a host country's culture--art, music, architecture, theatre, holidays--rather than the mundane, daily ones. He loses contact with the anchoring points of daily life both in the United States and overseas.

Such conditions foster the development of a rich fantasy life, that may flow over into the creation of a fantasy life difficult for others to comprehend. An adolescent girl told me that, when she was in Paris, she had lived out a vision of herself as a turn-of-the-century beauty, strolling through museums and stopping along the Champs Elysees for a cup of coffee. No one questioned the role she was playing out, least of all herself.

On return to the United States little support can be found to nurture international fantasies, and, in addition, the returnee has lost track of the events current in this country. Bafflement and frustration may ensue on all sides.

11

Communication of Experience

Much of our experience is primarily nonverbal. It is difficult to translate into words certain of our touch, taste, smell, or sight perceptions, even though these perceptions may exert a potent influence on one's consciousness and self-definition. A businessman lamented:

> You simply can't describe the feel of the hot wind on your skin in Sicily or the noise and commotion of traffic in Rome. It just can't be reproduced in conversation. When I try to tell people what it was like, it probably sounds like I just want them to envy me. But it's not that. I just want them to know what I felt, who I am.

This large component of experience, nonverbal and unshared, creates a painful barrier to comfortable communication, and the person returned from overseas, isolated from the world around him, may find that he becomes a prey to all kinds of distorted perceptions and disturbing fantasies.

Though we possess a time-honored tradition of farewell parties to send people overseas, and a considerable literature of adventure and self-discovery to guide them, we are endowed with very little ritual and writing to help them on their return. Thomas Wolfe's *You Can't Go Home Again* emphatically warns the traveler not to do what he must do, and Malcolm Cowley's *Exile's Return* praises the timeless, dreamlike pleasures of life in Europe, rather than any creative satisfactions to be discovered in the United States. We are in great need of a literature that will interpret America to returning Americans and, at the same time, explain them to those who have remained at home. Similarly, we need to devise societally recognized events that will reintroduce travelers to the people of their home country, and guide them to a recognized place in their community.

Symptomatic Problems of the Returnee
Many returnees describe feelings of discomfort and vague dissatisfaction with their lives, though they cannot pinpoint the basis of their difficulty. They are able to adjust to the United States, but are not comfortable with that adjustment. Most of the problems I have encountered fit into this category of vague adjustment reactions, rather than any more traditional psychiatric diagnosis. Long-lasting feelings of being restless, out of place, rootless are typically recalled, even by those who are overtly well-adjusted to their return from overseas.

Nostalgia for a Lost Way of Life

12   A teenager will often remember his time overseas as one of having fallen in love, not only with a girl friend, a boyfriend, or a culture, but as a time in which he engaged in an exciting love affair with a foreign way of life. Such a love affair is recalled as an ideal time, the disturbing, boring or unsatisfying moments forgotten, in which he gave all of himself to an experience. A wise teacher recalled the syndrome in this way:

> American teenagers who come to our school develop strong attachments and sometimes intense crushes with Italian youngsters. They become inseparable, for each sees in the other, at a time when both are bursting with vitality, an opportunity to fulfill all of life's wishes. The breaking off of these friendships when the American goes home can be devastating for the visitor and the Italian child alike. Both suffer the effects of separation for such a long time.

Young people who have had such an experience may find themselves unable to become involved with a new school and new friends. They make intolerable demands upon teachers and friends, demands that cannot be met no matter how hard new acquaintances try, because the teenager is yearning for an ideal person, an ideal time, that probably never did exist. These feelings of loss and disappointment develop into a kind of nostalgia for a great and perfect past. Sometimes this nostalgia takes on the proportions of a true disease, a yearning and grieving that seemingly has no end. A high school student in the United States wrote to his cherished friends in Tunisia about his sense of longing as follows:

> Vienna, Virginia is about as middle class as it can be. Our school is gigantic, made up of commuters and freaks, with no sense of spirit and a lot of people just trying to get it over

with. It is tough to rise above the general sense of apathy. I set here with your yearbook and am so envious of all of you there in Tunisia and think of how lucky you are to be isolated from the mass education we have here in the homeland.

This idealization of memory occurs because of the mind's wish to ignore unpleasant reality--the discomforts and uncertainties of the past--and to recall only the blissful fulfillments. A preoccupation with nostalgia succeeds in helping one forget the frustrations of the present and the efforts necessary to engage in a new life.

A Different Self-Concept

Attitudes of teenagers overseas about themselves and others were examined in a recent research study (Werkman & Johnson, 1976). Differences in attitudes and values between teenagers reared overseas and those reared exclusively in the United States were studied by comparing 172 teenagers who lived overseas with 163 teenagers matched for age, sex, and socioeconomic status who had lived exclusively in the United States. Using the Semantic Differential technique, the subjects' reactions to certain concepts were rated on the dimensions of evaluation, activity, potency, and sensitivity. The groups were separated at a statistically significant level in rating the following concepts.

Teenagers who had lived overseas rated themselves as less strong, good, or happy than those in the United States. The future was not so strong, colorful, stable, or close to them. Friends were less important, close, strong, and colorful. Loneliness was more interesting, close, stable, and comfortable for them. Restlessness was more interesting, good, and happy for them.

13

The results suggest that overseas teenagers are unusually searching and open about themselves, and especially capable of acknowledging potentially disturbing affects. They appear to be less secure and optimistic than adolescents who live exclusively in the United States, but in many ways more psychologically sensitive. The self-concepts of overseas teenagers appear to be less positive, and they seem to show less of a feeling of security and optimism about life in general. These results do not suggest that teenagers who have been reared overseas are less psychologically healthy than those reared in the United States, but rather that overseas experience does have a significant effect on their values and attitudes.

Roots

Because of the attitudes described, it well may be that overseas teenagers are candidates for becoming restless, possibly rootless people, who have a constant need to be on the move. Indeed, it is a general clinical impression that the majority of people who have grown up overseas do not want to settle down in one place during their adult lives. Approximately two-thirds of the people seen in the Boulder sample, as well as in my clinical and consulting practice, hope to return overseas, and expect to live geographically mobile lives. The following statements describe their views well:

> I just think of myself as belonging to the world: not any one place, not Pennsylvania, but anywhere I can do what I want to do. I doubt if I will ever settle down or if I will ever need to.

> I want to belong to a creative and openminded group of people who are interested and concerned about the world. Everywhere I stay is home because I don't need a single home, just a sense of the place where my family lives.

Recommendations for Successful Reentry

The findings from a number of studies (Borus 1973b; Hamburg & Adams, 1967; Silber, Coelho, Murphey, Hamburg, Pearlin, & Rosenberg, 1961; Werkman, 1977) have agreed that the following attitudes and strategies appear to be central to the achievement of successful transitions. The person who makes life transitions successfully seeks out advance information about the new situation to be mastered, finds ways to try out the new behaviors and attitudes required, and utilizes peer-group interactions to gain support, test out new behaviors, and learn about values needed in a new situation. He recalls successful experiences in the past when confronted with new challenges.

These conclusions were substantially confirmed in the subjects studied by the author. In addition, it should be noted that the person in transition does better if he is able to recognize and grieve over the losses involved in moving to a new situation.

14

The Importance of Goodbyes

In the United States it is rare for friends to part forever, but the overseas family must say final goodbyes repeatedly. Many families, finding the experience of leavetaking to be an increasingly wrenching one, slip into the unfortunate habit of evading the rituals of farewells. Though an effective short-term pain reliever, such evasion may result in a legacy of anxiety and guilty sadness. Unfinished farewells may return to haunt the memory of returnees.

Integrate the Past with the Present

A mother described her experience as follows:

> The first year home we bought an expensive barbeque grill, grilled steaks every night, and dressed in "mod" clothes. It was ridiculous. Then we began to realize that we didn't need to have a color TV or sugar-coated cereal every morning. My husband and I realized that we had learned some things overseas, and decided to keep those things we had learned for ourselves and our children.

Another put it this way:

> When you get back, you can't expect people to want to hear about your travels, but you do bring things that people need—the sense of community you notice in small towns in Greece; the humane way people deal with each other in villages; the slow pace of people who take time to be with each other.

Overseas Life Leaves Its Imprint
Recognize that living overseas has long-lasting effects on personality. Several returnees described those effects as follows:

> My experience in Germany has made me a much more reserved person, a more quiet one than I would have been if I had stayed here. I don't make quick judgments about things, but stand back and really look at them.

> Living overseas has given me a chance to look at things from a different perspective. Now, I want to know more about everything. I am more involved in searching and in finding, and know that there may not be a pure truth.

> You end up with a double concept of yourself. There is this sense that you have an extra talent, your knowledge of another language and another culture, that has no value except in planning your own later life. I think where people get in trouble is that they tend to come back and know they have this asset, but think that everybody else should know about it and feel "you should respect me because I've got this extra experience," but it doesn't apply. What you gain from experience abroad is going to be maintained, but it's better to tuck it away. What you have learned not only doesn't get you anywhere, but it tends to threaten or irritate people.

> It makes a person much deeper. You see that there are different kinds of people. I think here in America people are only what they are in relationship to others, instead of being what they are to themselves. The people in the school that I am in now seem to care so much what other people think about them. For example, when there are girls all crowded together in one part of the room you have to sit with your best friend or they think you are weird. But it doesn't bother me in the least.

A common theme running through these reports is a recognition of a deep sense of aloneness together with a need for individual self-definition. Returnees tend to view life in comparative terms and characterize themselves as observers rather than active participants in social experience. Their reports contain many themes of existential alienation described succinctly by Maddi (1967).

The Need for Support Systems
A parent described her family's successful efforts to find support systems in this way:

> We helped our 13-year-old get into the Boy Scouts through a talk with the boy who delivered papers. My daughter immediately looked for a place to rent a horse, and found friends around the stables. We joined a community swimming pool where our children made lots of friends. Our kids didn't have any real problems of reentry into the United States, but it is something you have to work at. It doesn't just happen.

A young woman spoke about what she felt she needed on returning:

> Nothing helped too much, but I wish I had been able to get in touch with friends who had shared my experience. The problem was that those friends were in a different part of the country. The only friends I have in high school have never been abroad and can't understand these things. They couldn't understand this cultural shock. It seemed so fake to them that I was having trouble readjusting to my own culture. I needed to talk to someone and tell them about it, so I wrote letters to friends and family. They helped because they had culture shock when they came back. I have always had this yearning to get back to Europe after every tour, but this time I almost wanted to give up my citizenship because I felt so lonely.

15

Emotional Cost of Adjustment

Transitions and reintegration take time, and inevitably are accompanied by pain. The various curves of adaptation to geographic mobility devised by researchers (Gullahorn & Gullahorn, 1966) all emphasize that periods of loneliness and discomfort alternate with periods of effective coping. They comprise part of the cost of adjustment.

Programs

People moving from one culture to another need advance information that can be offered through seminars and discussion groups before they move. They need guides and mentors in their new homes. The use of peer counselors (Hamburg, 1974) has been recommended as a useful way of helping students effect transitions successfully.

   Schools, colleges, businesses, and government agencies would do well to set up transition groups to aid in the integration of returning Americans. However, such programs should last more than a weekend, and include more than a welcoming ceremony. As one returned college student observed: "It would have been helpful to have someone show me how to locate friends and find my way around here, someone who could have taken care of me during the first month back. I mean someone just to watch out for me."

   The task of readapting to the United States demands the best efforts of people who have been away, and those present to welcome them. Some of the pitfalls of this transition have been described in this chapter. Useful strategies for dealing effectively with the stresses of geographic mobility have been summarized. The challenge that this transition be recognized as a serious rite of passage for many people remains to be taken up in the future.

16

References

Borus, J. F. (1973a). Reentry. I: Adjustment issues facing the Vietnam returnee. *Archives of General Psychiatry, 28,* 501–506.

Borus, J. F. (1973b). Reentry. III: Facilitating healthy readjustment in Vietnam veterans. *Psychiatry, 36,* 428–439.

Bower, E. M. (1967). American children and families in overseas communities. *American Journal of Orthopsychiatry, 37,* 787–796.

Cleveland, H., Mangone, G. J., & Adams, J. C. (1960). *The overseas Americans.* New York: McGraw-Hill.

Gullahorn, J. E., & Gullahorn, J. T. (1966). American students abroad: Professional versus personal development. *The Annals of the American Academy, 368,* 43–59.

Hamburg, B. (1974). Coping in early adolescence. In G. Caplan (Ed.), *American handbook of psychiatry,* Vol. II. New York: Basic Books.

Hamburg, D., & Adams, J. E. (1967). A perspective on coping behavior. *Archives of General Psychiatry, 17,* 277–284.

Kenny, J. A. (1967). The child in the military community. *Journal of the American Academy of Child Psychiatry, 6,* 51–63.

Maddi, S. R. (1967). The existential neurosis. *Journal of Abnormal Psychology, 72,* 311–325.

Silber, E. Coelho, G. V., Murphey, E. B., Hamburg, D., Pearlin, L. I., & Rosenberg, M. (1961). Competent adolescent coping with college decisions. *Archives of General Psychiatry, 5,* 517–527.

Smith, M. B. (1966). Explorations in competence: A study of Peace Corps teachers in Ghana. *American Psychologist, 21,* 555–566.

Werkman, S. L. (1972). Hazards of rearing children in foreign countries. *American Journal of Psychiatry, 128,* 992–997.

Werkman, S. L. (1975). Over here and back there: American adolescents overseas. *Foreign Service Journal, 52,* 13–16.

Werkman, S. L. (1977). *Bringing up children overseas: A guide for families.* New York: Basic Books.

Werkman, S. L., & Johnson, F. (1976, May). *The effect of geographic mobility on adolescent character structure.* Paper presented at annual meeting of the American Society for Adolescent Psychiatry, Miami, FL.

2

A Strategy for Managing "Cultural" Transitions: Re-Entry from Training

Art Freedman

Each person is a *member of* and *lives in* a number of very different social "worlds" or "cultures." People are members of their respective family worlds, community worlds, work worlds, and religious worlds. In the work world, people may be members of some special "subculture" like the hourly workers' union, first-line supervisors, middle management, or the executive group. Some may belong to several work subcultures at once; for example, a manager may also be a member of a professional association.

Usually people live in only one of these social worlds at a time. That is, at work they tend not to be conscious of the fact that they are, simultaneously, citizens of their respective communities and also members of their respective families. Occasionally, however, people do live in two or more worlds simultaneously: for example, when an employee asks the boss for a raise in order to maintain the family's standard of living in the face of spiraling inflation, or when work for his employer begins to conflict with his union contract or with the ethical standards of her professional organization, or, perhaps, when the disposable by-products of the company's manufacturing processes are found to be contaminating the community.

At times like these, people become uncomfortably aware of real conflicts among their own various vested interests. It becomes apparent that what is

Reprinted from: J. William Pfeiffer and John E. Jones, (Eds.), *The 1980 Annual Handbook for Group Facilitators*, San Diego, CA: University Associates, Inc., 1980. Used with permission.

acceptable to believe and say and do in *one* world is often quite different from (and can be in direct conflict with) the values, attitudes, and standards of *other* worlds. We become conscious that what is O.K. in one setting definitely is not O.K. in another. However, most of the time, people do not spend much time thinking about this paradox, probably because many people have been trained from early childhood to expect (without being consciously aware of it) that life *is* different in the different social settings among which individuals have to move as they engage in the process of living. Because such differences are expected, they are not surprising. When experience in life corresponds to expectations, there is usually little reason *consciously* to think about the paradox.

However, there are times when an unexpected conflict between what is expected and what is actually experienced is jolting. For example, a young man is surprised by just how much he is expected to allow his thinking, behavior, and style of life to be controlled by his superiors when he enters the military. A person put into prison or a mental hospital is shocked by the unusual, strange, and unexpected way in which the staff responds to his or her behavior--usually disconcertingly different from the way any other person has ever responded to that individual. Similarly, the tourist is often shocked by the enormous differences in expectations of behavior between citizens of a *foreign* culture and the citizens of his or her *native* culture.

20   Participants of a residential workshop often experience "culture shock" when they pass from their predictable, "real-life" worlds of family, work, social relationships, and religion into the temporary, artificial "foreign" workshop world and then back. Since most people who participate in such an experience do so voluntarily, presumably they hope to derive some personal learning from the event that they can use in their respective "back-home" worlds. However, the extent to which such learning is effectively and appropriately *applied* and *maintained* in participants' back-home environments is not clear. It has been demonstrated that, although participants derive a great many personal learnings from their workshop experiences, these learnings do not always hold up over time (Freedman, 1963).

Applications
The concept discussed here may enable internal and external consultants, trainers, organizational managers, personnel specialists, and human-service providers to facilitate people's negotiation of a number of different types of life transitions. These could include temporary migrations into and out of such institutions as, for example, mental and general medical-surgical hospitals, prisons, residential rehabilitation centers, companies, foreign assignments, and residential communities, in addition to intense, experiential "cultural island" training experiences or the military.

Some examples of functional work groups might be (a) off-shore oil/gas drilling crews; (b) crews for long-distance ocean-going vessels; or

(c) engineering/construction crews working in a third-world nation. Other application possibilities could include such situations as (a) taking a first job with a company after having completed college or a training program (e.g., for the hard-core unemployed); (b) being promoted within the organization; and (c) being transferred from one geographical-cultural location to another (e.g., the headquarters of a multinational company moves from New York City to Houston). Modifications could also be developed for one-time-only migrations such as permanent moves to a foreign country, a nursing home, or a hospice for the terminally ill.

Entry: Migration from "Native" to "Foreign" Culture
Most often, when people find themselves in a "foreign" culture with which they have very little past experience, they generally--quite naturally--behave in ways that are familiar to them. They do what they are already skilled in doing. When they discover that their behaviors--the things they say and do--and their expectations are not acceptable to the residents of the foreign culture, they first experience a sense of disconfirmation of *their expectations or hopes*. Then they are faced with a complex decision that cannot be avoided. They must decide whether to (a) continue to behave in the same ways they are used to, comfortable with, and skilled in (regardless of whether or not these ways are acceptable or tolerated in the foreign culture); (b) leave the uncomfortable foreign culture (either by returning to their native culture or by becoming "psychotic"); or (c) discover and adapt to the expectations of the citizens of the foreign culture--even if that means giving up, suspending, or modifying previous attitudes, values, and behaviors. If they choose the last option, they place themselves in the awkward and uncomfortable position of knowing little, if anything, about the new culture and having to learn *everything* about what it takes to get along there.

Many inexperienced participants in intensive workshops expect that their trainers will function like the leaders of the traditional, goal-oriented work groups with which they are familiar. When they realize that these expectations are not going to be fulfilled and that the trainers will not set agendas or tell them what to do or how to do it, participants tend to become extremely uncomfortable. In an attempt to allay their discomfort, participants frequently attempt to cajole, threaten, or implore the trainers to act according to their expectations. When these attempts fail, participants must assume responsibility for themselves in order to make sense of their experiences.

The "Pioneer" Experience
Those who choose to explore the foreign culture and adapt or accommodate themselves to it soon learn that their experience is analogous to that of the pioneer or explorer. What is not known about the new environment (the "foreign" culture) is much greater than what is known. And most of

what *is* known consists of the individual's increasing awareness of his or her own restlessness, uncertainties, fears, hyperactivity, social errors, or misunderstandings.

Nontypical Behaviors
An increasing sense of tension develops, and out of this tension certain nontypical behaviors evolve. *Attention narrows.* Whereas in their familiar and comfortable native culture people may allow themselves to be open to all the sights and sounds and events that occur constantly around them, in the foreign culture their vision becomes selectively constricted (a sort of "tunnel" vision) and focused on only those events that correspond most closely with whatever their preoccupation is. For example, a person may feel unattached to and isolated from the foreign culture and may experience the need for a home base (a "safe" place to "live") from which to venture forth and explore the new environment and to which he or she can withdraw when feeling overwhelmed or overextended. For this person such places as hotels, motels, rooming houses, apartment houses, YWCA's, hostels, etc., will be most prominent, while other aspects of the environment will blend into the background.

22
Having established a "safe" home base, a person may now get in touch with the tensions that relate to being (or feeling) socially isolated, unattached, and alienated. In response to these feelings, the individual may initiate a search, perhaps by trial-and-error or in a frantic or calculating manner, for candidates who might be able and willing to serve as companions, escorts, guides, behavior models, and/or interpreters. Such people might be friendly citizens of the foreign culture, other caring migrants who are more familiar with the host culture, or simply other uncertain and searching migrants who seem to have similar needs. Schutz (1971) refers to this phase, in the natural evolution of personal-growth groups, as the "inclusion phase." This might also be called a search for a "mentor."

Decrease of Tension
Once one or more supportive persons have been found, the tensions and inner turmoil of the "pioneer" will probably decrease. This release will probably be experienced as joyous and freeing, enabling the individual to expand the limits of his or her vision enough to begin to *see* the way life in the foreign culture unfolds for its natives. This less-restricted vision will, in turn, assist the immigrant to identify and then modify or eliminate those aspects of his or her behavior that conflict with the host culture's norms and standards of acceptable behavior.

At first, attempts to experiment and practice with behaviors that are new will feel (and appear to others to be) awkward. People will probably feel visible, vulnerable, ungainly, and embarrassed. However, with practice, they will become rather proficient at the new behaviors and the new language.

Even the new style of thinking will become natural, and they will almost automatically think, feel, and act in a way that is at least acceptable to the host culture's citizens. When this plateau--virtual automatic proficiency--has been achieved, people have adapted or become *socialized* to the foreign culture to which they have migrated.

Re-Entry: Migration from "Foreign" to "Native" Culture
If the migration is permanent, a major cross-cultural hurdle will have been successfully negotiated. However, when people have been temporary, transient residents (more than just tourists) and return from the foreign culture to their native culture, they will soon discover that their cross-cultural problems are far from over.

Conflict
Upon re-entering their native culture without adequate preparation, people are likely to discover, much to their surprise, that they cannot simply pick up where they left off. Their friends, family members, and work associates did not go into hibernation when they were away. Not only that, those who stayed behind have no way of knowing what the migrants went through or how they were affected by their experiences. Friends remember them more or less as they were when they left. In all likelihood, they are expected to be very much the same. However, to the extent that they really did allow themselves to become immersed in the foreign culture, they will *not* be the same people they used to be. They will walk, talk, think, and feel in ways that are strange and perhaps unheard-of to the citizens of their native culture. Thus, a situation with a surprisingly high potential for conflict between "foreigner" and "native" is created.

23

The conflict results from common human needs: people strive to create their worlds in ways that are comfortable to them. Comfort--relatively speaking--is what we feel when the world and the people in it behave in ways that correspond with our expectations: our world is predictable, and we feel comfortable. When a discrepancy occurs and people act in an unpredictable manner, we become uncomfortable. Thus, as people try to put potential solutions for some of their back-home problems into operation, they are actually creating new problems for other people. The returnees are no longer predictable, and the citizens of the native culture become uncomfortable and attribute the cause of their discomfort to the migrant.

Disconfirmation
Very much like the feelings of the pioneer entering the foreign culture, the hopeful expectations of family, friends, and associates may be disconfirmed. However, the citizens of a person's native culture--to a much greater extent than those of a foreign culture--can be expected to exert a considerable amount of pressure on the returning culture-crossing traveler to give up his

or her strange and unpredictable behaviors and to return to the comfortably predictable person they once knew.

It is a simple fact that our family, friends, and co-workers can have power to influence us only if and when we give them this "power" to determine our choices. We care about them, and we are concerned that our behavior might be displeasing to them and that they might withdraw from us. Our own human desires for acceptance and affiliation set us up to be perfect targets for subtle forms of blackmail and bribery. People who are important to us inform us that unless we return to our culture's traditional norms and standards, we risk being excluded and isolated. We may be asked to feel bad or guilty about what our behavior is "doing to" people about whom we care. But if and when (but not until) we "shape up," all kinds of nice things will happen to us.

During this re-entry process, individuals' levels of comfort, effectiveness, and satisfaction dip down almost as far as when they first migrated to the foreign culture. However, after going through the same cycle of cultural-shock impact, recoil, and accommodation, their equilibrium becomes somewhat restored, low levels of effectiveness and satisfaction "bottom-out," and new but increasingly secure relationships begin to be established with the citizens of the native culture.

24   **Renegotiation**
To be enduring and meaningful, new relationships have to be based on the creation of new and mutually acceptable expectations: what can both sides legitimately expect of each other? This process becomes an explicit renegotiation of what used to be an implicit contract between people who want or need to live with one another in home, community, or work settings.

It becomes clear that the re-entering, culture-crossing travelers will have to be prepared to modify their recently acquired "foreign" behavior. Most people would prefer that citizens of their native culture not reject, isolate, or expel them. However, in order not to give up the benefits derived from their travels, they will attempt to model their newly acquired behavior for their fellow natives--inviting their native culture's citizens to tolerate, then accept, and then, maybe, experiment with the new behavior themselves. This is the process by which transcendental meditation, Tai Chi, the martial arts, Zen, acupuncture, and other aspects of Eastern cultures were probably introduced to the Western world.

The W–Curve Hypothesis
In order to prepare people to leave a foreign culture and return to their native, back-home cultures of family, community, and work, it is helpful to explain the concept of transitions by presenting it in the form of a diagram (see Figure 1).

There are two points that the diagram illustrates that have not been discussed. One is *hope:* without that, few people would bother to try anything new. They might be terribly dissatisfied with the current conditions of their lives, but without the hope that life does not *have* to be that way, people would tend to say something like "Better to live with the devil I know than the devil I don't." And they would sit dead still and endure chronic dissatisfaction or suffering.

The second point is that, in terms of levels of comfort, satisfaction, and effectiveness, the dips tend to be shallower and the peaks higher as people move from their foreign culture back to their native culture. It is this curvature that lends its name to this concept.

This model is especially helpful in providing workshop participants with some conceptual handles that they can use in re-entering their "native" culture. This concept helps absorb a great deal of the tension and anxiety that participants tend to experience toward the end of a workshop when they begin to anticipate the re-entry process. They begin to ask themselves, "How are my people back there *ever* going to understand me now? How can I let them know what I've been through here?" This model allows participants to anticipate the re-entry "dip" and develop a plan that will reduce its depth.

Conclusion

In presenting this material, the facilitator might wish to point out that these concepts relate to all of us who find ourselves moving, with increasing frequency and rapidity, from one temporary social system to another (Toffler, 1970; Bennis & Slater, 1968). The unprepared individual can be expected to experience chronic migrational shock. However, through the use of the concepts presented here, people can learn to cope with and then overcome the impact of constant cultural migration so that the dips flatten out and a rising slope of satisfaction, effectiveness, and comfort gradually replaces the temporary peaks.

25

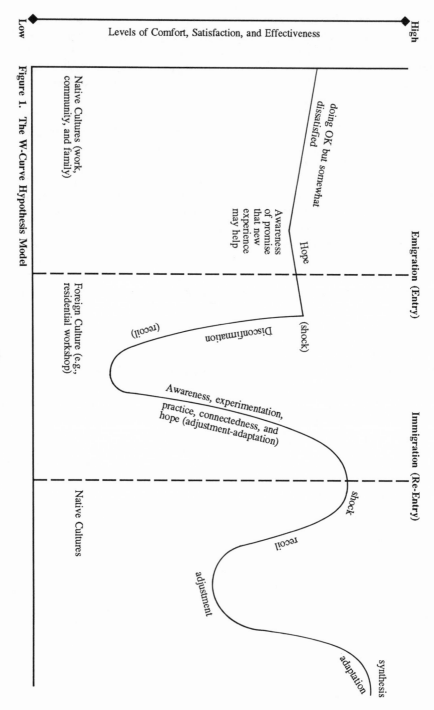

Figure 1. The W-Curve Hypothesis Model

References

Bennis, W. G., & Slater, P. E. (1968). *The temporary society.* New York: Harper & Row.

Freedman, A. M. (1963). *Changes in perception of on-the-job problems following human relations laboratory training: II.* Unpublished master's thesis, Boston University.

Hall, E. T. (1976). *Beyond culture.* Garden City, NY: Anchor Press/Doubleday.

Schmuck, R. A., et al. (1977). *The second handbook of organization development in schools.* Palo Alto, CA: Mayfield.

Schutz, W. C. (1971). *Here comes everybody.* New York: Harper & Row.

Toffler, A. (1970). *Future shock.* New York: Random House.

Tyhurst, J. S. (1957). The role of transition states--including disasters--in mental illness. In *Symposium on Preventive and Social Psychiatry.* Washington, DC: Walter Reed Army Hospital Institute of Research.

27

3

Managing the Overseas Assignment Process

Nessa P. Loewenthal and Nancy L. Snedden

The movers arrived on schedule and packed the family's belongings very efficiently, down to the last shoe rack. Visas, passports, medical exams and shots were handled in record time, and no slip-ups plagued the family en route to the foreign country where the employee had a new assignment waiting. The employee's expertise seemed to fit the new job's requirements exactly.

Yet, within six months he and his family had requested a transfer back to the States. The company granted it reluctantly, having already spent many thousands of dollars on the overseas transfer and now finding itself in the position of having to arrange for a replacement--far ahead of the original schedule.

This is an all-too-familiar scenario, even in organizations with many years' experience in multinational operations. The number of things that can go wrong on an overseas assignment is enormous. However, most of these disasters can be avoided by proper planning and for a relatively minimal cost. It has been estimated that it costs between $55,000 and $150,000 to transfer someone to an overseas post. For a fraction of that amount, $500 to $1,000 per family unit, a company can design and implement a program to protect its investment.

"Managing the Overseas Assignment Process," *The Bridge,* Spring 1981, pp. 14–15; 41–43.
Used with permission from the Intercultural Press, Inc.

The major reason for overseas assignment debacles is the failure of the organization to take what is called, in contemporary terminology, a "holistic" approach to the subject. The foreign assignment process begins with selection and ends with repatriation; in between is the pivotal element of orientation. Insufficient attention to any one of these phases can have adverse consequences.

Still, it is a rare organization that devotes adequate planning and resources to all three. Many companies select employees because of their technical skills, with no regard to their ability to adapt to a foreign culture. Some do not prepare the employee--much less the employee's family--for what awaits them in terms of culture, attitudes, climate (weather and political) and the details of how one takes care of day-to-day matters. Others ignore the reality of the "reverse culture shock" that greets the employee and the family on their return to the home office and the home country.

In years past, multinational organizations could survive this sort of inattention far better than they can today. The prevailing attitude used to be that the employee belonged to the company and would be at its beck and call, no matter where the assignment; his family would go along to the new locale or not, whichever was more practical for the company. The job was the most important element in life, and other elements were accommodated to it.

30 But times and personal values have changed. No longer are employees content to be shifted around for the company's benefit--unless they see some benefit to themselves. "Quality of life" has come to mean more than "quality of job"; and if a proposed assignment enriches one's wallet but impoverishes one's life and family relationships, the employee will opt out.

Who Should Go Abroad?
This brings us to the first consideration in managing the process of foreign assignments: selecting those who should go. Although technical expertise and capability are essential in a foreign assignment--where the person is not only doing a job but also representing the organization--the person who has been a resounding success in the home office is not necessarily the one who will perform best overseas.

For example, a young executive's aggressiveness and openness might earn him high praise in the U.S. but resistance and hostility in Japan or Taiwan. What might be viewed as constructive criticism on a jobsite in Texas would be interpreted as a severe and profoundly embarrassing putdown by an Algerian worker. An American who is unaware of such differences in cultural values--and is unable to adapt his or her behavior accordingly--will have problems in a foreign environment. Such difficulties can cause costly delays and/or problems on the job, not to mention the harm done to a firm's image or success in a host country.

Another factor important in selection is the impact of the assignment on the employee's career. Many employees are sent on a series of assignments abroad; if the series is structured so that each assignment builds on the previous one, the employee's attitude, productivity and loyalty to the company are going to be far better than it will be if he or she sees no progression, no career benefit and utilization of previous experience.

Not only is this sense of progression important in the job assignments themselves, but adaptation to a second culture is facilitated by the employee's ability to use knowledge of one culture in adapting to the next. Suppose a manager's first assignment abroad is Jakarta. When he returns to the U.S. to a position dealing strictly with U.S. personnel, there will be little use for the specialized knowledge he has gained about the Muslim culture. However, if his next assignment is Kuwait, or working with others going there, this knowledge can be most useful. Sending him to Korea instead, although it will use some of his "new" knowledge, is not making the most of his cultural expertise. Frequently, an employee, although unaware of the cause of his dissatisfaction, will leave the corporation for another multinational organization where his previous experiences can be used. Therefore, career planning is an essential element of the entire process.

Age and experience should also enter into the selection process. Some executives report that those who have the least difficulty in adapting on foreign assignments are in the 50–60 year age range. These employees usually have established their identities and their relationships within and to the company, have developed some expertise in technical and human relations matters, no longer have children in school, and have passed the midlife crisis.

Of course, if a company were to restrict itself to sending only people in their fifties, the choices of candidates would be severely limited. Younger candidates can also be highly qualified and highly successful. However, maturity and life situation are definitely factors that should be considered during the selection process. In fact, human resource planning at the highest levels of a multinational organization should include an analysis not only of key employees' career paths but also of the ways in which the organization can best use the knowledge and expertise these employees gain, or have gained, in their overseas assignments.

When considering a person for an international assignment, it is important to look at that person's own reasons for accepting an overseas assignment. Is he going in order to save his marriage or to get his children away from drugs? These problems are probably not going to disappear. Is he going because of the high pay the company offers an as inducement to accept an overseas post? Although this is one of the key reasons given for accepting an assignment, it should not be the only one. If, however, the employee seeks the overseas assignment for the challenge, combined with the opportunity for career advancement, he has the right perspective and will probably be successful.

One of the most important--and most often overlooked--factors in selection is the employee's family. A major reason for the premature return of an employee on overseas assignment is the inability of the family to adjust to the conditions of living abroad. Since it is not practical to select only single individuals for overseas posts, or to send employees away for years at a time without their spouses and children, family considerations are of the utmost importance. The spouse must be aware of what awaits her in the new locale and must be as capable of adjusting as the employee.

How can an organization determine who best meets the requirements for overseas assignment? There are, as yet, no objective measurement instruments capable of taking all the relevant factors--including family issues-- into consideration and unfailingly selecting the best candidates. Although there are tests to determine potential in nearly every other key function of a business, most multinational organizations have not found tests that accurately evaluate overseas effectiveness.

Although no formalized screening vehicles are available, the candidates' immediate supervisors have a number of mechanisms at hand for aiding in selection. For example, performance history will indicate a candidate's organizational ability, flexibility, self-discipline, technical ability and ability to work independently, as well as his supervisory skills. Health records offer information regarding the person's ability to meet the physical demands of travel and of the new climate.

32

Additionally, an evaluation of the candidates according to the following profile of the Effective Overseas Employee (developed by Frank Hawes and Dan Kealey in their 1979 study *Canadians in Development* for the Canadian International Development Agency) will provide an indication of the potential success of an individual on an international assignment.

Interpersonal Skills

Interpersonal Skill is the capacity to relate effectively with others. The effective individual overseas is open to and interested in other people and their ideas. He is cooperative, friendly, respectful of others, and an attentive listener; in short, he is capable of building relationships through interpersonal trust. He is aware of cultural factors when living overseas, and takes them into account. He is calm and relaxed in stressful conditions. He communicates well with his family.

Self-Assertion/Identity

However, the individual has a sense of self which he can express appropriately without disregard for others. He can be frank and outspoken, direct in his dealings with others. He asserts himself with confidence, he is able to take the initiative and say what he feels. He is not afraid to take risks when necessary.

Realistic Pre-Departure Expectations

Prior to departure, the individual expresses doubts and concerns about overseas assignment, but overall expects the assignment to be a rewarding experience. He is realistic about the constraints, yet optimistic about success.

Ideally, the candidate--and the candidate's family--should be interviewed to determine motivations, attitudes and expectations.

Preparing for the Relocation

Orientation for the employee who is to be sent overseas should cover a broad range of factors: *job specifics* --scope, responsibilities, labor relations, length of project, rate and conditions of pay, perks, vacations and so forth; information about *people, government, and customs* of the area; *living conditions* --medical care, housing, handling of household and personal effects, local transportation, schools, recreational opportunities, taxes, group insurance and benefit plans; *language;* and, particularly for those at the management and supervisory levels, information concerning *interactions* with U.S. and local government representatives, clients and other company employees at the site.

Considering the variety of detail involved, it is not too surprising that organizations often fail to provide some essential bit of information. For example, one U.S. family was sent to Quebec, which seemed a relatively easy relocation--until they discovered that their sixteen-year-old child could not graduate from high school without a knowledge of French, and no information on alternatives had been provided. Careful investigation at the foreign location is a prerequisite to effective orientation.

A pre-departure orientation program should be both informational and experiential. It should include current, accurate printed and audio-visual materials on living and job conditions, combined with the information on the cultural differences and similarities between the home and host countries. Additional on-site orientation should be provided to reinforce pre-departure learnings.

One key element, too often overlooked, is a specific orientation geared towards the spouses. This aspect of preparation for an overseas assignment is particularly important, as family adjustment is essential to the employee's effectiveness. The spouse holds the key to the family's adaptation to a new culture. A man who arrives in the new country has, waiting for him, a job that will absorb his energy and make use of his talents. (In fact, he was probably wanted four weeks ago.) Often the assignment will be more or less an extension of the home office. English will be the language that is used most often. A secretary, an aide, a telephone and all the tools necessary are provided.

The wife, on the other hand, is suddenly thrust into a vacuum. (Generally, the wife is the non-working spouse in this situation.) She knows no one and has no pre-established identity save that of being a wife. She may have given up a job or community activities in order to accompany her husband. Additionally, she has given up her entire support structure (family, friends, etc.). She is the one who will have to deal with the unfamiliar culture and language on a daily basis in order to get things done. Her role changes from that of a participant in household management to that of manager or supervisor.

The Bechtel Group realized several years ago that orientation for families was a critical factor in overseas success. The program Bechtel adopted is more than justifiable on bottom-line terms: orientation for 100–300 families can be provided for what it would cost the company if just one family returns prematurely.

The orientation, varying in length from two hours to two days provides area- and culture-specific information to both employees and spouses. At one point during the program, employees and spouses are separated, with the employee receiving job-specific orientation while the wife is given information on managing a home and family in the new area. Ample time is provided for questions. It has been found that, when they are in a group of their peers and apart from their husbands, women will ask questions that their husbands would be embarrassed to ask but which are nevertheless important. Generally, these concerns are about minor rather than major issues. One woman was extremely reluctant to go to Riyadh, Saudi Arabia because she had heard that the water was undrinkable; she was worried that her young daughter might get water in her mouth while washing her hair in the shower. When reassured that in Riyadh the water is not poisonous or harmful, although it has a brackish taste because of the high salt content, her concern was alleviated.

The family support process extends beyond the home shores to the new location itself. At Bechtel we have developed a method that benefits both the spouses who are new to the foreign culture and those who have lived there for awhile--and is virtually cost-free to the company. We involve the spouses who are already abroad in the process of acculturation and evaluation. We inform a wife that Sue Jones is coming with her four kids; this area contact then writes to Sue, welcomes her pending arrival, gives her the pertinent information she's discovered since living in the location, and tells her to let her know if she has any questions. This is not only reassuring to Sue, it is also a service the wife on site has gladly volunteered to provide. The spouses also serve as an important information source for the company. After three months on site, volunteer spouses fill out questionnaires regarding the adequacy of the pre-departure orientation program and of the arrangements for the move. They also provide up-to-date information on costs and availability of goods and services.

Language is an important part of the orientation process for both employees and their spouses. An effective orientation program should include language training for the employee, with provision for additional training by means of tapes, books and/or lessons when the family arrives at the new locale. Even in situations where English is the major language spoken on the jobsite, it is difficult to get a true feel for people's motivations and behavior without an idea of what the language is like. Spouses who must shop, manage servants, take their children to school or visit medical facilities in the new country frequently need more language instruction than the employees themselves.

If several employees are going to the same location on a company assignment, the company can conduct a one- or two-day group orientation consisting of get-acquainted exercises; discussions of pragmatic details (maintaining corporate benefits while overseas, shipping household effects); visual materials presenting a vivid picture of the new locale; descriptions of medical and educational facilities; and lectures and exercises designed to ease culture shock.

In addition to providing orientation, Bechtel gives the departing employees "Assignment Books" that describe the conditions to be found in the new environment. These books discuss everything from geography and climate to social customs, from community facilities to necessary travel documents. Differences between different sections of the country are noted. The employee is given practical information that is designed specifically to prepare him for a change in lifestyle. For example, in *Assignment Indonesia,* he is told that "Indonesians are difficult to get to know . . . you must make the first overtures" and that "The electricity supply is 110–50 cycles, so most of your U.S. appliances will work without a transformer, except those that must operate at a given speed, such as clocks and record players."

The information presented in these books is continuously updated, as one of the most important criteria is accuracy. It is better to present no facts than erroneous facts.

Evaluation is an essential element in any program for managing overseas assignments. At Bechtel, this includes pre-departure questionnaires and, if possible, on-site interviews as well as the previously mentioned "3-month questionnaire." The line managers who supervise the overseas-bound employees should play a part in designing the evaluation process to ensure that the company's specific needs are met.

During the orientation process, the employee is learning what is in store regarding the job responsibilities, career implications, and everything related to living abroad in a particular environment. It is always possible that the employee could decide somewhere along the line that he or she is not enthusiastic about the overseas assignment after all. That employee should be allowed to withdraw gracefully. This process of self-selection prior to the actual relocation will save the company money and should be possible without negative career implications for the candidate who has made an honest self-assessment.

35

Re-entry

Just as the orientation process must honestly confront the probability of
culture shock resulting from moving overseas, the organization should also
prepare the expatriate for another kind of culture shock: that of returning
home after months or years abroad. Frequently, the re-entry problems are
greater than the initial transfer problems. Most people expect to make some
major adjustments when going to live abroad, but they are quite unprepared
for the adjustments they will have to make upon their return to home soil.
This of course makes the adjustment more difficult.

Consider the case of Joe X, a manager who has been on assignment in
Indonesia for two years, accompanied by his wife and son. The family returns
home to California--to find that much has changed. First, because of soaring
real estate prices, they cannot afford housing equivalent to the home they
sold before they left. Second, Joe's old job has disappeared. The company
is willing to put him to work, but the available jobs make no use of his
overseas experience and are not as challenging as the one he had before
going overseas. He feels as though he's been put on the shelf. Besides, his
income has suddenly shrunk drastically (the incentives for the overseas assignment are generous) and the cost of living in the U.S. has leapt upward.

Joe's wife finds that, although learning to get along without servants again
is only a minor problem, she does find it hard to get used to being a nobody
as far as the company is concerned. Abroad, she had been "Mrs XYZ
Company," an important person in the company-dominated environment.

When the son re-enters school, he finds that it has changed. He has been
used to small classes and individualized instruction; now he faces large, less
personal classes. Many of his old friends have moved or graduated. Everyone says, "Tell us all about Indonesia." As he hesitantly reveals some of his
experiences, they listen politely for awhile, then interrupt with, "Say, did
you hear what happened to the Giants last week?"

There are several things a company can do to ease this re-entry shock. A
debriefing in the country prior to departure for the U.S. would help
employees and their families integrate what they have experienced in the
foreign assignment, define what they expect to find when they return to
the U.S., and prepare them for conditions which will have changed during
their absence. A support system in the U.S. could aid the wives in getting
resettled. This should include a "reverse buddy system" of wives who have
recently returned and gone through the experience, as well as company support services sensitive to the needs of relocated families, staffed at least in
part by personnel who have had an overseas experience.

In managing the process of overseas assignments, the term "holistic" should
be applied not only to the programs aimed at the departing employee, but
also to the involvement of management outside of the Corporate Personnel
Department. In designing career paths, in selection, in training and evalua-

tion of training, and in re-integrating the employee into the home environment, the participation of line managers and executives is essential.

Deciding which departing employees should receive orientation is an executive issue, and an important one. Many companies agree to sending their middle managers and supervisors through orientation prior to overseas assignments but do not provide such orientation for senior management, lower level management, or for the business development representatives who are seeking new contracts. As a result, many of these important company representatives--unaware of cultural subtleties--alienate the host country nationals. When this happens, the foreign nationals may well conclude that using American technology is not the only way to meet their needs. Competition in a world of multinationalism is getting stronger; the shots can no longer be called by Americans.

Therefore, close cooperation is necessary between the various staff departments responsible for the overseas transfer process, the candidates for overseas posts, the families and the supervisors of these candidates, and the company's multinational policy makers. If overseas projects are worth the investment in company planning and resources, some percentage of the planning and resources should go toward ensuring that the human element is managed as well as the technological.

4

International Relocation:
A Comprehensive
Psychosocial Approach

Coralyn M. Fontaine

39

Relocation through a job transfer is an adventure for some and a nightmare for others. This is true for the companies requesting the transfer as
well as for the individuals and families concerned. A successful relocation
experience depends largely on psychological and interpersonal factors; these
often receive less attention from employers than compensation, foreign language instruction, and socio-cultural training. EAPs can help employees at
each stage of the national or international relocation process: 1) selection;
2) pre-departure; 3) on-site adjustment; and 4) repatriation.

About two years ago, Corporate Services, a division of Western Psychiatric Institute and Clinic (WPIC) of the University of Pittsburgh began to apply
its mental health expertise to helping families and companies in national
and international relocation processes. The psychosocial issues and needs
in both are similar, but they are intensified in the international case. The
psychosocial concerns of the family and the company at each of the four
stages of the international relocation process are examined as are some mental health interventions developed by Corporate Services to address these
concerns.

From "International Relocation: A Comprehensive Psychosocial Approach" by C. M.
Fontaine, 1983, *EAP Digest*, March/April, pp. 27–31. Copyright 1983 by the Performance
Resource Press, Inc. Reprinted by permission.

The Selection Phase

"We need somebody to go to South Africa to supervise the installation of the new computer system. Jim is the one with the expertise. Get him."

Technical competence is typically the basis for selection of an employee for a foreign assignment. Yet, as many veteran expatriates and international personnel specialists know, psychological and social coping skills are just as important. And what about the spouse and family? Few companies routinely consider them in the selection and decision process. However, a successful assignment is impacted by the spouse's and family's adjustment to the culture--job success and family adjustment are interrelated.

Some executives recognize the impact of the psychosocial factors in making a good selection. Limbach International is a construction firm that sends skilled craftsmen, engineers, and managers to work sites in Saudi Arabia, Germany, and Japan. The firm has brought psychosocial factors into the selection process with the goal of reducing costs. Limbach's president explains, "If I have to replace someone overseas, my direct costs are $30,000–$40,000; indirect costs in consequence to a complex engineering project can add up to $100,000 or more. Just as a person must be screened for engineering or technical skills, so should they have a psychiatric screening to learn about their strengths and weaknesses. I'm a business man and good mental health and good business are not conflicting goals."

To meet selection needs, clinicians at WPIC developed a comprehensive assessment procedure in which the employee and the spouse are assessed by a team individually and then together. The outcome of the assessment is a "suitability score" and eligibility estimate from one to ten indicating the degree to which the person or couple can successfully cope with the foreign assignment. This suitability score is provided to the employer who can decide and weigh whether the potential risk in sending these people is tolerable.

What do clinicians look for in the relocation assessment? Dr. Carol Anderson, one of the designers of the assessment procedure, says, "I think the key issue is not to look for the mentally 'healthiest' person or couple to send, but, rather, to look for a good fit between the person or couple and the assignment. Some of the best adjusted couples that we saw were not recommended to go because it would have been quite devastating for them in terms of what they wanted and what they saw as their goals." One couple, for example, assessed for an assignment in Saudi Arabia, were middle-aged, had a very solid marriage, and were part of a close group of friends. Their strong ties here plus their unrealistic expectations of Saudi life increased the risk of poor adjustment, stress, and possible early repatriation. The man that was sent instead was extremely isolated and had a marriage that was on the lower end of normal in the sense of companionship. Because the company wanted to send him without his wife and he wanted the assignment strictly for the money to buy a house, we felt he was an ideal fit. Clinicians performing these assessments must adjust to looking for "fit" instead of looking for "health."

In another segment of the assessment, each person receives a health risk evaluation, developed by Dr. Richard Jennings, who has researched the impact of the "Type A" personality on susceptibility to stress-related illnesses such as coronary heart disease and hypertension. The effect of a simulated stressful situation on blood pressure and other physiological indicators of stress responses are measured. A medical history is also taken.

Following the "health risk evaluation," each person's coping styles under stress are evaluated. What is the effect of stress on daily habits? Does he or she eat more, drink more alcohol, sleep less, exercise more? How does the person react emotionally to stress? Is he or she energized by the added stimulation or does he become anxious or depressed? Actual behavior in times of stress is explored. Does he or she withdraw or retreat from others or become more irritable and hyperactive? Is he or she able to make use of leisure time as a method of coping and in what ways? A Corporate Services clinician and member of the assessment team, points out that the presence of a significant drug or alcohol problem is predictive of erratic work performance and possible disruption of interpersonal relationships. It can also contribute to the development of significant medical problems.

A comprehensive selection assessment of the kind described above lasts several hours and is something that most company personnel specialists or managers may have neither the skills nor the time to conduct and may feel it inappropriate for them to do so. The mental health professional, on the other hand, can bring expertise to bear in helping the company to weigh the risks of the transfer. He or she can also maintain substantial privacy and confidentiality for the assessed individual or couple. In the Corporate Services assessment, the only information provided to the company is the suitability score and one paragraph describing the pros and cons of the individual or couple succeeding on that particular assignment.

Limbach's selection assessment program and its cost-effectiveness is summed up by its president, "Employers pay for the program whether they have one or not--they pay more for it if they don't have it."

The Pre-Departure Phase
Once an employee is selected for an overseas assignment, stresses may begin to increase as the family faces the implications of the transfer. Young teenagers, who are beginning to cement relationships with peer groups, can have a particularly difficult time making the break from friends and school. Harlan and Jan Holdorf with their four children accepted an assignment to West Africa where Harlan was to install computers for a mining company. Their teenage daughter cried all the way to the airport accompanied by a carload of red-eyed friends. Says Mrs. Holdorf, "The whole neighborhood was crying. Of all of us, she probably had the hardest time saying goodbye."

It is during the pre-departure phase, between the time of having been offered the assignment and leaving, that the unresolved marital issues or family concerns may surface. A family may feel the need to clarify their decision and plan together how they will handle the stress of relocation. An option that some experienced personnel specialists offer is the opportunity for transition counseling with a mental health professional.

The Corporate Services approach to transition counseling is to meet with the couple or family and help them to clarify their expectations of each other and of the cross-cultural experience, to anticipate the stress points in their relationships during the assignment and to begin to plan and prepare for them. In transition counseling (as distinct from relocation assessments), no information is sent to the company and the purpose is solely for the individual's or family's own self-exploration, decision-making, and anticipatory stress planning. This confidentiality consideration can produce a dilemma for the transition counselor especially if a psychosocial assessment was a part of the relocation selection process. For example, during the single transition counseling session that a company had offered, the clinician became aware that the wife had a serious depression, drank excessively and that she and her husband were about to be sent to a very isolated overseas situation where access to professional help was minimal. This combination of factors was identified by the clinician as a serious potential problem for them; and, had it been a selection assessment rather than transition counseling, the clinician might have recommended to the company that they not go.

While a selection assessment is the most effective way to avoid such unfortunate situations, the company might provide the option for more than one transition counseling session so that issues raised can be more fully dealt with by the family. Another intervention technique during this pre-departure phase is an experiential workshop for two or more families to provide perspective. Using case examples and discussions of expectations and coping mechanisms, participants have a chance to share their hopes, fears, and learning in a non-threatening, educational setting.

While the pre-departure phase can be a time of psychological stress and uncertainty, it can also be a time of great excitement and anticipation. Many families experienced in international relocation have found that a vacation on the way is a very effective way to relax and manage the transitional stress because it provides time between home and arrival at the new location to assimilate the changes of the move. The Holdorfs, in preparing for relocation to West Africa, saw the transfer as an opportunity to visit Europe and Africa with their four children. In the author's experience of relocating to Australia for three years, a stopover of several days in Polynesia helped to slow down the rapid transition produced by a move now made in hours by air as compared to weeks by ship.

On-site Adjustment Phase

International relocations intensify stress reactions because they may combine the extremes of cross-cultural impact, distance from social support systems, and the greater dependency of family members on each other for emotional support in the foreign environment. Yet, the families interviewed for this article met these challenges in creative ways and turned the foreign experience into a rewarding adventure.

One of the creative approaches that Britisher John Stening of U.S. Steel and his wife have found is to avoid comparison. As veterans of several overseas assignments and currently expatriates in the U.S., they "made a pact that we would never compare home with the new culture. There is no direct comparison. Once you compare, you become dissatisfied. It's a no-win situation." Appreciating the influences of each cultural experience rather than succumbing to the temptation to compare "better" and "worse" lends a freshness to the experience and helps the expatriate family to avoid the destructive complaining of some expatriate communities.

Most families who go overseas for the first time are unprepared for the emotional impact of adjusting to a foreign culture. Experts in the cross-cultural field have identified a predictable "up-and-down" emotional cycle that seems to occur for expatriates regardless of the particular foreign culture. On arrival, there is a "high" period lasting a week to a month or so, followed by a "low" period of two to three months characterized by irritability and hostility. Under optimal circumstances this is followed by gradual psychological adjustment to the cultural differences. Typically, a little over halfway through the span of the assignment comes another emotional "low" point often of greater severity, in some cases a depression. This emotional cycle is so predictable that families can be prepared for these otherwise inexplicable and frightening changes through pre-departure workshops or transition counseling.

How do people who are not prepared for the psychological impact try to cope? One of the more dangerous ways of attempting to cope with the cycle is alcohol. In reflecting on their two and a half year stint in Africa, the Holdorfs note that, among the scores of expatriate American families in their town, "There was an awful lot of drinking. I can't think of anybody who didn't drink at all. You can't imagine how cheap it was and it was always there. One couple we knew went through a serious problem that unfortunately still exists. What added to the problem was not only was there nothing else to do, there was nothing else to spend the money on."

Raul Suarez, vice president of Limbach International, and his wife observed alcohol being used as a "refuge" by expatriates in such countries as the Philippines and Singapore. Unfortunately, as Suarez points out, "On many foreign assignments, there is no access to help and the problem goes unrecognized." The Holdorfs add, "If it got bad enough, the boss might tell the guy to watch it, but there was no systematic, organized way to help. It

43

was between the boss and the employee. Sometimes, people would go on medical leaves if it got really bad."

Exacerbating the problem is the fact that, as Dr. Carrol Curtis, Director of Health Policies and Practices for Westinghouse Electric Corporation and himself a former expatriate in Ghana and Guatemala puts it, "In such situations, drinking is viewed as 'understandable'; i.e., it's a hard place. Thus, the expatriate community atmosphere is often very permissive about alcohol. This is combined with a greater opportunity to cover up and get away with an alcohol problem since the boss may also drink too much."

Dr. Curtis estimates alcoholism in expatriate communities to be at least twice as high as in the home country. Out of concern for these human and organizational problems, he developed a corporate alcoholism program at Westinghouse. He recently returned from the Philippines where he and a recovering alcoholic presented a program to raise awareness among expatriates on how to recognize and intervene in alcohol problems through performance documentation and referral for treatment.

The accompanying spouse may be particularly at risk for alcohol as well as stress-related mental health problems overseas, since there is less opportunity for effective intervention with her. As John Stening says, "All problems are harder on the wife." The stresses of an international relocation present unique challenges to the spouse who is usually not allowed to work in the foreign country due to lack of a work permit and does not have the built-in support structure and company identity of the employed spouse. At times, the sense of uselessness is aggravated by company attitudes towards the wife as "excess baggage." The psychological impact can be quite significant. When Rosemary Suarez was in Singapore, she says, "It reflected my self-esteem and I experienced feelings of dependency on my husband. So I began teaching English privately and acquired a car to provide me with some independence."

For many accompanying spouses, especially those who are used to working outside the home, having little to do during the overseas assignment can intensify the emotional "down" cycles or disrupt adjustment to the culture. Says Mrs. Green, a librarian who accompanied her husband on a year's foreign assignment to a university in Israel, "I had nothing to do. After three months, I was depressed and found myself sitting at home and staring at the wall. Of course, this also had an impact on my husband." She resolved the situation by starting to work on a voluntary basis at the university library as a librarian and by taking intensive Hebrew language training courses. While in Ghana, Dr. Curtis' wife worked in an orphanage and taught in a missionary school. As a result of this successful coping strategy, both women consider the foreign experience to have been very positive. Mrs. Green is looking forward to an upcoming assignment in Switzerland with her husband. Now that she knows what to expect psychologically, she plans to look for volunteer work at the outset.

44

Another important coping skill on a foreign assignment is being able to take the initiative in forming social relationships. Again, this is particularly crucial for the spouse since the transferred employee's job provides a basis for some of his relationships. The non-working spouse faces the challenge of having to establish her own social-psychological supports. Doing this effectively has enabled some people to experience the assignment as a holiday, as Jan Holdorf did in West Africa and South America through an active involvement in community sports and group activities which involved the whole family.

Relocation services are of special interest to Lee Faught, director of Corporate Services at WPIC. She lived overseas for ten years in both Europe and the Middle East. As the spouse of an international business consultant, she found that "creating a positive home and family atmosphere is what makes relocation an adventure in living and learning." She notes that it often becomes the spouse's role to be "substitute doctor, teacher, recreation consultant and foreign culture expert. The decisions have to be made alone because the father and husband is incommunicado on a work-site."

Living an expatriate life often puts additional strains on a marriage. As Rosemary and Raul Suarez say about their experience in expatriate living, "It can split people up, especially the wife's hardship. There were lots of problems that could have broken us. Yet, we also have more to share, and this draws us closer."

45

One challenge to a relationship comes from the tight-knit quality and frequent isolation of the expatriate community itself. Jan Holdorf, reflecting on her experience in West Africa says, "There were quite a few of the people that we knew who either split up or exchanged partners because of the closeness that everybody had there. Other than sports and being with each other, there was no other outlet. There were other attractive couples in the community as well as single males and females for whom it was a lonely life. With no other diversions, we saw a number of basically very young marriages go down the drain."

While these potential stresses do exist, the expatriate period can also draw families closer together emotionally. As Harlan Holdorf says of his experience with his four children in Africa and South America, "I wasn't that close to the kids and probably have not been that close again since we've come back to the States because I get all wrapped up in my own work. But one thing I found out over there is that I could get closer to my kids and get along better with them than I had anticipated."

Children, at least those below the teenage years, typically have the easiest time adjusting to the cross-cultural experience. Todd Holdorf, now seventeen, who was eight when he left for West Africa, says, "I suppose I was against it at first, wanting to stay here with everybody I knew. But it was great over there. I'd go back in a minute."

Younger children usually adapt relatively well to being uprooted from their friends and peers. However, the teenager who is beginning to cement peer relationships and develop an adult identity often has the most difficult time. Besides leaving friends at home, overseas they must assimilate into a school where groups are already formed. By college age, however, an international move may become easier again, as a greater independence from the high school peer group is attained and a stronger sense of personal identity is formed. By and large, a lot can be learned by adults and teenagers from young children's attitudes and flexibility.

The Repatriation Phase

Surprisingly, coming home is often the most stressful phase of an international relocation and is the least recognized as such by companies, relocation consultants, and novice repatriates. Returning expatriates experience an unanticipated "reverse culture shock." The new experiences and perspectives gained abroad mean that home is never the same again. Family and friends who have not been overseas ask what it was like in the foreign country and as the person begins to share the experiences, the listeners' eyes glaze over and they begin looking around distractedly. Well meaning as they may be, they cannot relate to the experience.

In fundamental ways, being abroad for extended periods of time changes people. As Harland Holdorf says of his return after five years overseas, "Suddenly I became aware of how much our perspectives, our observations, our sense of values had changed. And to this day, though it's not as acute anymore, I still notice it." The Holdorfs, like the Suarez family and others now socialize mainly with former expatriates or foreign nationals who share their perspectives.

In the repatriation phase, the high school age teenager typically has the most difficult time, again for the same reasons as in leaving the peer group initially and adjusting to a foreign culture. Miriam Green returned with her parents from a year in Israel at age fourteen. She had become very attached to her peer group in Israel after a difficult initial adjustment. She sums up her repatriation experience well: "I didn't want to come back. When I did, the groups in my high school were closed and difficult to break into. Not only that, but they asked me such things as whether we rode camels over there and then didn't want to listen to what it was really like. I went to a counselor who said I had outgrown the kids here, but things didn't really get better until a year later when I went to a private school that was more cosmopolitan." Still, Miriam views the international relocation as having been very positive for her. Now eighteen, she attributes her choice of a university major in international studies to her cross-cultural exposure. She is enthusiastically preparing to take her junior year of college abroad in Switzerland during her parents' next foreign assignment there.

Most returning expatriates don't expect the reverse culture shock syndrome, and, therefore, often don't know how to cope with it. Companies and returning expatriates alike seem to turn a blind eye to this phase. As Barnes of Westinghouse says, "I try to tell people about what to expect on return, but they don't listen. Few people are interested in this most difficult phase because of the excitement associated with coming 'home'." Psychosocial interventions through workshops involving veteran repatriates can be particularly valuable at this point.

The returning employee typically faces some hurdles back on the job stateside. One of these is "job shrink." As Stening points out, "On an overseas assignment, you typically have more decision-making power and autonomy and you don't realize that until you get back to less." Barnes adds, "You're unique overseas, special. Returning home often means a reduction in status. You're now one of many." Sometimes, returning expatriates feel that they are called upon by management to prove themselves again even though they may have been rated overseas on the same performance rating system as the United States employees.

Despite the stresses and challenges of an overseas assignment, most people view the experience as a unique opportunity for growth, especially when given adequate assistance in the psychosocial aspects of relocation. As Stening puts it, "Going overseas is a great opportunity; yet the positive elements may not be apparent until your return."

How EAPs Can Help

47

EAPs are in an ideal position to provide assistance to relocating employees and their families. Presently there are very few relocation service providers and almost none that approach the problem from a psychosocial framework. Most services available are usually oriented to cross-cultural training, languages, or housing. Consequently, approaching the human issues of relocation through adjunct or additional services of broadbrush EAPs is a logical avenue through which corporations and mental health providers can help.

Drawing upon the resources of WPIC and the University, Corporate Services is in the process of developing a relocation center having the ability to coordinate the expertise of the University of Pittsburgh's schools of business and international relations as well as the language departments. With this growth in mind, contacts have been made with counseling centers in other countries that could provide mental health services for overseas American personnel. Also planned are some much needed educational films to help families and managers handle the psychological aspects of relocation.

EAP practitioners and providers can assist individuals, families and companies through their mental health and human service expertise at all stages of relocation, from the selection of low-risk candidates for transfer, to predeparture counseling or workshops, to international treatment resources, to repatriation workshops or counseling. From Corporate Services' experience, it is evident that mental health professionals have a definite and important role to play.

5

Return to Society: Problematic Features of the Re-Entry Process

Diane P. Jansson

Countless individuals leave the social system in which they were living, and often do not return until a prison term is completed, a prolonged hospitalization is finished, or a period of voluntary service in another country is completed. Regardless of the person's reason for having left, a relatively common process takes place when he attempts to re-enter his former social system. During his absence, the person changes, for presumably he is carrying on his life in a way unlike the lives of those he left behind (Miller, undated; Lifton, 1973). His self-system and the former social system are each moving forward, though on divergent paths.

Re-entry is the process that occurs when the individual attempts to return to the social system of which he was once a part. In re-entering the former social system, he may try to regain his former status, or because his values have shifted while away he may reject his former position and try to redefine his relationship to those around him. In either case, the re-entry process is likely to be slow, painful, and under certain circumstances, terrifying.

As a graduate student in the Ohio State University Psychiatric Mental Health Nursing Program, I had the opportunity to observe the behavior of a group of people undergoing the re-entry process. I worked with the staff

From "Return to Society: Problematic Features of the Re-Entry Process" by D. P. Jansson, 1975, *Perspectives in Psychiatric Care, 13*(3), pp. 136–142. Copyright 1975 by Nursing Publications, Inc. Reprinted by permission.

in the general program and in group therapy sessions in three community agencies and collected additional information through interviews and personal experience as a returned Peace Corps volunteer. The re-entrant population included ex-convicts at a halfway house for former offenders, former mental patients at the Intermediate Care Unit of a local community health center, six returned Peace Corps volunteers, and two ex-nuns. In my work with these re-entrants I was able to identify certain behaviors and problems that appeared to be shared by most members of the group. I will describe here some problematic features of the re-entry process, and suggest ways to assist the re-entrant during this difficult and crucial period.

Re-Entry Issues and Suggested Intervention

The Deviant Identity

The person about to re-enter a social system can be viewed as one who has deviated from that system's social norms, regardless of whether his departure from the system is judged commendable (as with armed forces and Peace Corps overseas service), or unacceptable (as with imprisonment or psychiatric hospitalization). In most cases, there is a shift in values, a portion of "history" that is not mutually shared, and behaviors which differ from those expected within the social system. The re-entrant is in the minority and is, in a sense, defined by those who remained in the group. It might be more obvious to identify former offenders or mental patients as deviant, but the label can be applied to others, such as the veteran who has clung to his "war ethic" in peacetime, a Peace Corps volunteer who has adopted the values and customs of the host country, or the ex-clergy, who refute society's expectation of "life-time commitment."

50

> Social groups create deviance by making the rules whose infraction constitutes deviance, and by applying those rules to particular people and labeling them as outsiders. . . . Deviance is not a quality of the act the person commits, but rather a consequence of the application by others of the rules and sanctions to an "offender." The deviant is one to whom that label has successfully been applied; deviant behavior is behavior that people so label (Becker, 1963).

The re-entrant may incorporate this label into his self-concept, thus acquiring a deviant identity. Scheff (1966, p. 54) labeled this phenomenon "residual deviance." Labels such as "ex-nun," "ex-con," or "former psychiatric patient," and the like testify to the fact that the former status is used as the point of reference when identifying many re-entrants. Thus, the re-entrant to a social system is confronted not only with a different world from the one he knew, but also with a different identity, in his own eyes and others'. All these changes, whether for commendable or unacceptable reasons, compounded by the loosening of social bonds caused by absence, can produce anxiety in the re-entrant and in members of the social system.

Goffman (1968) suggests that if the re-entrant has access to a "significant other," who can put in a "good word" for him and help him to develop a "once deviant, now well" (or at least "reabsorbed") identity, the stage could be set for a stable community career. Goffman also enumerates three other social system elements that are necessary for successful re-entry: (1) equipment, that is, a place to go and a source of support; (2) a strong "significant other," who will constantly reassure the re-entrant that he is able to resume active family and community life and is capable of being a whole and adequate person; and (3) a spontaneous environment in which the re-entrant is neither patronized nor protected. Such social-system supports are designed to counteract the negative effects of the deviant identity, especially the subtle expectation of failure.

Euphoria/Denial
In some cases, the feeling of freedom, the anticipation of beginning a new life, or the sense of having paid a debt to society can cause the re-entrant to experience elation, or even euphoria. "I'm free--a new person!" In his elation over the prospect of a new beginning, the re-entrant may go to great lengths to conceal all traces of his former, that is, deviant, identity. I have often seen re-entrants who desired a completely new wardrobe. Prison shoes are discarded, though there is nothing about them that would indicate that the person had been incarcerated. One man said, "I know this is silly but I feel that if people see me with cuffed pants, they'll know I've been in prison." Another man went to expensive and painful lengths to eradicate the tattoos he had acquired while in prison. Frequently, rigorous efforts are made to take off the weight gained while out of the system in order to conform to the standards of the reference group. In *Stigma, Notes on the Management of a Spoiled Identity*, Goffman (1961, pp. 41–48) refers to these gestures as efforts to convey or hide certain social information. They are efforts to "fill out" an image in a particular way, and to disassociate oneself from elements in one's past.

51

During the period of euphoria, the re-entrant tends to focus only on the positive aspects of his return to the social system, while denying the potential problems of adjustment. This is often the period when he will try to prove to himself that nothing has changed in his absence, or if changes have occurred, that he has at least kept pace with them. In most cases, however, the re-entrant has not shared a common history with others in the social system to which he is returning, and there is some "catching up" to do. As Miller points out in her monograph,

[The re-entrant] . . . must pick up the main threads of his life again after several weeks, months, or even years of community moratorium. He is forced to be, in some degree, dependent upon others and to an extent to define himself as others define him. He comes from a previously established routine of living into a world which has been functioning without him. In a sense, he finds himself tangential to the central life of the social system. Following a brief period of optimism, the salient and significant others are confronted with austere realities and conflicting expectations.

Although this period has been described as a critical one, it can be a period of change and growth. Obviously, each person will face the re-entry situation differently and with his own fears and expectations. Although it is important to intervene in the network of relationships, which include the re-entrant's family, significant others, and the community, Tyhurst (1957, p. 168) maintains that the most effective intervention can be accomplished *prior* to re-entry. The nurse and other helping persons can assist the re-entrant to define the new situation and to identify specific things which need to be done in order for him to cope with the outside world. Tyhurst advocates "trial settings" to bring the individual's assumptions closely in line with reality. In prison, for example, the offender anticipating release could role-play a situation in which he is frisked by a local policeman while his date stands and watches. The hospital patient could be encouraged to imagine a stressful situation and helped to "walk through" problem-solving techniques. Pre-release and weekend programs also provide an opportunity for the transition to be made, but I believe that unless personnel intervene directly to analyze potential difficulties and provide situational supports for the re-entrant and his family, pre-release efforts can amount to little more than a weaning process.

The main difficulty of intervening at this stage is that the re-entrant may be denying what is about to happen to him. Tyhurst notes this difficulty in trying to prepare people for imminent stressor events in their lives. I, too, observed this phenomenon in ex-convicts whose main concern was getting out of prison and "off-paper" (finished with parole). They paid little attention to what this process would entail; the difficulties of re-establishing family relations and finding employment were often avoided until the last moment before release.

52

Anger
When the re-entrant begins to confront the harsh realities of returning to the system, such as lack of personal successes and inability to find a job, his euphoria may be replaced by anger--at himself, at others, and at the system he believes has victimized him. In speaking of transitional states, Tyhurst maintains that "actions in the new setting lead to an increasing sense of incongruity between the individual's frame of reference and the society around him. Characteristically, there is increasing anxiety and depression, self-preoccupation, somatic symptoms, hostility and suspicion" (p. 149).

Unfortunately, society does not always recognize anger as a constructive mechanism which allows the individual to express his feelings, then go forward in meeting other needs. To many people, anger indicates loss of control and reinforces preconceived notions that the re-entrant is deviant. Lifton (1973, pp. 140–45) identifies anger as the dominant feeling among the Vietnam veterans he studied. Some veterans were able to ventilate their anger directly through "rap" sessions; others transmitted it through art or other modes of creative expression.

That anger must be ventilated is well-known to members of the helping professions, yet re-entrants are offered little opportunity to deal with this emotion. For example, many former offenders state their intention to remain on "good behavior" until they finish parole. Certainly this idea is pragmatic, yet one wonders what happens to the anger resulting from discouragement when a job cannot be found, and to unexpressed feelings dating back to the prison experience.

Intervention at the time when reality hits can make the difference between regression and growth. When the re-entrant realizes that his expectations cannot be fully met, he can be helped to establish more realistic goals. The helping person can convey acceptance of the re-entrant's anger by allowing him to ventilate it, and can encourage its expression through acceptable forms, such as the arts and the media. Channeling anger through these forms can serve to educate the public about the needs and feelings of many groups of re-entrants.

As the re-entrant becomes discouraged and angry, emphasis should be placed on his accomplishments. In the midst of coping with the great obstacles placed in the way of successful re-entry, small accomplishments are easily overlooked. The re-entrant should be encouraged to review his gains and evaluate their contribution to his long-term goals. For example, a former psychiatric patient became angry when members of the intermediate care program which she was attending told her to paint a mural. She regarded her anger as a regression to "old ways." As a staff member in her group therapy session, I allowed her to express her anger at the demand to paint and at herself, then helped her to realize what she had accomplished since her discharge from the hospital. She was, on her own initiative, working as a hospital volunteer, preparing to take a high school equivalency examination, and negotiating enrollment in a commercial art school. It was necessary to keep the reality of these accomplishments in the forefront, since she tended to deny them whenever her behavior did not meet her own expectations of "wellness."

Sense of Powerlessness
Nearly every re-entrant I spoke with mentioned a sense of powerlessness in coping with a world that had continued without him during his absence. First, the re-entrant must face physical changes in the environment. The sight of tall buildings and heavy traffic amazes all, and is terrifying for some. The inflationary economy further reinforces feelings of powerlessness, since the period of transition is usually one of limited financial resources. Such feelings may be equivalent to a "fall into helplessness," the term used by Seligman (1973) to describe depression. Since the re-entrant first depends upon previous patterns of behavior which were successful in the old

53

environment, the realization that these are now unsuccessful in dealing with the present environment can reinforce the sense of powerlessness. His frustration increases through unsuccessful attempts to act.

Attachment to a reference group can be a beneficial experience at this point. Through the sharing of his experiences and feelings with others who have been in a similar situation, the re-entrant can gain perspective, receive support, and learn of tested solutions to common problems. For some re-entrants, access to a group such as Recovery, Inc., a self-help program for former psychiatric patients, can have much more meaning than professional intervention. This organization systematically integrates the concept of self-help into its group meetings. There is no pitying, no pampering, and no "giving in" to feelings. Self-endorsement is required (Lee, 1970).

One patient, who had been hospitalized for psychiatric difficulties, experienced terrifying feelings of inadequacy and threatening impulses after discharge. One day, while doing the laundry, she realized that even this task was too great for her. After a period with Recovery, Inc., she stated that she learned to go on in spite of her feelings, and to understand that although these feelings would remain with her, she could control and overcome them and not consider them evidence of a need to return to the hospital.

The Seventh Step Foundation, a group composed mainly of former offenders, also relies on the reference group as its mode of assistance. Group meetings are held weekly within the prison prior to the inmate's release. Upon leaving prison, the re-entrant can attend group meetings of the local chapter of the organization. This group has been quite successful in job placement for former offenders, and appears to supply them with situational supports without violating the philosophy of self-help to which they are committed.

Fear of Rejection, Regression, and Guilt
Self-help groups such as those described can also assist the re-entrant to cope with fear of rejection, regressive behavior, and guilt feelings associated with the deviant identity.

Underlying the re-entry process from the very beginning is the possibility of rejection. Some re-entrants cope with the fear of rejection by assuming a deferential posture. For others, withdrawal is more comforting. If the re-entrant involves himself only minimally with others, the possibility of rejection is reduced. The danger here, however, is that extreme withdrawal, whether motivated by actual rejection or the fear of it, can lead to regressive or backsliding behavior.

Wiseman (1970) illustrates the concept of backsliding with the example of the recovering alcoholic, who finds his probationary status as a family member or employee more than he can handle upon return from treatment. When the stress becomes too great, and the threat of rejection is imminent, he seeks solace in an environment (such as a group of drinking buddies) where there is some comfort from the struggle to change and from the expectations of family or employer.

For many guilt plays a significant part in the dynamics of the re-entry process. Lifton (pp. 128–29) differentiates between *static* and *animating guilt*. He defines the former as "self-condemnation for one's responsibility in the breakdown of human connection and order. Animating guilt involves probing the roots of failure and exposing the self to the self." He believes it is better for the individual to come to grips with the past and use the situation as an experience for learning and growth than to engage in self-condemnation and try to numb the shame.

A 59-year-old man, who had spent most of his adult life in prison, was a re-entrant whose behavior was dominated by static, rather than animating guilt. He rarely used the term "prison," but would refer to his incarceration as "when I was over there." Only twice in the twelve times we met did he ever refer to how he viewed himself. In both instances, his statement was succinct: "Sometimes I get disgusted with myself," after which, without speaking further, he would leave the interview with tears in his eyes. His usual behavior was consistently deferential and dominated by his need to please other people. It seemed that he had not had the opportunity to face and accept his past. His self-image was based on how others viewed him in the present.

55

Immobilization/Recidivism

Many re-entrants are returning to the social system after a period of institutionalization. In *Asylums,* Goffman (1961) has developed the concept of the "total institution," a label that can be applied to mental hospitals, prison, the armed services, and so on. He defines the total institution as a "place of residence and work where a number of individuals in similar situations are cut off from the wider society and lead an enclosed, formally administered life. The key fact of the total institution is that many human needs of whole blocs of people are under bureaucratic control. The staff is concerned with surveillance; the inmates with conformity." This conformity is often the key to insure survival within the system. It also partly explains recidivism in mental and penal institutions, and the rate of return of some former members of the armed services to career status (Shiloh, 1968).

A member of a total institution is required to make few decisions relative to his everyday life. Within his institutional world, regardless of how unpleasant and devoid of amenities it may be, he is assured of shelter and food. He pays no bills, nor does he worry about making a monthly paycheck stretch to cover all necessities. It is small wonder that a return to the fast-paced, urban, American culture can cause immobilization in some re-entrants and recidivism in others.

Immobilization is often a period of recoil after being bombarded with continuous and unexpected stimuli. A wife of a career Navy officer, who spent most of her married life in military housing installations, is a case in point. Following her divorce, she was hospitalized for confusion and depression. Upon release from the hospital, she found it exceedingly difficult to carry on the basic duties of everyday living, including managing the checking account, furnishing a household, and shopping. She depended on her son to perform all household necessities. On learning that he would marry within the year, she began to exhibit many of her pre-hospitalization symptoms. She was enrolled in the Intermediate Care Program, and in addition to individual and group therapy, was helped to practice basic life-activities to prepare her for her new, but reluctantly accepted, independence. As a product of two bureaucratic socialization systems, the armed services and the psychiatric hospital, her re-entry and relearning were more complicated than most.

Intimacy Problems
Lifton (pp. 267–279) views difficulty with sustained intimacy as an additional consequence of institutionalization. He attributes this to the fact that the psychological work as a survivor (of a previous system) is so demanding as to preclude, at least for a time, sustained intimacy or long-range personal commitment. "Drying out" is the term frequently used to describe the process.

56   In assisting the re-entrant to develop or redevelop a capacity for intimacy, the helping person can serve as a role model of one who cares. The nurse especially, perhaps more than the social worker or the parole officer, can represent the accepting, non-authoritarian person in the life of a re-entrant. Glasser (1972), like Goffman, maintains that acquisition of a successful identity is contingent upon involvement with at least one successful person. In the stress-filled period of re-entry, when family members might not be able to fill this role, the nurse can provide the involvement that will validate the client's new self. As Glasser states,

> The person being helped must begin to understand that there is more to life than being involved with his misery, symptoms, obsessive thoughts or irresponsible behavior. He must see that another human being cares for him. . . . Any subject can provide the warmth and give-and-take relationship that help a "failing" person learn that he can be accepted by and accepting of another human being (p. 108).

There is no doubt that the re-entry process is difficult under the best of circumstances. Obviously the duration and degree of difficulty will differ as each re-entrant faces the situation with his own fears and expectations. Goffman's three requirements of a source of support, a strong "significant other," and a spontaneous environment serve as a practical guide in planning intervention. Re-entrants need to define for themselves who and what will be their source of support, but for most, a reference group is found to be most helpful. The reference group can serve as a forum for exchange of information, expression of feeling, and support from those who have had a similar experience. This is especially important if the re-entrant is some-what skeptical that a professional could have an understanding of his problems. Recovery, Inc., Seventh Step Foundation, and Dr. Lifton's "rap groups" serve this purpose. Also, quite simply, there is need for socialization, which is more easily accomplished with a reference group than with a sin-gle individual as a source of support. At least one caring person or "significant other" can provide the validation of the re-entrant's ideas, aid in problem solving where necessary, accept occasional backsliding, and minimize discouragement.

A spontaneous environment is perhaps more difficult for the re-entrant to achieve, although larger social-system changes along the lines of public education, job placement programs, and community-based facilities are just beginning to initiate change in this direction. As a further step, I would sup-port legislation that would have the record of a first offender expunged after a period of five years so that he not over-identify with the label of "ex-con" for the remainder of his life. The difficulty experienced by the stigmatized person of any kind in trying to find employment speaks to the therapeutic value of such legislation.

References

Becker, J. S. (1963). *Outsiders* (p. 9). New York: Free Press.

Glasser, W. (1972). *The identity society.* New York: Harper & Row.

Goffman, E. (1961a). *Asylums.* Garden City, NY: Anchor Books.

Goffman, E. (1961b). *Stigma, notes on the management of a spoiled identity.* New York: Anchor Books.

Goffman, E. (1968, Spring). Unpublished lecture. University of California at Berkeley.

Lee, D. T. (1971). Recovery, Inc., Aid in the transition from hospital to community. *Mental Hygiene, 55,* 194–198.

Lifton, R. J. (1973). *Home from the war.* New York: Simon & Schuster.

Miller, D. (undated). *Worlds that fail, Parts I and II.* State of California Department of Men-tal Hygiene, Bureau of Research, Research Monograph No. 6.

Scheff, T. J. (1966). *Being mentally ill, a sociological theory.* Chicago: Aldine.

Seligman, M. E. (1973, June). Fall into helplessness. *Psychology Today,* pp. 43–48.

Seventh Step Foundation, National Office, 28 East 8th Street, Cincinnati, OH 45202.

Shiloh, A. (1968, December). Sanctuary or prison--Responses to life in a mental hospital. *Transaction, Social Science and Modern Society,* 28–31.

Tyhurst, J. S. (1957, April). The role of transition states--including disasters--in mental illness. In *Symposium on Preventive and Social Psychiatry.* Washington, DC: Walter Reed Army Hos-pital Institute of Research.

Wiseman, J. (1970). *Stations of the lost: The treatment of skid row alcoholics.* NJ: Prentice-Hall.

Unit B

Federally Employed Citizens

Federally Employed Citizens

Federally employed citizens live in a complex and often hostile world overseas. Many officials, officers, and their wives must participate in elaborate and demanding social circles. Terrorists may blow up their pets and mailboxes in a series of harassing attacks, or worse, the lives of these public servants might be threatened at spasmodic intervals.

Some military personnel live on a designated base; others live "on the economy." Their children may attend a Department of Defense (DOD) school, international school, or private national school. The drug problem may be overwhelming in any of these schools. Vietnam veterans walking along Main Street may be asked, "How many women and children have you killed today?" RPCVs may be told that their PCV experience is "not relevant" for an unexpectedly large number of civilian jobs. It is against this vivid and unforgettable backdrop that the authors in Unit II discuss their comrades.

The plight of the diplomatic returnee, as cleverly described by Boley in Chapter 6, revolves around four problems: (1) he has become "intellectually highfalutin"; (2) he has met celebrities while living abroad; (3) he is a speaker of foreign languages; and (4) he must learn "how to graft the bloom of Europe upon the stem of the United States and produce that rare flower, the good life, his own hybrid."

Perry gives fascinating attention to the diplomatic home leave in Chapter 7. In a captivating manner, home leave is exquisitely defined as a"'floating' --trying to be home and not making it." In part, diplomats are appraised as being "campers," experts on cultural relativity, addicts to information, professional aliens, but recipients of the gifts of wonder, independence and friends. Those who have lived overseas will find this article identifiable and emotionally touching.

In Chapter 8, Sidey, in heartrending eloquence, etches on the reader's heart the meaning of affluence. He narrates the "plunder of China" by the American reporters during President Nixon's 1972 China odyssey. His diminutive interpreter hovered over him day and night, patiently answering his questions. Although she was the wife of an official in the defense ministry, she was "on hand" daily in her blue cloth coat and black pants. He contrasts the silent, unforgettable welcome and farewell granted by Chou to Nixon with the kingly fanfare accorded Nixon in Washington.

In Chapter 9, Longsworth explores the contribution of the RPCV to his own country. The deep-seated, enduring influence in the volunteer's life occurs because of the element of challenge and the resulting self-confidence; the confrontation with poverty; the experience of cultural relativity; the demand of the PC to do one's best; and the opportunity to see yourself as others see you. Like jewels in a tasteful necklace, Longworth's series of exemplary anecdotes provide "flesh and blood" to the homeward flow of PCVs. The study reveals that the most significant contributions of RPCVs have been in the field of education.

As a result of her own experiences with reverse culture shock, Koehler in Chapter 10 is led to conduct a study of the problem among military families. She found that she was not alone in believing that once "back home," life again would be perfect and problem-free. Service wives indicate that recovering from reverse culture shock takes from six months to two years or longer. Reentry shock appears to affect military wives and children far more than their active duty husbands and fathers. None of the women in the study received any form of reentry orientation prior to reentry.

62

Sobie, in chapter 11, astutely draws on her family's overseas reentry from Scotland and selected interviews with DOD representatives to depict vividly returnee stresses. Specific efforts of the U. S. Navy, Air Force and Army to deal with the issues of relocation are noted. To underscore the magnitude of the challenge, Sobie records that 81,000 soldiers and their families moved back to the United States in 1984 after an overseas tour.

In Chapter 12, Faulkner and McGaw, on the basis of observations and interviews with twenty Vietnam soldiers, capture the essence of the homecoming experience. The authors affirm that three interrelated concerns constitute the reality of their homecoming: (1) disengagement and the process of "moving from" the war, (2) reentry and the process of "moving back into" "The World," and (3) reintegration and the concern with "moving toward" the consolidation of social involvement and binding separations. Homecoming is seen as a status passage which is affected by the veteran's feelings and perceptions. His emotional world may be severely impacted by the death of several buddies. It may be difficult, if not impossible, to describe their loss. Because his psychological development was interrupted by the war, upon reentry he may struggle with identity concerns while grappling with issues of intimacy in marriage. He may be excluded from once-secure social groups. He is often denied the support of extended social networks.

6

On the Art of
Coming Home

Jean Boley

It is certainly appropriate that we as a nation are represented by a matron
in New York harbour. It should surprise no one that in America, Liberty is
immortalized in bronze by a dignified figure on fire with the cause. She is,
in fact, the ideal clubwoman, the supreme example of the national genius,
carrying that fervour which begins humbly in any small town where the
ladies, considering Reciprocal Trade Treaties, bog down slowly in a morass
of angel food cake--carrying that fervour to its logical conclusion, a salute
to the world.

Now the Statue of Liberty ought to restore confidence and a sense of security in any American returning after years abroad. To look at her is to
remember suddenly the details of liberty, as well as ice cream, warm houses,
and that sorely missed lust of the flesh, the hearty breakfast. But the art of
coming home is, alas, not just a matter of the old stimuli reviving the old
response. Living abroad for many years there creeps over the simple American the most indecent complexities. Once straightforward, he now feels
devious. Once open, he is now obscure. A decade ago he sailed away in a
polo coat and a buoyant red necktie. "Today he returns in a chesterfield
with a mysterious foulard cravat" upon which one of the more obscure one-
celled organisms has been rendered by the hundreds in diluted shades of

From "On the Art of Coming Home" by J. Boley, 1948, *The American Foreign Service
Journal*, 25 (8), pp. 12–14. Reprinted by permission.

mustard and rust. A decade ago he shrieked "Kill the ump!" and passed out afterwards in the Astor Bar. Today he plays a spot of tennis at Hurlingham and remembers to pour the milk first in his cup of tea. And now, passing the Statue in New York harbour, while the eyes of all sound persons are filled with tears he finds himself facing that tireless female with the same trembling bravado he always hopes will be effective in a fight with his wife.

When a husband returns to his old wife, after a long stay abroad free of restraint he is apt to develop new resolutions about independence. There is to be no more dishwashing in ruffled aprons, and the guest bedroom is not to be inhabited by Aunt Lou and her false teeth resting like some grotesque marine life at the bottom of a glass of water. . . . And so he attacks, too desperately, as befits one who is doomed before he starts by the enemy's mere tonnage and poundage.

To the astonishment of the American, coming home is just such a problem in conjugal adjustment. He finds he has built up an elaborate defense against the ancient domination--a defense he has not admitted to himself.

But this morning he is disenchanted. In the billowings of that mountainous old wife he will not, by George, lose his small identity. For this precious identity has cost too much and is his pearl formed by the million irritations of life abroad: the cold breakfast roll, sub-titles in the movies, and the thousand nights on damp and mended sheets. He fancies himself, this returning traveler, he has been lucky, he has had the chance to suffer from a more heterogeneous collection of itches than less fortunate persons in more homogeneous surroundings. Out of this character-moulding martyrdom has emerged--himself, the fine fellow, the cosmopolite, the citizen of the world. Now there should be no catch to this. Ordinarily it should be a starting point to enjoyment, a sort of jumping off place to the Higher Life, the threshold to all cultural inner sanctums. But what do we find instead? . . . that this citizen of the world is concentrating his educated energies not upon Bach or the peacetime uses of atomic energy, but upon the mere continuance of himself as a citizen of the world. Instead of living he is trying not to die.

When we study him we find him to be suffering from four main troubles. In the first place, sitting over there in redolent old Europe where every cobblestone, he was pleased to note, kept reminding him of somebody esoteric like Pascal or Lope de Vega, wallowing in all that he got rather intellectually highfalutin. Where he would normally read golf fiction in the Post, he took to reading Phillip Wylie or I. A. Richards, or Salvador Madariaga on what was the matter with the United States. But instead of digesting it all, he would just scream, "Yes!" or "Oh, wonderful!" or "If that isn't Cousin Billy to a T!"--underline it with a red pencil and base a whole philosophy of life on it. He became, in other words, a labeler, which has always been a good port for anybody foundering in an intellectual storm. Being a labeler didn't matter in Europe where he admired everything anyway, but when he came home to the U.S. it was very limiting. When he saw any woman over twenty-five he automatically fled her maternal claws. When anyone mentioned the Middle West he said 'isolationism,' and looked pained. And before the ubiquitous cocktail he was ashamed and stood empty-handed knowing it was useless to call for sherry.

Now one sad part of such a perspicuous attitude is that it requires a tireless vigilance lest one miss a cue--and upon being faced with such typical Americana as Forest Lawn Cemetery in Los Angeles, or a rodeo in Ox Butte, Wyoming, have no idea what should be said and thus be brought to the point of having to think for one's self. And thinking for one's self is a justified terror of mankind, and the absolute anathema of the highfalutin, for in it lies the unspeakable disaster of approving what this year is being disapproved of. One wouldn't wish on one's worst enemy the intellectual oblivion that descends on a fellow who, for instance, actually enjoys Longfellow in his ignorance of what more furious and exalted minds have said of Hiawatha. But to avoid such pitfalls is not easy, and particularly worrysome for the traveler returning to the United States. It's a big country full of a number of things. How difficult to be remembering all day long what the Right people have said about everything from radio commercials to the salt box architecture of New England! At best, it's a shorthand philosophy, a question of adjectives, whereby salads are 'insane.' New York is 'neurotic,' labor is 'spoiled,' and anything west of the Alleghenies is 'adolescent.'

Another trouble that besets this world citizen is that he has met celebrities while living abroad. He has been to parties at his Embassy and shaken the hand of several foreign secretaries, Lily Pons, and at least one Viceroy. No decent celebrity can have any idea of the damage he has inflicted upon the soul of, say, one Mortimer Small, Willow Grove, Idaho, by shouting at him through the cigarette smoke, "I say, you there, would you mind awfully passing that plate of shrimps?" Nothing could seem more casual, and yet in time it produces a periodic craving which we can call shrimpism, or a desire for a brush with famous people at fashionable festivities. Shrimpism derives its name from the most successful ruse of its sufferers to obtain satisfaction: a serving of hors d'oeuvres. If one must chat with an ambassador the least offensive approach is via the curly shrimp and the deviled egg. Shrimpism is endurable in Europe where there are always notables, but in the United States it keeps him circling between the East Fifties in New York and those corners of Connecticut out of reach of the commuter. Here, with luck, he may find a few famous names, but the circling takes most of his time and all of his money and does not allow him even one sneaked trip to Willow Grove, Idaho. And so he is deprived of the true joy of coming home, which is to shed one's pretensions like tight shoes, have coffee and dough-

67

nuts at the kitchen table, and boast of wonderful adventures to the familiar tune of Grandpappy champing his gums in the mahogany rocker.

Now the third difficulty of this prodigal son is that he is a speaker of foreign languages. In the field of foreign tongues there are strange extremes. Consider the neophyte. No one is so meek as the American who has had three lessons at Berlitz and can manage, with idiot brightness. ¿Comio Ud.? Si, comi una banana." It is the nether point in humility, but be it ever so humble it is home for the spirit, a place of infantile gregariousness, where cuteness has its hour and grown men are suddenly beloved for the little noises they can make in their throats. Now consider the initiated. No one is so proud, no one so silent upon a peak as the American who can not only speak but even think in Spanish. What is he to do in the United States? There are so few to whom he can talk, for of course, as in Norman times, English is a vulgar idiom useful for those nasty passages with bus drivers but certainly inadequate for the pleasures of conversation. He is lonely and in his spare moments comes to haunt that Spanish-speaking section north of Central Park where he can understand what is being said. The golden sound pours forth and he stands on the corner of 7th Ave. and 118th St., his eyes closed in a kind of Iberian seizure, and hears once again that immortal dialogue of the fruit peddler and the housewife: "Ladron! Yo no voy a pagar . . . Thief! Go to the devil with your prices." "But lady these bananas are cheap . . . "

But all these are side issues compared with his central problem--how to graft the bloom of Europe upon the stem of the United States and produce that rare flower, the good life, his own hybrid. This is the gist of his independence, and quite a decent sort of aim, if only he could concentrate on the product instead of the process. But his belligerence about effecting the graft so exhausts him that he would be too tired to enjoy the double chrysanthemum if it did burst forth.

Consistently negative--although this is the only consistent thing about him--he begins by listing what he will not accept in the United States. When we examine this list of what he has outlawed we find everything on it to fall under the heading of Unjustified Indulgences. This world-citizen takes his pleasures hard, they must be purposeful and are decidedly to be endured for Culture rather than enjoyed for escape. Heading his list are American movies. He will not go to them, except, of course, Shakespeare who being over his head is thereby worthwhile. He is very firm about the movies, wholly persuaded once again by Mr. I. A. Richards' fascinating theory that the movies being false art with their clumsily contrived solutions are subconsciously frustrating and lead away from that sense of order and rightness which true art gives. He is very firm in spite of impertinent memories of certain evenings, long ago, when he slouched in the last row of the Willow Grove Palace, ate peanuts, kissed his girl, and applauded when another redskin bit the dust. What he felt then, he reminds himself sternly, could not have been pleasure--even though it seemed so at the time--but was only a nasty disintegration of the nervous system through his sensitivity to the artistically worthless celluloid experiences of William S. Hart.

He is also very firm about not reading the cheaper American periodicals, even in barber shops. "Their slanted prose, adjusted at the feeble-minded level, is very persuasive in the long run and conducive to the gradual loss of good taste." Maintaining his taste by a conscious effort is the world citizen's original idea. Or at least he doesn't remember where he got it. At any rate it's in the sound Puritan tradition of avoiding what you can't resist. And the heroics of Puritanism have always been wonderfully satisfying to the ego. So he stands before the news-stands in railroad stations, during those winter waits for trains, studies the covers on the magazines, clucks, and says, "shocking!"--referring not to morals but to taste. At train time he buys the Christian Science Monitor which he doesn't have to read, being so happily engaged in gloating over his strength in not buying pulps and his breadth in objecting to them not on moral but on aesthetic grounds. "Oh Culture, Oh Perfection," he whispers in a little ecstasy.

He is not quite so firm about the question of central heating. On the whole he is against it because its so comfortable. And here we touch upon one of the returning American's most significant convictions--he considers comfort to be synonymous with rot. That is, certain comforts. The oil burner is effete but the open fire is virile. Packaged foods obscure life's meaning while the tired vegetables in European markets show forth the Lord's purpose. The private car degenerates but the bus invigorates the soul. . . . And on it goes encompassing all manner of unrelated elements in a determined philosophy by which he prefers rain to sun, gravel to concrete, cold baths to hot, and, in short, sums up the good life as one lived under conditions of reasonable adversity at a mere step from the Louvre. Translated into American terms this would mean a pre-Revolutionary farm in Connecticut where winters, he hopes, will be severe, and if his luck is really good there will be a complete breakdown in deliveries of food and fuel.

But all these eccentricities, these refusals and rebellions, are after all merely the outward sign of the inner dream. From abroad he has brought an ideal, an idea of a way of life--the positive for which all these negatives have only been a defense. From Spain and France and England he has brought the basis of his new independence: the essence of Europe. For he is sure he under stands what Europe is, and all he does or does not do is to the end of preserving that essence. Or so he will explain it to you, with gulps and spasmodic soarings of talk and the shyness a man feels when he tells you about what to him is poetry. What is Europe? Why the essence of Europe is complexity, and complexity is more truly related to human life than simplicity. The American, mourns the cosmopolite, his finite--his character, his house, his method is knowable at a glance. This is how the American wants it. This is the great American dream that life is simple and honest and understand-

69

able and determinedly cheerful. So he papers his bedroom wall with full-blown roses and never senses that their unchanging gayety, so insistent, so doggedly proclaiming like the soap operas that life can be beautiful, sets up the most aching frustrations. But the European is more realistic, cries the world citizen. There is something obscure in the European character, he feels, something in the end infinite and inexplicable. American tourists--and here he sighs--call it a lack of straightforwardness, slyness, circumlocution, inefficiency. They say that Europe is not functional.

Functional? Take a chair. A chair has two uses: for sitting and symbolizing. It should support the body but, more gloriously, it should exalt the soul by suggesting the history of chairs, centuries of chairs. It should remind us of human dignity, of pageantry. Before our eyes should pass a parade of the glorious chairs: the chair of Zeus with winged sphinxes and the feet of beasts, St. Peter's chair with the ivory carvings of Hercules, the English coronation chair with its "stone of Scone." Why even the foolish revolving office chair might lift the Monday spirit if one remembered that he was sitting upon an aristocrat with a family tree of 400 years. Complexity, the intricate suggestion of tradition, the hint of infinite causes behind a result, this is Europe and this is truly functional for the life of the spirit. America comforts the muscles, but Europe--Ah Europe comforts the mind! It matches a man. It is multiple-valued like life. It is obscure, like the mind. . . .

70   Now if one can prevent the soaring citizen from disappearing in the upper regions of metaphor and pull him down to the despised facts, it all becomes a matter of interior decoration. The European spirit can be expressed in the Connecticut living room, we find, by means of the Cultured Clutter. For of course the returning American is far beyond the stage of period rooms and authentic reproductions, which he considers the commercially fixed levels of bourgeois uncertainty. Now the 'period room' is a false whole because there is no truth in any of its parts. But the Cultured Clutter is a true whole because there is truth in each of its parts. The period room is a lifeless generality, but the Cultured Clutter is a group of lively particulars. The period room is a demonstration of furniture, but the Cultured Clutter is a demonstration of man. The period room can be bought by the ignorant from a catalogue, but the Cultured Clutter must be gathered piecemeal by the educated.

To make the Clutter: take a shiftless sofa and chairs, which, mercifully, do not snap to attention every time you climb out of them. (These are best bought in England.) Add books which overflow the shelves. (The overflowing is the important part of the books, as there is paucity in the period room but plethora in the Cultured Clutter.) Some of the books can be in English but a percentage must be in foreign tongues. Now mix an old Portuguese pulpit with a Dutch table, Biedermayer cupboard and the white rocker from Willow Grove. Sift over the whole with odd *objets d'art*--ivory knives from Spain, silver from Peru, porcelain from Germany, besides those homely bits which give such a flavour of spontaneity: opened letters, stubs of pencils, crumpled papers, and a half-eaten candy bar. On the floor put too many Persian rugs which lap over, on the wall hang great art, and then garnish the jumble with an old sweater, a battered hat, the offspring's fire-engine, and several crystal decanters. Here the world citizen inserts a note of caution to the American housewife--the genuine effect cannot be achieved by the sacking of department stores, nor, indeed, by any direct method whatsoever. In the words of Lao Tse, he would casually add, "will is not the way at all," but in the words of Shakespeare "by indirection find directions out." The clutter, like happiness, is soonest found in looking for something else.

Which brings us right back to the art of coming home. If the earnest world citizen could only apply his potpourri of epigrams about life to himself, he might see that, like the clutter, his identity is best asserted by indirection. If he didn't make such an issue of it the old wife might never notice the essence of Europe. And in fact none of his daft habits would bother anybody if he didn't keep reminding people of them. The best way to maintain the essence of Europe in America is to practice it as a secret vice. But the world citizen has no secrets. He confronts, he asserts, he denounces. Which only goes to prove that the world citizen is not a world citizen at all, but the same American who once long ago passed out in the Astor Bar. For such a belligerent honesty is only bred on this side of the Atlantic. Such relentless straightforwardness exists only in the sons of Mom. The very finiteness inherent in his epigrams is but another expression of that finiteness he so hates in other Americans. So that, if he but knew it, he needn't fear that female in New York harbour, since under his chesterfield and foulard cravat there lives still, unshaken after a decade, not the essence of Europe but the essence of Willow Grove.

71

7

Commonplace Thoughts on Home Leave

Jack Perry

Home leave is peculiar to diplomats. It is the coming home between stays abroad, the time of finding out that home is alien and the last Embassy is home. It is the time of recognizing that America has moved ahead and left you behind, even while you have moved ahead and left America behind. It is the seeing of the familiar through eyes grown foreign. It is the thrill of being back among kin and the shock of finding that old ties go slack. It is a suspension between rediscovery and rejection. Home leave is a floating.

Anyone can have a vacation, you say to yourself, and you watch the tourists around Washington and tell yourself that you are merely a tourist in your own country. But this is a lie. They do not have alien eyes, they are not floating. They can go home again. You are desperately trying to be home and not making it. Home leave is the time you cannot get home.

I walked outside the State Department building into a summer heat haze and stared up at the cool windows with all their inhabitants trapped inside schedules and programs and commitments. What a wonder it would be if one of them could walk outside and shed his schedule like a snakeskin; but he cannot. He is being paid to wear a snakeskin, but I am on home leave. And even I, feeling uncommited, unscheduled, even unshackled, did not feel free. Floating, but not floating free.

From "Commonplace Thoughts on Home Leave" by J. Perry, 1970, *Foreign Service Journal*, 47(12), pp. 39–41. Reprinted by permission.

I went down to the fountain by the Federal Reserve, where I used to slip away at lunchtime to be solitary and dream of joyous things, poems, trips, going to Bukhara. The sound of water falling on water was as good as ever, but I felt not so free as before. Not so ample and undefined. In the intervening years I had diminished not only in years left to live but in things I might do with those years. I had experienced joyous things, had taken trips, had seen good times. Now the potentialities were diminished by that much, the possible seemed less probable. I had already been to Bukhara.

Home is the place where you worry about money. Washington is the ingathering homecoming place where middle class people return to the middle class. Overseas there are perquisites and allowances and servants and general services and all of that, but mostly it can all be subsumed under the heading: no worry about money. We are not rich, overseas, not even close to it; but like the rich, at least the rich of legend and envy, we are free overseas from having to fret about dollars. The alien currency is so quaint anyway, spending it seems unreal. Things can be bought on the spur of the moment. Larks are possible. It is a life of using money for what it was meant for, to buy things, not to worry about.

But in Washington the greenbacks are familiar and real, like the dollars of one's youth but worth inconceivably less; and those dollars demand to be spent not on larks but on necessities. You find your friends talking about money and soon you find you are too. Home is learning how to worry about money again.

In France the smaller villages still have signs that say "Vagabonds may not camp here." These signs make me uneasy for as a diplomat, a vagabond of career, I feel sympathy for all those gypsies who cannot find a place to camp. Floating through home leave, I am constrained to recognize that we are all merely camping out. Some of us are in standardized government quarters; some in plush town houses; some within the housing allowance, most above it; some in palaces, some in suburbs; but all of us are merely camping out. That is what the Foreign Service is. We visited friends at one of the famous Foreign Service residences, a jewel of a mansion; but they were there only until the new Consul General arrived, and were hardly unpacked: just camping out. We visited a Service friend at a splendid Washington apartment; but he vaguely felt he might go abroad again on short notice, and was living in the apartment from day to day only: just camping out. Even those with enviable Washington homes in a mowed and shaded suburb were, after all, only between foreign assignments and had about their homes a vague aura of temporariness: just camping out. After a career of this, retired diplomats probably keep trunks handy and are always emotionally prepared to move on. I can see the whole lot of us arriving in heaven after judgment day--if that could ever happen to diplomats--and collectively eying the heavenly mansions with the suspicious eye of the short-termer. We will still be camping out.

74

Not only Americans have trouble finding home on home leave. An English diplomatic friend went home and spent what sounded like an idyllic month on a remote sheep farm in Wales. But he was disturbed--this was his first sojourn to Wales--to find anti-English slogans lettered up around the neighborhood, and to encounter in his rambles some local patriots who insisted on trying to make him speak Welsh. My English friend got that uncomfortable feeling, all too familiar to diplomats, that things were shifting out from under him.

Diplomacy is the apotheosis of dilettantism. It looks at life with highest regard for form, and history is an art rather than a sermon; moreover, there is more to consider than one can consider, and so amateurism is unavoidable. Those who think they can go beyond this and understand the infinite processes are, in the Tolstoyan sense, inviting the mockery of history.

At its height, diplomacy is the hourly brooding over of a universe of constantly shifting interrelationships and the formation of judgments about the emerging patterns. This is good hard work. But in its daily endeavor, diplomacy is doing more than is possible as well as possible; trying to read too much, to know too many people, to interpret too much, to consider too much, and trying to fit all this halfwayness into some coherent pattern. That is diplomacy, and thus we are all dilettantes. Home leave catches us up short. Cut off, unproductive, floating between a home that is alien and an alien home, the diplomat retreats from a feeling of irrelevance to a nostalgia for fading concepts. He erects an image of Foreign Policy as refuge-- then realizes that for those around him in the streets, foreign policy is what you do when real work is finished. Home leave is a time of truth and unease.

Glamor, romance, joy. If we do not have time for them what is time for? Kenneth Grahame said, "Mankind's most precious possession is the wonder of the world." Home leave is a time not given to most professions, a time when a hand is clapped on the head and one is forced to gaze at the passing of life. Under this forced gaze, truths come out that the settled man, the nondiplomat, the dweller-in-one-place, might avoid throughout a lifetime. But this kind of gazing is not only disconcerting, it is devastating; we were probably not meant for it. We struggle until we succeed in averting our eyes.

Instead of becoming wise, therefore--which we might do if only we could keep from averting our eyes--we become sophisticated, and we become worldly-wise. Home leave is a good time for this kind of bittersweet wisdom, for by our very travel in the world we can see its illusions and deceptions. Being diplomats, we are always going inside new rooms, instead of standing back all our lives and looking through the windows. Emily Dickinson, who somehow could look at truth without blinking, wrote about standing outside windows and the folly of going in:

. . . Nor was I hungry. So I found
That hunger was a way

Of persons outside windows
The entering takes away.

The diplomat, both in going abroad and in coming home, makes the mistake of entering the room he should have looked at through the window.

Diplomats are experts on cultural relativity. They know that sunrises look different depending on which side of the International Date Line you come at them from.

My favorite example is Helsinki, which can look like a rather charming provincial capital, or else like the Paradise of the Western World, depending on whether you come to it from Western Europe or from inside Russia. Or take a Howard Johnson motel. I have seen American diplomats, back from tours in an underdeveloped or unfriendly place, watching their children swim in a spotless pool while they watch baseball on color television and their wife bathes in a gleaming bathroom, greet Howard Johnson as a sturdy friend and fine host. I have seen other American diplomats--or the same ones a few years later--back from service in a venerable European capital, find Howard's service non-existent, his food inedible, and his taste execrable. In our business, most things vary depending on where you are coming from going to.

Diplomats are addicted to information. On home leave, the American diplomat, deprived of his massive daily intake of information, flounders and gasps and much resembles a drug addict deprived of his drug. Especially if he goes off into the hinterlands, out of reach of the NEW YORK TIMES, cut off from the more serious periodicals, having no Eastern Establishment types to converse with, he finds himself gasping. And he must take care. If he stays too long, he may begin to realize how much of his diplomatic personality is composed of those hot cables and profound Intelligence Community insights and secret sources. He may begin to notice that after a month away, talking to a bright young skeptic, his own conclusions begin to sound thin, not nearly so solid as when he discoursed so earnestly last month with the Rumanian chargé. He may begin to feel like a voice without a body. He may wonder if he feels anything to go with what he knows. He may recall George Kennan being asked why he did not write novels and replying that his whole training as a diplomat was to conceal feeling rather than to express it. He may begin to wonder what he is. Another peril of home leave. So we hurry back to our offices and devour stacks of cables and TIMES and instant knowledge, eager to become someone again.

Coming back to Washington is like coming back to a house and finding all the furniture changed, or coming back to a hometown and finding Main Street the same but all the old familiar people gone.

The streets in Washington change little, and if Foggy Bottom is renewed, still much is familiar, including stiff, sterile, glassy-eyed New State. In fact the trees and the grass of Washington are welcoming. But the friends are not there. They have gone. They just left for Caracas. They are in Rome, or Brussels, or left behind in Paris. Not here. Or those who are here will not be part of our lives as they were overseas. They will be busy, and no one entertains, and if you do you do not let your hair down, and anyway we are older.

The Foreign Service is where you find out that there is nothing to anything except friends, but the friends are usually somewhere else.

The diplomat is a professional alien. He tiptoes through life for fear of sinking too deeply someplace. He must be American enough to go up on the Hill and explain what we are up to in Quixotia, but foreign enough to explain to a French Minister in Paris what the essential aims of our long-term policies--not prejudicial to French interests but based on a pooling of resources and returns--are in that same Quixotia. He is an interlocutor in the old-fashioned sense of the middle-man in the minstrel line who questions the men on the ends; and often he must feel as false as a man in blackface. The longer he stays home, the more American he gets, the more he can set aside the daily habit of looking through another man's eyes.

The shock is at the start of home leave, upon first arriving, when the eyes are still alien, and the country seems strange but it is yours.

The other side of home leave is the recognition of independence. The diplomat comes home and finds his friends living in sumptuous homes with pressed lawns and driveways full of sculptured automobiles, knowing where all the country clubs are, occupying executive positions, drawing salaries to make Foreign Service people gasp, leading a tax-deducted social life, doing very well indeed. Those first few days, the diplomat feels like a rootless, windblown thing, maybe a tumbleweed, blown by chance into a forest of flourishing oaks. He feels bad.

77

Thankfully, there is a statutory minimum for home leave. The diplomat stays on, and looks harder, and impressions change. He finds pretty soon, to his surprise, that his contemporary stay-at-homes envy him. Looking closer at his home town, he finds patterns he had overlooked--barriers, limitations, constrictions. He sees that his old friends do not have the privilege of moving every few years into a new environment, with new acquaintances, new opportunities, a new language, a new culture--maybe even, one may always hope, a new life. Or to put it another way, he sees that his friends are incapable of getting out of their old patterns, and his freedom becomes more real. And he feels good.

I became infatuated with Gandhi, the Great Soul, when I was young, and have never got him out of my system, including the idea that India, with its overcrowding and its poverty and its famished environment, may be the image of the future, not California as we knew it twenty or thirty years ago. Gandhi said, "The woes of Mahatmas are known to Mahatmas alone." I think that the woes of diplomats, even those who have not great souls, are known to diplomats alone. And perhaps for a root-losing, drifting, teeming, cosmopolitan world, where Heathrow looks pretty much like Dulles or Sheremetyevo or JFK, where a superhighway to Caracas looks pretty much like one to Rome or Pittsburgh, where a suburb is a suburb, a crowd a crowd, perhaps we uprooted cosmopolitan diplomats are the image of the future.

To think about home leave without thinking about the technical impossibility of the thing is most difficult. I mean the moving around of a whole family without the means to do it comfortably, squeezing into places not big enough physically or spiritually, putting everyone out, feeling so homeless that the term home leave becomes a sour joke. But in this sense home leave is a microcosm of the diplomatic life, which on the surface cannot be done, or at least cannot be done without frequent disaster. Yet some people do it.

Home leave makes us aware of the high opportunity of the diplomatic life and the usually sad realization of it. Our friends envy us the opportunity, and we mourn how sadly we fall short. If both the chance and the missing of it are somehow grand, I suppose we had better not complain.

8

Coming Home to Affluence

Hugh Sidey

Coming down through thin clouds somewhere over Maryland, we reached the end of the 20,000-mile China odyssey. There was an endless plain of incandescence. Streetlights, neon signs, car lights, home lights, all gulping energy from America's thick river of power. I thought of the night flight from Peking to Hangchow only a few days before, and the lights across that vast land--a dot here and a flicker there, great black deserts between them.

So here we were. Surely one of the dividends of freedom was warmth and light, and horsepower to do the work. And yet I was struck with faint guilt. Absurd, I thought, my old Presbyterian soul rising up again, calling to mind all those self-sacrificing missionaries that I used to hear about along with the brimstone.

The Pan Am 707 touched earth at Andrews Air Force Base and applause erupted among those of us inside. Then it was time to gather together the baggage. Down the aisle went the American reporters, their pockets stuffed, their satchels bulging, with more packages under their arms--rugs, jade, gold, silver, silk, sculpture. Still plundering China, I suddenly thought, recalling some of the books I'd read about the way the West dealt with the Orient in the old days. There was a little twinge of inner pain.

From "Coming Home to Affluence" by H. Sidey, 1972, *Life*, 72(9), p. 12. Copyright 1972 by Life Picture Service. Reprinted by permission.

With a short jog across the tarmac to the floodlit hangar, the twinge passed. Fifteen thousand people waited there for the President and Mrs. Nixon to arrive aboard the *Spirit of '76*. There were acres of automobiles parked on the landing field. Men, women and children, in luxurious coats and sweaters, jostled closer. Glistening jets sat silently in rows in the distance. The wives of the dignitaries were elegant in furs and tailored coats, their hair meticulously tended, jewels sparkling in the intense light. I remembered my diminutive interpreter for eight days in China, Mrs. Lin Shang-chen, wife of an official in the defense ministry. At 6 or 7 every morning she was on hand in her blue cloth coat and black pants, no jewelry, answering my questions patiently and adjusting to my idiosyncrasies without any complaint, going all day. I never saw her eat. She hovered over me, worrying, as I wrote past midnight, and then saw me off to bed before disappearing into the bleak gray of Peking. I remembered wondering why she had to suppress her femininity. Chairman Mao and his joyless scripture was one reason, but surely there was another. Style takes energy. In China there is no energy to spare, not yet. Mrs. Lin talked only about helping the people, always the people, those others off there somewhere.

Here at Andrews, Vice-President Spiro Agnew was the master of ceremonies. He was flawlessly tailored, combed, manicured, polished. There was about him the smell of power, position and possessions.

80

The *Spirit of '76* roared up to its assigned place, the door was pushed back, and there were ruffles and flourishes from the army's special heraldic trumpets, followed by *Hail to the Chief*. A journalist next to me turned away. He muttered, "It's like the arrival of the king." Others apparently had the same readjustment problems.

I remembered how the small figure of Chou En-lai had greeted Nixon in silence eight days earlier. The effect of that understated welcome was shattering. Chou had sent Nixon off quietly, too. A joke or two on the ramp, a handshake, a wave. No band, no crowd. I'd thought then that I saw in Nixon's face something akin to gratitude for the simplicity.

But these thoughts were swept away as Nixon began shaking those pudgy official hands. Then he was on the podium, bathed in special lights calibrated at 3,200° Kelvin to render true skin tones for the national TV audience. "I want to express my very deep appreciation and the appreciation of all of us for this wonderfully warm welcome . . . " More memories from the past days crowded my mind. In Peking's timeless and graceful Forbidden City, gently powdered with new snow, Nixon had observed: "It snows like this in Chicago." His host, Marshal Yeh Chien-ying, vice-chairman of the Military Affairs Commission, saw the same sight and said, "The snow has whitewashed the world." At the end of the tour, which included a museum filled with priceless objects, Nixon joked with his guide: "You ought to search everybody now to make sure they don't have anything in their pockets." On that occasion the marshal said: "We hope that the people of the two countries and of all the world will enjoy peace and good harvests." Perhaps it *was* boilerplate, but the contrast was painful. How, I asked myself, can inner beauty survive in the grayness of Peking, the repression by the state? And how, with our own heritage of simple eloquence, from Jefferson through Lincoln to Truman, can we end up with silver trumpets?

Leaving the air base, I sat in a massive traffic jam for half an hour. China was there with me again, disturbing the quiet purr of the 245 horsepower up front. My dinner companion at the last banquet in Peking had been a 40-year-old magazine editor, Meng Chi-ching, father of two, living in two rooms, owner of a bicycle. Did he have a dream? I'd asked him. Wasn't there something he would like to do, or be, or some place he'd like to go? Wouldn't he like to own a car so that he could take his children to see their grandmother in Shanghai or show them China on the holidays? He paused, and looked at me with something near pity. "I never have thought about it," he said. "I have enough. My bicycle is good. I live near my work."

Driving up to my home near midnight, I had to park in the driveway. The second car's place in the garage was blocked by sleds, skis and bicycles. It occurred to me, as I looked at that beloved patch of Maryland suburbia washed in bright moonlight, that Meng should have a little of what I've got and I should have a little of what he's got. The same might even be true for Chou and Nixon.

9

The Returned Volunteer:
A Perspective

Sam Longsworth

The following article grew out of the Peace Corps' inherent curiosity about itself and its performance. One aspect of the Peace Corps, and it may represent the Peace Corps' most significant contribution to history, remains relatively unexplored: that is, the role of the volunteer come back home. The singular importance of the "third purpose" of the Peace Corps, the contribution of the returned volunteer to his own country, has always been recognized. It has not, however, always been clear just what was expected of the returned volunteer, or just how that experience of alien culture was to be woven into the American social fabric.

The principal source of information for this study was a four-part questionnaire sent by mail to all returned volunteers. Nearly 3500 responses were received, or about 10% of the total mailing. It should be noted that a significant percentage of the addressees failed to receive the questionnaire, presumably due to the inaccuracies of current address lists. In certain instances the questionnaire was supplemented by interviews.

To the naked eye a returned Peace Corps volunteer is indistinguishable from any other kind of American; indeed, one has the impression that his wardrobe is likely to be slightly less exotic and eclectic than that of the average

From "The Returned Volunteer: A Perspective" by S. Longsworth, 1971, *Transition, 1,* pp. 11–17. Reprinted by permission.

middle-class American. Folklore notwithstanding, he usually wears shoes, eats with a knife and fork, pays the rent, sends his kids to school, and votes every time he gets a chance. Clearly, his tour as a volunteer was one of the most extraordinary kinds of experience to which a person might willfully aspire. It often involved one of the most radical changes of social environment that the planet had to offer. He came from one of the most rapidly changing societies on earth and he spent his time in some places where little but the weather ever changes. He was usually a middle class representative of the most bourgeois society on earth, and he chose to live with some of the most isolated and underprivileged people of the earth. He came from the most highly developed technological nation on earth, and he went to places where the industrial revolution had never happened. He was thoroughly schooled in western thought and tradition, and he was expected to learn to behave in a thousand non-western ways. There is little wonder that the National Society, Daughters of the American Revolution, took alarm in August, 1961, when the Peace Corps legislation was under consideration, and expressed some urgent misgivings about this adventuresome proposal:

> The fact that these young people will be living under abnormal conditions and encouraged to take part in the life of the nation, tribe, or community in which they may be working may prove greatly to their disadvantage. This is especially true where they will be living with foreigners as individuals and not with their fellow compatriots in barracks as is customary in the armed forces. Separated from the moral and disciplinary influences of their homeland, serious consequences can be anticipated.

Returned volunteers state with near unanimity that the overseas experience has a profound and lasting influence. To describe that influence, diffused as it is through the lives of forty thousand individuals, finally requires recourse to the broadest kind of generalizations. There are, however, several important ideas that constantly recur: the element of challenge and its offspring, self-confidence; the critical encounter with poverty and the vast range of understanding that results; the experience of cultural relativity and the reflection upon one's own cultural umbilicus; a certain "Peace Corps ethos" that demands a quest for one's outer limits and accepts no excuse for not trying; the personal growth that comes from stepping outside of one's cultural cocoon to see yourself as others see you. The experience is a powerful educational process.

The return to the States is a critical process in the determination of the relevance of the experience overseas. Coming back can be adventurous, educational, treacherous, amusing, confusing, rewarding, relaxing, humiliating, and inspiring all at once. Whatever, it is rarely a smooth process in which continuity is readily apparent. It may take weeks, months, or even years to complete the transitional process as the integration of new and old, and seemingly disparate experience goes on. Judgments and decisions are made that cast perspective on experience; new responses and expectations grow out of new awareness, directions become clear, sometimes only by accident. However disoriented a returning volunteer may feel, he is deter-mined above all to make it on his own terms. In such circumstances the "hang loose" flexibility, legendary among Peace Corps people, is clearly a very useful tool for survival. While his story is quite atypical in every other respect, the return of Francis J. Reidy from Pakistan to become the Vice-President of Applied Technical Services was an exemplary exercise in flexibility.

> *I retired from the Peace Corps in August, 1965 to lead the carefree life of a traveller. I had four changes of clothes, an airline ticket from Dacca to Philadelphia with twenty-two stops on it, and 600 dollars in my pocket. I made it through India and Burma without doing too much damage to my wallet; but the next stop, Thailand, proved to be my undoing. The first night I slept in the Peace Corps hostel (the Peace Corps was kinder to its volun-teers in those days), and the second in a bar around the corner called "Dinos." Six weeks later I was broke, tired, and happy. When I discovered I could not collect my unemploy-ment insurance overseas, I went to work for Pacific Architects and Engineers in Saigon. The company had trouble keeping qualified people in Vietnam. Actually, I found the condi-tions much better than my last quarters, and I was able to work easily with the Vietnamese. In eighteen months I had acquired enough money and knowledge to form my own company. All it takes to start your own company is the patience of Job and the mind of a genius. Lacking both of these it will cost you money; in my case it cost.*

Another man who relishes the independence of self-employment discovered that within the system, initiative and drive are not always sure-fire vehicles to the attainment of responsibility. Robert Kalien, a former volunteer in Liberia and Somalia whose career as a stockbroker was nipped in the bud by the bear market, found some interesting social speed limits on his return:

> *. . . My first job was with the U.S. Customs. My job consisted of sitting at a desk in a large room where several other men spent most of the day drinking coffee and chatting with one another. No work was given me and nobody told me what I was supposed to be doing. When I asked for something to do I was told to take a coffee break. After about a week of this I begged the supervisor to give me something--anything--to do. He finally brought me a large book, a rubber stamp, and an ink pad and proceeded for about ten minutes to show me how to press the rubber stamp to the ink pad and then to stamp each line on each page with this single stamp. . . . After about half an hour I was asked to slow down my pace by one of my co-workers who had to prepare the book before it got to me. 'Take it easy,' he admonished, 'go get some coffee.' I only lasted four weeks on that job, and that was because I gave two weeks notice.*

The question of continuity is probably the most difficult. For many, the link between overseas and home experiences is very personal and subjective. Many volunteers return feeling like some new breed of immigrant and quickly discover that the mythical American melting pot is in reality a blast fur-nace that can smelt the integrity out of any cultural import.

Bud Blakey, former head of the Transition Center experiment, has developed an understanding of returning volunteers from his experience with the transition process:

> *At least two distinct societal environments shape the returned volunteer . . . his adolescent home and college life which is basically white and middle-class, and his Peace Corps experi-ence which brings him, probably for the first time, into direct and continuous contact with non-white members of another culture or sub-culture. This cultural and racial revelation is probably the prime mover in the establishment of a socially oriented conscience about jus-*

tice and the worth of the individual. His commitment to social and institutional change is, I suspect, more often an immediate product of his overseas experience and not his perception of the socio-economic ills afflicting America. The proximity of the individual to his concern usually raises his consciousness and understanding of it.

Surely there can be no more assured way of raising awareness of a given condition than to live it. While experience may not be the best teacher, experiential learning may be the best education.

Many returned volunteers would agree with Bud Blakey's analysis of awareness. Gilbert Lopez came back from Ecuador to become a program assistant in the Department of Health, Education, and Welfare working on special projects in bilingual and bicultural education:

The Peace Corps experience was invaluable to me. Although I didn't realize it at the time, it awakened my social conscience by forcing me to question my involvement in Ecuador while ignoring the plight of my own people here. After undergoing the conditioning of our educational system, the Peace Corps was the initiator of reinforcing a positive self-identity. Military service further reinforced my individuality by attempting to eliminate it. I am a Chicano, and I will work for Mi raza, wherever and however possible.

Leonel Castillo speaks even more specifically of that awakening experience. As the Executive Director of the Catholic Council on Community Relations for the Galveston-Houston diocese, Leonel is a dynamic worker for the civil rights of Mexican-Americans.

Through a fortunate bureaucratic accident I was assigned to serve as a volunteer in the Philippines because of my fluency in Spanish. Of course, Filipinos speak eighty-seven dialects and only very few speak Spanish.

However, the Philippines was settled by Spain through Mexico, as was my own state of Texas. The cultural characteristics which the Filipinos and the people of the Southwestern United States have in common are many and pervasive. I remember as I read the anthropological studies on the Philippines how strangely familiar the country seemed. After several weeks in the training program I realized that the reason the material seemed familiar was that it could have been written about the people that I had lived with all my life.

Of course, when I joined the Peace Corps I had no notion that I would be going to a place that was, as I later learned, probably too much like home. I didn't expect that techniques which worked in introducing change abroad might have great relevance for the Mexican-American in the United States.

The most popular return route is via school; over half (57% according to the Harris survey) the volunteers return to school soon after service. The academic community is a good transition site, familiar ground from which to survey the changing scene. But more importantly the return to school represents a recognition of the need for additional skills and professional credentials. The educational pursuits of returned volunteers reflect career decisions; by far the majority of students answering the questionnaire are seeking professional degrees. Two out of three students indicated their educational interests and career plans were directly influenced by Peace Corps service. The direction of influence tended to favor the fields of education, economics, linguistics, international relations, agriculture, and the social sciences. Nearly a third of the students expressed the intention of using their skills overseas, usually in the area or country of their Peace Corps service.

The Returned Volunteer: A Perspective / Sam Longsworth

One of the common activities of returned volunteers on campus is a formal or informal involvement with foreign students. It is not unusual to find an American conversing with a foreign friend in Thai, Hausa, or Tagalog on the steps of a campus library.

Bill and Betty Baumann are agents of change. After their tour as cooperative development agents, they remained in Colombia for six months to help run an emerald mine in the mountains. Back in the States they have sought the kind of mental and physical challenge they found in Colombia, and they have found plenty to challenge them on the rugged streets of West Philadelphia. Bill is a drug counselor and Betty is a case worker, both working out of community mental health centers. They find that skills and techniques they learned in relating to a small rural village in Colombia are effective in relating to their neighborhood in Philadelphia, albeit the problems they face are of totally different magnitude. They are particularly insistent on the necessity of living in and sharing the life of the community they serve. Not only do they feel that most of the solutions to the enduring problems lie in the hands of the community, but also they enjoy the reward of community participation. The problems they face are enormous and they are not even sure that there are lasting solutions, but they set for themselves attainable goals. They know they are not going to save the city, and they know they will not break the cycle of poverty in their neighborhood, and they know that crime and drug abuse may well continue to increase in spite of their efforts. But they reach some people and in that encounter lives are changed. They recognize that any real change must come through the remaking of institutions, and that institutions change through the will of the people.

The magnitude of problems at home is a shock to most returning volunteers whose only first-hand contact with poverty was overseas. Many remark that in a developing society an individual's psychic needs are fulfilled and his material needs frustrated whereas the reverse is the case at home. It is easier, they feel, to fight poverty than despair, and the two together are a formidable enemy.

By reason of numbers alone the most significant impact of returned volunteers is now in the field of education. One of five returned volunteers is a teacher, and the majority of them choose the challenging spots in city schools where the action is. One RPCV teacher in a rugged classroom described his job as "laying it on the line every morning at nine." Merely having been a successful teacher in the Peace Corps does not, however, ensure success at home. The tranquil classroom in Africa where students hold education to be a privilege bears scant resemblance to the American classroom where attendance is often seen as a form of involuntary servitude. The first four to six months are always the worst; descriptions of the "breaking-in" period are usually colorful: nerve wracking, excruciating, trial by ordeal, culture shock, non-violent combat, and target practice, to name a few! Not every-

87

body makes it. It takes a lot of endurance, perseverance, tolerance of frustration, self-confidence, patience, energy, and compassion.

> *It's like squeezing two years as a volunteer into six months. You swear every day you're going to quit. But then one day you wake up and realize you like the kids and you like the job. That's when you have made it.*

Returned volunteers are attracted to the field of education for many reasons. It offers independence and responsibility, latitude for innovation, constant challenge, variety, mobility, and human encounter. It is, above all, a job worth doing. One suspects that the Peace Corps experience will one day be most clearly evident in the attitudes of a new generation of Americans.

After having read more than 3,000 questionnaires, talked to more than 200 returned volunteers, and conducted 25 interviews, there remain for me more questions than answers about returned volunteers. There are 40,000 of them strung out all over the globe doing every imaginable thing. It is hard to isolate them for study since they tend to weave themselves into the fabric of their society. It is exasperating to try to fit them into categories or to find among them common characteristics because they tend to be uncommonly strong individuals with enough self-confidence to resist pressures to conform to anything. They tend to be restless enemies of the status quo who are as much concerned with the process of change as with the product. They place low value on material goals, prestige, and upward mobility, but seem to share a strong faith in the redeeming virtue of human encounter. Almost to a man they are contemptuous of bureaucracy as an obstacle to, rather than a tool of, human achievement; but they thrive on political action. They are agents of change who understand the importance of history and tradition. They are intellectuals who have been to the marketplace. They are a practical minded lot who would rather solve a little problem than complain about a big one. They are idealists who have tried their principles in action, and if one may judge, they have kept the faith.

88

10

Re-Entry Shock

Nancy Koehler

It was New Year's Eve, 1977, and I couldn't have been more excited. After two and one-half years of living in Japan, where my Navy husband was stationed on board *USS Midway*, I was on an airplane and on my way *home*. Blissful thoughts of being back in the U.S.A., long-awaited visits with family and friends, and two years, at least, of shore duty and settled living with my husband and two children outweighed any nostalgia I felt at leaving Japan, a country I had come to know and love.

My every thought told me that everything "back home" was going to be perfect and problem-free. Once again I would be able to be me, not a CO's wife, and free to pursue my own goals. Once again I would be no further than a phone call away from my family. Once again I would be able to speak the language, read maps and street signs, and shop at other stores if the exchange or commissary were out of the item I needed or wanted.

This euphoria was short-lived, however. Within a few weeks, following a whirlwind trip of East Coast family reunions and a move back into our California home, I found myself, unexpectedly, in the depths of despair instead of at the anticipated peak of ecstasy. Instead of enjoying the company of old friends and neighbors, I couldn't seem to find anything to talk to them about. Instead of enjoying driving on wide and familiar roads, I

From "Re-entry Shock" by N. Koehler, 1980, *Ladycom*, *12*(3), pp. 38–40; 70. Copyright 1980 by N. Koehler. Reprinted by permission.

was petrified because I often found myself on the wrong side of them. Instead of enjoying supermarket shopping, I was overwhelmed by the quantity and the variety of items available for me to buy.

What was wrong with me? Here I was, truly "back home," where I had dreamed of being for our entire overseas tour; yet, I was miserable--lonely, afraid, confused, depressed, lethargic. I didn't care whether the moving boxes ever got unpacked, even the ones containing our carefully-chosen Japanese treasures. What had happened? Even my husband asked, "What is ever going to make you happy?" I began to wonder that myself.

I now know that what I was experiencing was re-entry shock, the often unexpected and sometimes painful experience of readjusting to life in one's home country after living in a foreign country. I also now know that I was not alone in my experience.

Tentatively, at first, as I was experiencing re-entry shock, I began questioning other Navy wives, friends who had shared life with me in Japan, to find out whether they too were having difficulty adjusting to life back in the States. Encouraged by their affirmative answers, I wrote a paper on the subject for the Navy's first Family Awareness Conference in Norfolk, Va., in November 1978. The feedback from that paper was so positive that in the fall of 1979, feeling fully recovered, I began contacting more military wives who had lived in foreign countries, to attempt to gather more information. Through the use of a questionnaire and extensive conversations, I have come to understand better the experience of re-entry. This article is a result of these contacts.

90

When one moves from the United States to a foreign country--even if it is to a large military complex--at least a certain amount of culture shock should be expected, tolerated and understood. When returning home from an overseas assignment, however, one finds that re-entry shock is totally unexpected and is, therefore, difficult to tolerate or to understand. The underlying belief during the overseas tour, even with those who are enjoying their host country experience, is that all problems, even if they are service-connected, stem from living in a foreign country: Once "back home," life again will be perfect and problem-free.

Overseas, the home country environment becomes irrationally glorified. All difficulties and problems are forgotten and only the good things back home are remembered. Upon returning to the United States, people may be surprised to find that they not only miss their host country and its people, culture and customs, but also the people with whom they shared the experience. They realize how well they actually got along under a different set of living conditions and how much happened and changed back home in their absence. As one woman said to me, "Three years is a long time to be immersed in another way of life and I felt numb and kind of left out or not 'in' on things happening in the United States. It was a very unhappy time for me because I had expected to be ecstatic to get home."

Rosemary Dennison spent four years on Okinawa with her Air Force husband and their two children. Now living in Riverside, Calif., where her husband is stationed at March AFB, Rosemary described their return to this country this way: "We came back at the time of Watergate. We didn't feel as though we understood what was happening and had difficulties in conversation. Often we felt left out; sometimes we felt as if we had returned from outer space! The economy was such a shock. We were buying a house and could not believe the cost. We had had a water shortage on Okinawa and it disturbed us greatly to see how water was wasted here. Generally, there was a feeling of loss--of friends and of a lifestyle."

To those experiencing re-entry shock, the remote remains vivid and compelling because the immediate has not yet had a chance to come into focus. "I felt lost. I missed the States when I was living in Panama, but once I returned, I wanted to go back," commented Louise Adamson, an Army wife who lives with her husband and three children at Fort MacArthur in San Pedro, Calif. Although Louise had also accompanied her husband on a tour of duty in Germany, it was her life in Panama that she missed the most upon her return.

Ten years later, Louise recalled, "Panama was my paradise. I really missed our live-in maid. She was so good with the children. I didn't like having to find babysitters back home or doing my own housework again, for that matter. More than that, though, the whole close environment at Fort Kobbe made me feel good and at home. Everyone seemed to care, but when I got back to the States, I was very lonely because nobody seemed to care. Even the Army seems to care more about families overseas than at home. Overseas, I felt more informed about what was happening. In the States, I feel out of it all the time."

91

Re-entry shock is culture shock in reverse. Debbi McEwan, also from San Pedro, who accompanied her Army husband on back-to-back tours in Korea and England, said, "We came from a lovely rural area of England to the Los Angeles area. We were in an apartment and knew no one. Our son's bike was stolen and we had roaches. I reacted the same way I did when I arrived in Korea: I didn't go out and I wouldn't let the boys out. I felt threatened."

But why? Why is coming home from an overseas tour sometimes even more difficult for military families than moving to a foreign country?

"Who would ever expect to feel like a stranger in her own country?" asked Janet Batcheller of San Diego, a Navy wife who recently returned from Japan.

Janet added, "What I built myself up for in coming home just isn't here." Such unmet expectations also intensify the re-entry experience. Janet was shocked to find out that everything in this country was not perfect and problem-free.

Three years ago, Marilyn Brown moved back to her home town of Jacksonville, Fla., following a three-year accompanied tour with her Navy husband in Japan. Now living in Aurora, Colo., Marilyn described her re-entry this way: "I felt that once I was back home all my problems would disappear. I felt left out and behind the times. I had lived a totally different life for three years and had a very hard time readapting to life in the United States. My experiences were so different that I often felt that others thought I was exaggerating or bragging about them and my travels. I missed the friends with whom I had shared so much and had so much in common. I had a hard time making friends because I couldn't identify with new people. Often I felt as though I were living in a completely different world. It was a very difficult, sometimes lonely and unhappy time for me."

Recovering from re-entry shock in most cases is a gradual process and not easily defined. Some women I talked to were still going through it. Others remembered taking from six months to a year to recover--or couldn't remember how long it took. Others, two years after their return from an overseas tour, are still trying to sort out their thoughts and feelings.

Because re-entry shock is primarily a family problem, the realities of the experience have been slow to surface. With most of the women I interviewed, there was a certain initial reluctance to share their re-entry experiences. Foremost in their minds seemed to be that the good military wife is the "well-adjusted wife," and since they had experienced or were experiencing re-entry shock more than their husbands, the problem seemed personal and per-

92   haps indicative of a personal shortcoming to them. Some women who denied experiencing re-entry shock went on to describe just such experiences in great detail.

For many women, however, this initial reluctance was quickly replaced by feelings of relief that someone else had experienced or was experiencing the same problem and by the hope that perhaps if they shared their re-entry experiences, other women might benefit from them. Whether a woman had been "back home" for 17 years or a matter of months, the validation of her foreign experience was important to her and her re-entry adjustment was vivid in her memory.

Re-entry shock, as well as culture shock, appears to affect military wives and children far more than their active duty husbands and fathers. Military personnel have their work to occupy them whether they are living in a foreign country or in the United States. In the field, on deployment or at home, in this country or abroad, service personnel spend at least eight hours of each day in the familiar work setting. Wives and children, however, have nothing similar to help them make the transition from life in this country to another or from living abroad to coming home.

Coming home can be a very critical part of an overseas tour for service children, as well. Wanting to be accepted and not wanting to appear different, teenagers, especially, coming from overseas DOD schools to American schools in a civilian community, often find that their peer groups resent their worldliness and make fun of them for not knowing such things as the

current slang and the most current dress styles. Rosemary Dennison's daughter, Lisa, was 15 and a sophomore in high school when the Dennison family moved from Okinawa to Nebraska. "Socialization was very difficult," recalled Lisa. "The social life was more advanced and getting into high school groups was nearly impossible. I watched a lot of TV as a result--and also because I missed TV programming overseas."

One of the reasons that Debbi McEwan and her husband did not extend their tour of duty in England was because they saw their two children, ages 8 and 4, turning into little English boys and they felt it was time to get them back to their own country and culture. But, Debbi said, "My older boy felt English in an American society. He was usually outgoing but he became insecure and shy. He adjusted quickly, though."

Erika Hatch, an Army wife who moved to Fort MacArthur in Los Angeles with her husband and their three sons last July, after a four-year tour in Germany, agreed that younger children adjust quickly to an overseas relocation--more quickly than older children or service wives. "Our younger boys, ages 8 and 12, seem to have adjusted easily; and other than an occasional, 'I wish we had stayed in Germany,' they seem to be okay. Our oldest son, though, who is in high school, is really finding it hard to adjust. He feels like an outsider. His peers are already in groups and don't want to bother with a newcomer. He is very distant from his dad since he feels it is his dad's fault that he is here. He's blaming his dad for his feeling of not belonging."

93

Erika, who was born in Germany, has experienced culture shock in coming to the United States as a service wife, re-entry shock in returning to Germany for two subsequent tours, and is experiencing re-entry shock now in returning to this country again. "I feel like a piece of forgotten baggage," she said. "Leaving Germany again for California was exciting for me. I had loved living in California during our last assignment, but things here have changed so much in four years. This time it is very hard for me to adjust. I have the feeling that no one cares."

Time and support are needed for people--children and adults--to adapt to the home situation at the same time they are clinging to the values of the foreign experience. Generally speaking, service children seem to adjust rapidly, perhaps because they have the support and understanding of their parents, particularly their mothers.

Beyond casual conversation, service wives often find that friends, neighbors, new acquaintances and even relatives are not really interested in hearing about their life overseas, and talking about it is often interpreted either as boasting or as criticism of the United States. Not being able to share their foreign experience at the same time that they are not yet feeling a part of life at home leads to confusion. To make matters worse, they may also find that their spouses are also confused and unsupportive of their situation.

Janet Batcheller's husband, Navy pilot Peter Batcheller, agreed. He said, "I realized that something was not right with Janet, but I didn't perceive the problem as it was happening. Investment of my time became more of an issue. I was concerned enough to try to spend more time at home instead of at work, but hindsight tells me that because I didn't realize the significance of Janet's problem, I didn't spend enough time at home. Nobody appreciates the problem of coming back. There is no support system for re-entry shock here at home like there was for culture shock when we went to Japan."

Although understanding does not necessarily relieve the pain of adjustment, a great deal can often be gained by the realization that others have experienced a similar painful phenomenon and by having the source of the pain explained. None of the women in my study were prepared for their re-entry shock experience in any way and most agreed that some type of preparation would have been helpful:

"Anything," said Navy wife Dee Crouch of Lemoore, Calif., "even someone telling me that re-entry shock was to be expected and explaining it to my husband so he wouldn't think I was going crazy." Janet Batcheller added, "Some type of preparation would probably have been helpful. Although it may not have changed my reactions to returning home, it has helped a lot to talk about it and to find out that I am normal." Somehow, any painful experience is easier to tolerate when it is expected, understood and known to be a normal reaction.

94

11

The Culture Shock of Coming Home Again

Jane Hipkins Sobie

There were plenty of McDonalds in the highlands of Scotland. But none of them sold hamburgers.

For three years the only McDonalds I knew either played the bagpipes or raised sheep. Every day, Ian McDonald's sheep grazed in my front yard. Each spring I'd watch his lambs devour my daffodils. But in Scotland, sheep rule the land. My family and I learned to accept that part of the Scottish culture when we were stationed there from 1975 to 1978.

I anticipated some cultural adjustment when we went overseas. It took time getting used to having no ice in the drinks, calling french fries "chips," and remembering to drive on the left side of the road. But the more I learned about the Scottish people, their history and culture, and the more I assimilated myself into their lifestyle, the more rewarding was my highland fling.

I made it a ritual to have tea at 3. My husband became a regular at the local pub's dart tournaments. Our sons attended Scottish schools. Within a few weeks, it was difficult to tell them apart from the other five-year-old lads. Their trucks became "lorries," warm became "warrrrm," and I was "Mum."

America grew farther and farther away.

When orders to Washington, D.C. came in, I had mixed feelings. I was excited about going home to family and friends and getting back into the mainstream. As much as I loved the highlands, they were isolating. Yet it was painful to say goodbye to a country and its people, knowing I might never see them again.

I anticipated my adjustment to America to be a snap. After all, I was coming home, right? But America hit me like a tidal wave. As soon as I got off the jetliner at JFK Airport, I felt as though I were seeing technicolor for the first time. Someone had also turned up the volume and speeded up the film. America was in a hurry. Whoosh! Everybody talked, walked, ate as if there were a prize for the f-a-s-t-e-s-t.

I was shocked when I went to the airport newsstand. I didn't recognize one face on the magazine covers. What was Saturday Night Live? I thought Chevy Chase was a suburb of Washington, not a movie star.

Shopping malls overwhelmed me. All glitter. Pizzaz. In Dunoon, Scotland, I had two varieties of sunglasses to choose from. In America I had thousands. Pink tinted. Blue. Purple. It took me two hours to select a pair.

America was a smorgasbord. But within two weeks, I had indigestion. Then things began to make me angry. Why did Americans have such big gas-guzzling cars? Why were all the commercials telling me I had to buy this product in order to be liked? Material possessions and dressing for success were not top priorities in the highlands. And American TV? I missed the BBC.

Then I felt guilty about thinking this way. How could I possibly think America was anything but the biggest and the best? I was confused.

So were the children. They were used to a strict Charles Dickenish headmaster. Their Washington, D.C. principal strolled the corridors in a leisure suit and clogs. "You'll find American schools far superior to Scottish schools," he said. Yet I found Scottish schools two years ahead in math.

On the first day of school, as the other third graders stood up to say the Pledge of Allegiance, our son Steven, sat silent in his seat. The teacher scolded him for not joining in.

"But I neverrrr hearrrrrd it beforrrrr." His classmates laughed at this American with a funny accent.

That night at the dinner table Steven asked, "Mum, am I American or Scottish right now?"

Re-entry Shock

Our family was suffering from re-entry shock. It is reverse culture shock and has been around ever since Uncle Sam has been sending families overseas. It's been a "hidden family problem," until recently. In the past, emphasis was placed on culture shock for families moving overseas. Nobody talked about the "other" culture shock. Re-entry shock comes as a jolt to most Americans because it is totally unexpected.

"Overseas relocation is a major life stressor," says Sandra Mumford Fowler, head of the Navy's overseas duty support program and president of the International Society for Intercultural Education, Training and Research. "Closing out an overseas experience is very different than moving from Norfolk to Charleston. When you leave England, The Philippines, Italy or Germany, you are leaving a country and people you may never see again," she says. "It is a painful experience and similar to the mourning process."

Although returning to the United States is not as intense as experiencing the death of a loved one, the stages of denial, anger, grief and acceptance are very much a part of the re-entry process.

Studies indicate that those who have adjusted most successfully to their overseas country will experience the greatest reverse culture shock on their return home.

"You are a different person as a result of your overseas experience," says Fowler. "You have seen another way of life, and learned new values and attitudes. You must allow yourself time to process that experience."

Recovering from re-entry shock is a gradual process and difficult to define. It takes some people six months to a year to recover. Others need up to two years or longer to sort out their feelings and thoughts and blend the two cultures.

When you come back from overseas you see America as a foreigner does. You view America through a sharper lens, and are able to pick up the strengths and weaknesses of the country much more clearly. The reluctance for many people to speak about the experience is fear of being considered by family or friends as unpatriotic.

"When I came back to the states, I found Americans shallow and plastic," recalls Ann Tarzier, an Air Force wife who was stationed in Germany with her husband and two children from 1980 to 1983. She served as Army Community Services director in Landstuhl. "I felt hostile towards American drivers who wouldn't get out of the fast lane," she says. "I treasured the cultural experiences I had in Germany. Somehow, America seemed like Archie Bunker. Once back in the states, I missed Germany. I couldn't share this with my neighbors. They'd have thought me a traitor or snob."

Consequently, Tarzier, like other returnees, feel guilty about their feelings and keep them inside. This often leads to alienation and depression. Many don't talk about the difficulty they are having adjusting to America for fear of being seen as weak. (What sense does it make that you could adjust to a foreign culture, but have trouble adjusting in your own?)

"I thought I was going crazy," recalls Tarzier. "I had shortness of breath, felt panicky and was very depressed. I knew I needed professional help. But it was like going to a doctor with a hangnail, and yet that hangnail can cause more pain than a broken arm."

The therapist said Tarzier was suffering from "separation anxiety." "Having experienced nearly 20 years of military life and two other overseas moves,

I thought I had the whole thing wired," says Tarzier. "But moving doesn't get easier over the years. I tried to leave Germany with a stiff upper lip, and it didn't work. I was intellectualizing the entire overseas experience, rather than giving myself the permission to humanize my feelings. Getting help was the best thing I ever did."

Today, Tarzier is the Army's relocation assistance program coordinator. "In the past two years I have talked to many people who have gone through similar experiences," she says. "If just someone would have told me that what I was feeling was normal, and that this too will pass, I could have handled it better. One day, a bunch of us sat around and cried together about how we missed Germany. And that's o.k.!"

Even people who did not enjoy their overseas tour can expect to experience re-entry shock. Often they come back to America with unrealistic expectations. They think their problems will be solved once they come home. But when the taxi driver yells at them, and the streets are dirtier than they remember, and the plumber doesn't fix the sink on the first try, they become disillusioned.

According to Fowler, some returnees experience little re-entry shock. "There are Americans living overseas who never really penetrate into the foreign surroundings," she says. "They live, eat, work, and shop on the American-ized base. They don't miss the U.S., because in many ways, they never left it."

98

But for service members and their families who do live on the foreign economy, coming back to the states can be a financial shock. In October, 1985, the destroyer tender, PUGET SOUND, changed home ports to Norfolk, after a five year stay in Gaeta, Italy.

"Overseas, we had first class petty officers living in Italian villas and driving Porsches," says Captain J.F. McCarton, commanding officer of the PUGET SOUND. "In Norfolk, Navy housing and making payments on a Ford Escort are the realities. Overseas, a soup to nuts meal was $12. Here, that barely covers the wine . . . "

According to Sue Reno, a PUGET SOUND Ombudsman, over 50% of the wives have taken jobs since the ship's return. "We literally had to," says Sue, who has taken a part-time job. "In Italy we paid $230 for a two bedroom apartment. Now we're paying $500."

It can cost the military family nearly $2000 to relocate in the United States after living overseas, says Bobbie Brenton, overseas duty support program coordinator at the Norfolk Navy Family Services Center. "A family should plan for this before coming back to America," she says.

In addition to the financial adjustments the PUGET SOUND had to make to living in the states, Captain McCarton also notes a psychological adjustment. "In Gaeta, we (ship) were the big fish in the little pond," he says. "In Norfolk, we are just another grey hull amongst many."

This feeling of loss of identity is common for returnees from overseas.

"In Germany, I had a job and a very good sense of who I was," recalls Tarzier. "Coming back to Washington, DC, I felt faceless and empty. I don't think my husband could relate to my problem," she says. "He had a job waiting for him at the Pentagon, and a desk with his name on it."

Re-entry shock appears to affect military wives and children more than active duty husbands and fathers. "Men have their built-in support group," says Brenton. "They come back to a familiar job, they wear the same uniform, and their basic day's work is the same. The wives and children have a new medical and school system to enroll in. Shopping methods are different. And for wives seeking employment," she adds, "they have to start the job hunting process all over again."

Because their world changes faster than anyone else's, and peer acceptance is crucial, teenagers are very susceptible to re-entry stress. "They feel out of it when they come back," says Fowler, who conducts cross-cultural training for the state department and Georgetown University. "Some begin to feel that being overseas was a bad thing. Not many kids want to hear about their adventures in London or Naples," she says. "Instead of being able to process their years overseas, they have to pretend it didn't happen."

It is not uncommon for normally active teenagers to withdraw and become depressed after an overseas tour. Some use alcohol and drugs as a means of coping. Even a different grading system can cause tension for teens.

Seventeen-year-old Kristin Morgan recently moved back to the states after her Navy family had back-to-back tours in Cuba and Italy. "Overseas, 90–100 was an A," she says. "In Virginia Beach, 95–100 is an A. I really prefer the overseas schools," she says. "I knew practically everybody and had a better sense of belonging. Here," she says, "it's more difficult to fit in. Most kids have lived here all their lives."

Younger children also experience their own variety of re-entry shock. Nine-year-old Scott Reno, son of first class petty officer, Dick Reno and his wife, Sue, had never seen milk cartons with pictures of missing children on it before moving back to America. In Italy, it was perfectly safe for Scott and his younger brother, Bryan, to roam the streets at night. But one night Scott had a nightmare that woke up the rest of the family. "He dreamed that someone had stolen his brother," recalls his mother.

In working with families who have come back from overseas tours, Chaplain William Weimer, Lcdr. USN, PUGET SOUND, observes that sprawled out American communities can create a sense of isolation and tear at the once close-knit family unit that was fostered overseas.

"Here you get up at 5 am. You fight traffic. Go to work. Fight traffic again. Eat dinner. Watch TV. Go to bed," he says. "You've got to get used to driving everywhere you go . . . scouts, PTA, school, church, shopping. It can be a grind."

Experts agree that an overseas tour can strengthen a marriage and family. "The overseas marriage is more of a partnership," says Tarzier. "There are

[handwritten margin note: again w/ the topic of people not wanting to listen to their stories]

99

less distractions, like TV, and you do more things together. When you come home, you can share those memories together."

However, an overseas environment can put extra strain on a marriage. "If you have problems going overseas, such as financial difficulties, or family violence, it's like amplifying those issues," asserts Tarzier. "The added stress of coming back to the states, is like turning up the heat again."

Fowler, who has been instrumental in implementing the Navy's program on re-entry shock, believes families should be screened before going overseas by the family services centers. "Some families are simply not suitable for overseas living," she says. North Island Navy Family Service Center is currently involved in this project.

Keflavik and Siganella have excellent re-entry programs according to Fowler. Workshops are held in the evenings for families. In addition to a re-entry movie, discussions dealing with the practical and emotional aspects of relocating are addressed.

"It's unfortunate for Navy families," she says, "that their ability to adjust or know what re-entry shock is, depends on where they are stationed and what programs, if any, the base provides."

"A lot of ships still pay minimal attention to families," says Tarzier. "Even if you have a CO who is concerned about families, his operational commitments come first. Sometimes he has no choice. We need to bring the programs to them."

100

When the PUGET SOUND changed home ports, the Navy Family Services Center in Norfolk sent a team to Gaeta in June to conduct re-entry workshops. Captain McCarton then sent his own team back to Norfolk in July, to assist 500 family members relocate, while the ship steamed home.

"We did everything from pick them up at the airport to help them find housing," says Chaplain Weimer, who headed up the three-man team. Newsletters were sent to the families to keep up the communications, and picnics and inter-faith worship services helped to keep up the morale until the ship came home.

"Just knowing someone was there to help us and give us the straight scoop meant a lot to me," says Judy Morgan, who with her three teenage daughters, was assisted by the return team.

The Air Force is developing a handbook to deal with the issues of overseas living, including re-entry shock, according to Major Frank Goldstein, director of the Air Force Family Support Program. Although the Air Force has no official program to deal with re-entry shock, Goldstein notes that Moody, Luke and Fairchild Air Force bases have good relocation programs.

Like the Air Force, the Army has no official program to address this issue. They are starting an outreach program for military families, and relocation will be included in this effort.

For the most part, the military considers re-entry shock a "soft" issue, says Tarzier. "The ramifications of re-entry stress are not yet recognized.

But it can affect job performance, cause depression and lead to spouse and child abuse."

In 1984, 81,000 soldiers and their families moved back to the United States after an overseas tour. "I think the most forgotten group in the military today is the returnees from overseas," notes Tarzier.

But there are ways to deal with re-entry shock, even if your base does not sponsor a program. Recognize that re-entry shock is real and not just imagined.

Give yourself and your family time to process the overseas tour and home-coming experiences. Talk about it at the dinner table. Check on each family member to see how they are adjusting to work, school or new daily activities. Seek out other people who lived overseas to share viewpoints.

If adjustment becomes a problem, get help through a chaplain, counselor, or your family support center. Remember, children will adjust to their overseas tour in much the same way their parents do.

"Just as it took time to learn how to live in a foreign culture," says Chaplain Weimer, "it takes time and patience to learn how to live in America again."

P.S. It's been seven years since our family left the highlands of Scotland. Our 14-year-old twins laugh at the tapes we made when they had Scottish brogues. Today, they're as Americanized as any Virginia Beach teenager, zipping about on their skateboards. My husband, Rich, hasn't played darts since he left Scotland. His shelf is full of running awards now, a hobby he pursued in the U.S. And although I was the most laid-back person when I came back to the states, I now work at a pace that would melt the snow off the heathered highlands.

"Slow down," my mother warns. "S-l-o-w down."

When traffic is at a snarled standstill on I-64, I do slow down. It is then that I dig deep into my mental reservoir and recall the lush green highlands, Mr. McDonald's wee lambs, Inverary Castle, and the rest of my highland fling. That part of me will never change.

12

Uneasy Homecoming: Stages in the Reentry Transition of Vietnam Veterans

Robert R. Faulkner and Douglas B. McGaw

From Waller's *The Veteran Comes Back* (1944) and Cottrell and Stouffer's "The Soldier Becomes a Veteran" (Stouffer et al., 1949) to Lifton's *Home From the War* (1973) and Borus' "The Reentry Transition of the Vietnam Veteran" (1975), investigators have periodically, but irregularly, focused on the problem of reentry into civilian society, the meaning of passage from soldier to civilian, and the social psychology of homecoming.[1] Schutz's (1964) important essay on the homecomer uses the soldier-turned-veteran as the paradigmatic example. The return to an alien homeland reveals the interplay between self and significant others; not only does the homeland show the soldier an unaccustomed face, the soldier as homecomer appears alien to those within his social circle. Handling the imputations and actions of others becomes a key concern during the difficult period of early reentry. Not only are many of the practices and perspectives acquired in the war irrelevant to civilian life, but the person must reestablish relationships, reorient himself to the home experience from the standpoint of nonsoldier grouping, unlearn the war's moral order, and relearn the home's moral order. It is through the successful reacquisition of roles and symbolic meanings that identity and status as civilian are affirmed.

Faulkner, R. R., and McGaw, D. B., "Uneasy Homecoming: Stages in the Reentry Transition of Vietnam Veterans," *Urban Life*, Vol. 6, No. 3 (October 1977), pp. 303–328. Copyright © 1977 by Sage Publications, Inc. Reprinted by permission of Sage Publications, Inc.

Our aim is to offer some interview materials with a select sample of Vietnam veterans and to analyze, in interactionist terms, certain stages through which their homecoming typically passes. In late 1974, we observed and interviewed twenty Vietnam soldiers with an interest in the stages of their homecoming. The men we had talked to came back to urban society, decided to go to school, and enrolled in a major university on the East Coast. This is where we met them. Most are successfully "making it" as graduates or undergraduates. With a few exceptions, they are all men in their late twenties, who were either infantrymen or helicopter pilots. Half of them are married. Over half served their war time between 1967 and 1969, the rest between 1970 and 1973. Six were wounded. Interviews with them were tape recorded and ran from one-half to two hours.[2] We were particularly interested in case histories and their profiles of what happened in the war experience, problems subsequent to coming home, successes they have experienced, changes in relationships with others during reentry, and the features on which successful reorientation depend. As an exploratory, interactionist study of the Vietnam veteran, we focused attention on the way these homecomers order and make meaningful the objects of their experience, including themselves, during the critical stages of reentry. In focusing on the experiential turning points and contingencies of coming home, we shall write mainly from the *phenomenal world* of those undergoing this kind of status passage.

104

Reentry is shaped by sentiments and cognitive perspectives. These are brought from the war experiences as well as directly conditioned subsequent to the arrival back in the states. If home is the place to which a soldier intends to return when he is away from it (Schutz, 1964: 1907), then coming back to "The World," as it is called by Vietnam veterans, involves two things. First, the veteran has changed. Second, the home has changed with respect to the veteran. The homecomer has experiences he feels he cannot relate to the nonveterans. He also has to face some of the community's apprehensions, misunderstandings, and distinctive systems of relevance. This kind of interaction between the returning soldier and his social world is significant for what it tells us about reentry, both as it affects status transition and as it implicates general features of interpersonal process. We find that from the perspective of the Vietnam veteran, three interrelated concerns constitute the reality of their homecoming and stages of their reentry career: (1) disengagement and the process of *moving from* the war, (2) reentry and the process of *moving back into* "The World," and (3) reintegration and the concern with *moving toward* the consolidation of social involvement and binding separations. These three stages of homecoming as status passage (Glaser and Strauss, 1971) have to do with individual changes in social position. They are also lined with emotional and evaluative processes; thus, we pay particular attention to the active imputation of emotional importance and meaning to these changes. Each stage in the transition process imparts a characteristic stance and feeling toward the crisis and dilemmas of role and identity that arise (Becker and Strauss, 1956; Strauss, 1959; Becker, 1964). Although the process of reentry transition to be discussed here will focus on Vietnam veterans, the general relevance of the process of homecoming for a variety of roles will be pointed out.

Moving from the War

Coming out of the war experience is a process of disengagement, and among the features of any disengagement are the importance of social bonds in the setting from which one is moving. Also important are the meanings attached to that membership, the degree of shared experience there, and the affective character of those bonds. As has been noted in a variety of contexts, the transition from the war is problematic because the war itself has such a central role in the life of the individual (Lifton, 1973; Stouffer et al., 1949; Waller, 1944). The soldier has "tasted the magic fruit of strangeness, be it sweet or bitter" (Schutz, 1964: 116). For the men we have been talking to, it was both. For Stan, one of our exemplary respondents, "Vietnam is the biggest thing that happened to me since I was born." For several of his buddies, the centrality of becoming a soldier was emphasized. It was "a big thing," a way to manhood with all its attendant responsibilities, duties, pragmatic self-interests, and shared obligations. It was also, for them, exposure to combat risks and hardships. It was an adventure in winning and an adventure in losing. They won some friends and manhood; they lost important parts of themselves, often their friends, their innocence, and valuable time on the civilian job market. They also changed in important ways.

The sources of change can be traced to various themes that are commonly encountered in war, some of which are general, and some of which are more specific to the Vietnam experience. One theme, as Waller (1944: 111) noted in his report on World War II veterans, is that "they have learned to hate and kill. They have shot over. They have lost their reverence for many of the word symbols that formerly controlled their behavior." They have also occasionally found themselves used as bait in order to lure the enemy into attack in an ambush. Helmer (1974), in writing on the Vietnam war, also points out how commanders adopted the use of enemy body counts as an index of effectiveness and a means of rapid promotion in spite of their own losses. The soldiers have seen or heard of fragging of NCOs and officers in their own or nearby units. They have also been part of primary group solidarity which at times served to foster and then to reinforce dissent from and noncompliance with the purposes of the military organization. Innumerable reports have pointed out the ubiquity of the drug problem in Vietnam, where drugs were used by many to escape from the harsh realities of the war. These themes of war life do form a partially integrated pattern, working together to produce a state of experienced affairs in the life of many of the men. They are often ruling dimensions from which these former soldiers see themselves as disengaging. We touch briefly on the key problems of comrades, losses, and personal change, for they reach into the very stuff of reentry as moving from the war.

We asked Stan to talk about the war and some of the changes he had experienced in himself as a result of being in Vietnam. He responded:

There's a very limited number of people who have shared this experience with me . . . and I feel like I've been through something that was so intense, that unless somebody else has been through it, they're going to have a hard time understanding where I'm coming from. I've gone beyond the age of innocence and [the other kids in school] are still in that age, maybe passing through it. Somehow, they haven't seen some of the harsher things that can happen in life, and they're still naive to a great deal. Who was I then? . . . That I did what I did? You know, taking another human life. It's a hard thing to deal with. I feel like I was put in a position that, once I experienced it, I didn't want to be in, but, in order to make it all the way through, I had to play the whole game. There was no place to run. So I had to kind of see the thing through to its logical conclusion, absurd as it was. . . . I went through a lot of changes.

What makes this definition of the experience so central is that the war world is a very different one from the "Real World" in that it involves a different set of definitions, interpretations, and behaviors. It constitutes a different system of relevance (Schutz, 1964). This change in a system of relevance would be less central if it were not so sudden and dramatic. "One week you're in the States, dating, going to movies, working a 9-to-5 type job; and the next you're at war, sleeping in the rain, being fired at, living in almost constant apprehension." For most veterans, the war was a disruptive, traumatic, and largely unpleasant experience. Their definition of the war experience is central to an understanding of how they interpret their ability to relate to others, because, as many of them are aware, the war forced them to change or readjust certain behavior patterns and patterns of thought to which they had become accustomed. To repeat, it is this experience *from which* they are adjusting that needs to be taken into account. There is a change in identity as one moves from the war world. The civilian turned soldier has an acute sense of the war as having made him different through and through, not merely identifiably different. This is not a mere acquisition of knowledge, but a change in *being;* a change that comes from the expectation of personal loss, fear of one's own death, anxiety over being alone, and a sharing of terror. This loss can be expressed in at least three ways.

1. A sense of loss of *time* out of his life is expressed by Tony. "The hardest part was that, in essence, when you were *away* for that long of a time. It's just like someone comes along, and you have a banana, you slice two inches out of the middle and you put it back together again.

2. But not only is there the sense of having lost time, but some feel they have lost a part of their *selves.* This loss of self is expressed most strongly by Ricky, "I lost a lot of my personality through going over there and everything. I used to be a very open person. I used to be like, very good-

natured to everyone, you know? I found that, being over there, I became very questioning of people.

3. There is also the loss of *others*, especially of close friends. Stan, having lost close friends in Vietnam, says that now "In a lot of ways I fear getting too close to someone, because then maybe I'll lose them."

The unique qualities of the friendship or comradeship experienced in war, combined with the anomic atmosphere which is endemic to war and the veteran's return to a vastly different society than he found in war, arouse in the veteran the sense of loss of objects or someone intimate in a way that is not fully understood by civilian society.

Above all, the war entails two kinds of very conspicuous cost. Having nothing to do with fighting in Vietnam as such, but rather with the losses occasioned by it, values foregone through being away constitute an *extrinsic* disadvantage. On the other hand, the implications of facing death and slaughter are *intrinsic* to that war and can arise in few other ways than through being there. The peculiar thing about wartime death is a combination of the extreme violence of it, the intensely close bonds felt by the soldiers, and the intentional nature of the death. A very close friend dies a horrible death, a death which is witnessed by the veteran, and it is often harder to accept by blaming it on God or fate because of one's awareness that the death was consciously and intentionally inflicted by other men, enemy soldiers. (Parenthetically, a very common belief that arises, apparently in reaction to these contingencies, is exemplified by the statement, "Don't sweat it. When your number's up, there ain't nothing you can do. If it ain't up, you won't get hurt." In other words, there is a common and widespread fatalism that pervades as a legitimation of death in war.) These vital elements are usually lacking in nonwar deaths, so that the veteran's feeling of loss of another's life may be seen to be uniquely salient to him and to affect his later perceptions in a particularly sharp manner.

107

The transition back to "The World" also affects his perceptions very sharply. The pace of transition, in this case geographical transition, creates a lag in consciousness. Tony said:

> You're in the Army one day and out on the streets the next, bye now. . . . That's it. . . . You really need some pasture time to think about where you've been and where you're going. It just happens too quick, you're really not prepared, even though you're counting all the time for the day of leaving. It is the event, leaving and coming home. Over there in Nam I thought it would be great to be back, and home was a dream, a beautiful dream, and when you get home all of a sudden you're faced with it--right then.

None were divested of the habits of thought, feeling, and action learned in Vietnam. The actual and symbolic preparations for leaving the military did not prepare them for their returns, for their homecoming. Socialization for the home was inadequately programmed. This is in sharp contrast to the rites of passage into the service. As our respondents note, the anticipation of DEROS (date of reentry into the States), was intense; return now was the most important event in their lives.

But they were in a marginal situation; they were, as several put it, "in limbo." Their passages were traversed in aggregate rather than collective fashion where transition time between Vietnam and the United States (by jet) was extremely short. And as in other careers, pacing and timing are crucial. "Transition periods are a necessity," write Becker and Strauss (1956: 259) in their programmatic statement on careers, "for a man often invests heavily of himself in a position, comes to possess it as it possesses him. . . . If the full ritual of leave-taking is not allowed, the man may not pass fully into his new status." Akin to Tony's reference to "pasture time," some of the veterans indicate that more time in the army after returning either was or would have been helpful in moderating the shock of the transition. The mechanisms of restoring people to membership in civilian society that Becker and Strauss (1956) outline underlie the reported importance of "pasture time" as a transition period.

When we look at this stage concerning what the men bring out of the war to society rather than at what society offers these men, it is essential to keep in mind that the changes from civilian to soldier and from soldier to civilian mark turning points in the life of the people we have talked to. Some central features of this transition can be noted: (a) the acquisition of new goals and purposes while in the service, and of the newly discovered means to realize them; (b) a primacy of self-interest, but one often combined with deep bonds to one's closest friends in the military; (c) a shared meaning of the war experience among these friends; and (d) a loss of something valuable. The loss may be that of time, of buddies, or of the ability to bind the discordance in the individual's perception of the real "home" and the ideal "home." The "World" that exists is often in contrast to the "World" that the soldier expects or feels should exist. The issue throughout the interviews about loss involves the nature of the relationship between the individual and the object or referent of value: whether, for example, the soldier now becoming a civilian can control his life circumstances, whether he feels that the course of transition from the war is comprehensible, or whether he feels that he has the opportunity to undo the war within the context of his own life.

108

Moving Back into "The World"
The reentry into the "home" culture involves a readjustment in one's perspectives. The intensity of the war experience--especially for the infantrymen--combined with its alien set of values are what makes the reentry problematic. This reentry is difficult for several reasons: (1) a discontinuity in the systems of relevance, (2) and related, the unsharability of the war experience, and (3) various forms of exclusion by the "home" society.

1. By *discontinuity* in systems of relevance, we refer to the fact that many

of the typifications and norms governing behavior in the war situation not only are different, but are inimical and actively discouraged at home (Schutz, 1964). The returnee, the veteran, is bewildered to see that his conversational "others" do not understand the uniqueness of the experiences that have made him another person. He has to alter his patterns of behavior and his reactions to others. This problem is exacerbated by the speed of the transition and by the fact that most veterans did not experience a homecoming, a rite of passage akin to the one experienced by the bulk of the World War II veterans. There was no official boundary-marking ceremony, for instance, to collectively certify reacceptance by the veteran's home culture.

The readjustment stage is accomplished with varying degrees of success by these veterans. For most of them, some three-quarters of those we talked to, this stage is difficult, time-consuming, and often acrimonious. It was difficult for Ricky because reentry "was just bringing me right back into the rules of society so fast, in less than a day."

The fast-paced discontinuity in transition is closely tied to violence in the war setting. The legitimation and practice of violent acts as a soldier can be carried back to the home setting, where it is not a relevant or acceptable form of behavior. Many veterans report they have trouble--at least in the early months of reentry--controlling their violent "impulses" when confronted with problematic situations.

In moving back into the home world, the former soldier moves back into a different "symbolic universe," in Berger and Luckmann's (1967) words. He must as one soldier put it, "get his head out of Nam." As has been noted in a number of contexts (Schutz, 1964; Lifton, 1973; Waller, 1944), this requires an adjustment *from* the forced integrated setting of the military *to* a more "open" society, a renewal of his basic constitutional and civil rights, restricted relevance of the use of force threat in interpersonal action, nonlegitimation of violence, increased expectancies for control of one's life, and the wish to be free, to manage one's affairs with a minimum of interference from others. This state of affairs in the former home "universe," we find, can be transformed into one of open problematic possibilities.

2. This discontinuity between the war world and the home world is closely related to the second major difficulty in reentry, that of the *unsharability* of the war experience. The veteran has gone through an experience of personal change as a result of his war experience, and, because of this experience, he feels qualitatively different from the nonveterans around him back home. He has a different history, a history and experience which he finds difficult or even impossible to communicate to others, even though he often desires to do so. In other words, his "being different" is most often manifested through his perceived inability to adequately communicate either his experience or his feelings to others. We find that it is magnified by the fact that

most civilians often do not want to know what happened in Vietnam. And, even if they do, they are not credited by the veterans as fully understanding.

It is with this possession of the unsharable experience that the evaluative *and* emotive framework for veteran's later resocialization to home world perspectives assumes a certain rudimentary shape. Ricky discussed this at some length. We asked him about the problems Vietnam vets faced, and the problems he faced.

> When I first got back, no one cared, really, what went on in your head, what you experienced.... You got hit with the question that everyone had seen in every war movie. What did it feel like when you killed your first man?... No one seemed to really care how I felt, what had transcended in my mind.... Everything was face value, you know, "How you doing? How was your year? Did you see much action? What did it feel like when you killed your first man? I'm glad to see you're back; I'll see you later." It ... tended to disenchant the Vietnam veteran when he came back because no one wanted to really know. Either people were too afraid to find out your real feelings on the matter, or they didn't really care.... And it tended to set me into a shell that ... where I would never talk of my experiences at all ... when I first came home and I was at a party and someone really attacked me for going to Vietnam in the first place. [What was your reaction?] Violence. I went at her, she was a little girl--I went at her, and lucky it was broken up, but ... I just snapped. It was too personal for me to listen to an attack from someone who didn't know anything about it [the experiences in Vietnam]. They were part of me. They were there. It was just too close, too personal.

The problems here are that neither the veteran nor the home to which he is returning are the same as before. The home itself is seen by the veteran as being different.

110

3. The discontinuity in the systems of meaning and the perceived unsharability are some of the most difficult and salient problems of reentry facing the veteran. Another is dealing with *exclusion* from the home society. The Vietnam veteran not only feels different from other civilians, but also feels that society denies him access to events, objects, and processes that are important to him. This contingency is exacerbated for these veterans by virtue of the invidious comparisons they make to the treatment accorded to the veteran of World War II. As they see it, after the war the World War II veterans came home to popular support, to bands on the docks, to confetti, to adoration and affection. What is more, they came home--by and large--together. The war was over and won and the boys home victorious to a grateful nation.

By contrast, our respondents talk about a return *from* an unpopular war *to* an essentially silent, if not ambivalent, society. No bands, no cheering crowds were on hand. Moreover, much of the country--even most of it toward the end--opposed the war in which the veterans had fought and risked their lives for no discernible political purpose. They found little sense or purpose in what they were doing. They had given perhaps "too much" in a war in which America was not the victor. The emotive aspect of distributive justice flows directly from the labeled recognition of incongruity between effort and reward. They feel they have received inadequate moral compensation for the high investment they made. Andrew best articulated the fracture between dreams and deeds: "They blew their chance when they didn't have any homecoming parade for me." This imagery and stance is then compounded by the evaluation they have of being "let down" by society's and, specifically, the government's indifference to them subsequent to reentry. In short, there is discordance between what the "home world" *should be* and what it *turns out to be.* The veterans see themselves as the recipients of injustice. They all note the disjunction between what they claim they are entitled to and what they receive on return to the states. Their own treatment is compared with the relatively better treatment of veterans of World War II. Finally, they are keenly attuned to hypocrisy--especially the contradictions between public pronouncements and actual programs for these veterans and the dilemmas surrounding their own reentry. Invidious comparisons with the World War II veterans on matters of employment opportunity, scope of the GI Bill, and availability of VA benefits and complaints about the older veterans' blaming the younger for losing the war appear with regularity throughout their discussions as manifestations of the "shock" of returning home.

In summarizing the focal concerns at this second stage of reentry, four general elements stand out. In characterizing these veterans' outlooks, the elements discussed below are or have been present in most respondents: Of course, the relative prominence of each element tends to vary.

1. Vietnam veterans come to define initial reentry as involving   *111* *misalignment between their dreams and deeds,* that is, between home as it is recalled and longed for during their absence and what, in fact, home turns out to be at initial homecoming. The discordance between anticipations and subsequent reactions toward them by others (and these include World War II veterans, the VA, and, in many cases, employers) underscores a key dimension of their disillusionment.

2. The homecomer is neither the same for himself nor for his significant others. *The veteran is not the same man who left;* in trying to weave together the transformed threads of his biography, he finds that a new identity, a new set of announcements, must be recurrently made and validated (see Stone, 1962: 93). Trouble occurs here also. There is a painful disjunction between altered self-representations and placements enacted by others in encounters. This renders an identity precarious. The placements by others are inconsistent with the veteran's conception of himself as an autonomous person with goals, needs, beliefs, and abilities of value. The veteran at this stage may progressively overidentify with the role of civilian, but is not fully accepted in this role by others. This makes of him a marginal man, a person "in limbo" between two cultural identities--that of the *socialized soldier* and that of the *resocialized civilian.* Either he or other people or both do not quite know to what identity to refer him.

This stage, it can be argued, startles these young men into thinking about relationships, objects (including the self), and expectations for control in their home environment they have hitherto taken for granted. Reentry brings vivid and rapid awareness of those decisions and events for which he himself is directly responsible and those made by others which affect him.

3. Directly related to feelings of bitterness and confusion, there are frequent expressions of *frustrations and annoyance* at the content of everyday sociability. The veterans report that in many cases the attention of others toward them in sociable interaction is narrowly channeled. Their identity is circumscribed by the "deviant" and bizarre aspects of what came to be an unpopular war (e.g., My Lai). He is the recipient of resentment, both for not winning the war and for the "dirty work" he has done. He finds that often he is feared and that people are all too quick to label him as a "killer" or "potential psychotic." He is negatively typecast, tainted by his participation in the war. The labeling is done by people with little, if any, understanding of the Vietnam experience; these civilians do not share his inner knowledge of the deaths, dilemmas, and demand conditions of that war. He thereby comes to gain an identity through notoriety. Such treatment serves to reinforce his sense of exclusion by others; it also alters his symbolic framework for judging them.

4. Finally, the veteran is not only downcast by others, *he is cast adrift* in his former home world. He is fundamentally motivated to seek a reincorporation of his biography into the taken-for-granted social reality of home. But *anomy* occurs for him as events and processes cannot be subsumed under the formerly shared social reality (Berger and Luckmann, 1967: 102). It is precisely the taken-for-grantedness and refashioning of shared perspectives that are precarious at this stage. This is what makes the initial points of the homecoming career difficult, for the reactivation of recurring relations with persons and events is contingent on mutual sharing. Until the *nomos* of his common world is reestablished, the veteran is considered strange, feels out of place, and cognitively undergoes an erosion of his ability to control or determine the outcomes he seeks with his fellow men.

The relevance of one or all of these points is apparent in the phenomenal world of our informants and in the social situations and settings in which they find themselves. They are focal concerns that are part of any homecoming where the world to which one returns is by no means the home one left, the home one expects to have under control on return, or the home as nostalgic object that was longed for and anticipated. What the veteran does about these problems depends on the opportunities available to him, his ability to take advantage of them, and the implications these have for his self-image. This ushers in the third stage of homecoming.

Bootstrap Betterment: Undoing the War and Moving Toward Reintegration
Whatever the typical troubles of homecoming are for these veterans, the pattern of associated problems vary by one's stage in this career line. Each stage entails changes in the person's self and in the framework for judging

112

self and others. So it is that the problems of reentry bring in their wake inner demands for self-aggrandizement, reward, and sense of accomplishment. The problem is getting access to events and processes that will facilitate these wishes. A number of general opportunities for the reaffirmation of identity and binding of separations are available. In brief, these opportunities include (1) peer-group relationships that provide a perspective on "responsibility" and encourage an acceptable self-image through acting on that perspective, (2) the cumulative acquisition of valuables that result in crescive commitments to the social world, and (3) the presence of other Vietnam veterans at various stages of "making it" that provide role models against whom comparisons of success can be made.

1. The first of these opportunities is in many ways the most important first step toward "getting your head out of Nam" and "taking care of business." How quickly this new perspective settles in depends on how well it fits the new situation. During early reentry, for example, we hear many stereotyped laments (Goffman's "sad tales") about "not being taken care of" or "not being *compensated."* In this later phase, the veteran's primary focus becomes a search for opportunities for "taking care of number one, *by* number one." This refocusing of energies is often dramatic. If met with success in the occupational and educational sphere, it serves to dissipate the feelings of injustice that besieged them at first. By this we mean that the more access the veteran gets to things he wants by acting on this "responsibility" perspective, the less he feels he is owed anything, and the more he gains in the conviction that he and his performances are authentic. One of our exemplary respondents, Don, put it like this:

> You do it by your own bootstraps. Things must get done, life must be lived. The world is not peachy-keen to live in, OK, accept it for what it is. Success must be won, I think. Take the bull by the horns in spite of the obstacles set up by the Veterans Administration. If people don't always treat you so well, it does little good to cry about it. Stop the crying.

An attitude of self-sufficiency is fostered by the shift in the locus of responsibility. When things have to get done according to the schedules of other people, the easy path of waiting for your "rights" and "just due" as a veteran must be foregone in favor of the more difficult and, for many, efficient path of overcoming the obstacles.

Each *shift in responsibility implies a different imagery of self and others,* the final ideal being someone who can take care of himself and who is motivated to work hard at bootstrap betterment. This and other changes have been facilitated by the anticipation and then the change in the kind of object they make of themselves. Stan, who is perhaps less fully integrated than some, clarifies this point: "I've been back a few years and I've come to realize I can either let this [experience] continue to work on my head and be an impediment to what I want to do, or I can just come to accept it, and say, 'This is an experience I had, it was a bad one'."

The veteran, if he is to "get by" in American society, must effectively "deprogram" himself from his war experience, in his day-to-day life, in order to feel that he is tied back into his former home world.

2. The two areas in which separations are most successfully and commonly bound are in the educational-occupational and in the family-friendship spheres. If we look at those veterans who could best be said to have "made it" back in, we can see that they have experienced fewer economic and educational hassles on the whole than most of the others. Most of them have sources of income additional to the GI Bill, all are competent students, and all have some long-range plans regarding their future. In short, they feel that they are in at least partial control of their own destinies. These most "successful" veterans also hold jobs in addition to their going to school, a factor that contributes to their subjective perception of success. If "a man's work is one of the most important parts of his social identity," as Hughes (1958) writes, then important consequences for reintegration and building commitment ought to flow from fulfillment in that sector. Thus, the sense of disjunction that shrouds his beginning reentry efforts--the first order discrepancies between self and others in a similar "symbolic world"--grows less poignant as experiences for "making do" in work accumulate.

What is of equal importance as a condition of reintegration is the veterans' ability to bind separations in the familial and friendship sphere. There is a very high correlation in our sample between those who are married and have been married for a number of years and the relative degree of reintegration. Those who are most successfully reintegrated are not only uniformly employed, but are married and have children. The marriages of Andrew, Rod, Will, and Don date back to before their war experiences. Though many veterans were married before the war, not all stayed married. The importance of the family-marriage bond to reintegration is expressed by Don in describing his wife's attitude subsequent to his return: "her attitude was one of--'Come on, now, get your head out of Nam. You've got more important things to do than sit around and brood about your past. Stop being so silly.' I can't say I agreed with her entirely, but she at least helped me to get my head back to earth and realize that life had to go on." Close ties with a member of the nonwar culture, in other words, are essential for helping the veteran to regain his "civilian head" and to start once again to "buy into" the norms of the society he left a few years prior. Although we would not argue that marriage itself is essential in this pattern--in fact, many other friendship ties are seen to be essential to both the married and unmarried veterans--marriage is the most common form of intimate relationships sanctioned in our society that would involve contact between a veteran and a nonveteran in an exclusive atmosphere.

There are, in effect, fiscal and familial priorities which the veteran sees as having enabled him to tie back into the system. Having recognized his responsibilities and acted on them, having become used to the routine of executing these responsibilities, the veteran then may become committed to the furtherance and maintenance of executing these responsibilities--in short, he becomes committed to the lifestyle that has enabled him to "get by." He begins to accumulate valuables--both material and in terms of inter-personal relationships--that are difficult to relinquish (Becker, 1960, 1964). He has a good job or is getting the education needed to obtain the job, he has friendships and family relationships that he does not want to upset, and he is now beginning to get used to the routines of the home world.

3. Since "betterment" is based on some social comparison, statements about it must always take into account a reference criteria. Experiences with other veterans are highly salient to the veterans' coping with their post-Vietnam reintegration. First, the chance to talk with other veterans gives the person an opportunity to start "undoing" the war, through "purging" himself, as one put it, in front of others who really "understand." Second, he can com-pare himself with those who are either "doing good" or "messing up." This comradeship, with its familiarity, ease, and, we would emphasize, mutual outspokenness, markedly affects adaptation and view of self.

"I was somewhat luckier than most of the guys," Perry said to us.

There were three of us good friends, for a good two years we would get together, sit around, really talk things out, and we were able to specifically name places, people, things that hap-pened to us. That way it was a good sounding board. After a period of time, I've pretty much adjusted to it, but it took that time to really be calm. Whenever I had flashbacks, I was able to talk about them with friends, you know.

115

Peer-group relationships provide an excellent opportunity for the recon-struction of self. Coincidentally, and serving to augment the resocializing influences stemming from access to events out of which to build self-confirming rounds of activities, there develops a differentiation of success and failure. There are, in effect, positive and negative reference models from which to fashion and evaluate how well they, and others, are doing. Some see the slow workings of career fate on others and are making attempts to avoid a similar situation. Veterans who are living proof of the negative conse-quences of "having your head still in Nam" or "not being able to get started" serve as comparisons for one's own progress. This type of experience pro-motes a mental realignment with home values and standards and may be observed in the veteran's thoughts about himself in covert social situations, in his direct interpersonal relations with veterans, and in his work with repre-sentatives of the home culture.[3] It is in these various settings that a develop-ing sense of self as civilian is put to the test. It is in these settings that he judges how well he is doing vis-á-vis like-situated others.

Conclusion

Homecoming is a status passage, and among the features of any status pas-sage are the desirability of transition, whether or not the statuses have been occupied before, how much difference the passage makes to the person, length of time within statuses, the extent to which one can communicate and share

the experiences with significant others, and the amount of control participants exercise over their fates through the process (Glaser and Strauss, 1971).
These features are especially salient to the veteran. It is useful to think of
homecoming as an interactional process. Some homecomings are relatively
stable transitions; others are precarious. In some situations, status passage
as change from one position to another is relatively uneventful; in others it
is traumatic.

Self-conceptions of the homecomer should be considered a crucial dependent variable to which we should pay more attention. We have tried to suggest that "transformations of identity" become crucial, for personal identity
during reentry transition is not a fixed object, but rather a changing, emer-
gent quality.

The problems and pains of reentry as visualized here may be regarded as
simply one variant of a more general form of homecoming. Yet the interpersonal problems of communication, perceived sense of exclusion and loss,
sharp rite of transition, disjunction between announcements and placements,
and experience of self as different are key features of the veterans'
homecoming. Still, it is not difficult to extend our analysis, for example, to
treat the emphasis on precariousness implied by Irwin (1970: 107–148) in
his discussion of the world of ex-prisoners and their return, by Wiseman
(1970) in the cycle of making a comeback among Skid Row alcoholics, by
116   Ray (1964) in the relapse and return of addicts to the street, and, more
generally, by Erikson (1964) in his observations on the return of "deviants"
to society. Obstacles to the resumption of a normal life in the community
appear in all these cases. More generally, the analysis should apply to the
experiences of ex-mental patients, parolees, ex-alcoholics, prisoners of war,
and Peace Corps returnees. The emphasis on exclusion and loss is, for many,
a response to the failure of prevailing others to incorporate them as they
are or as they would be. As such, the stages of reentry may prove useful in
looking at the rigors of reentry into urban culture as moral career (Goffman,
1961b).

We have dealt primarily with an uneasy homecoming as seen through
the eyes of the veteran. An interactionist approach to homecoming emphasizes the primary role that subjective meaning plays in the interpretation of
reentry. Further understanding of these stages and their aftermath can be
gained through focusing on the definitions and experiences of the veteran's
social circle.

Notes

1. See also Levitan and Cleary (1973), Levy (1974), and Waldman
(1970).

2. The men interviewed and whose comments are contained herein have
been given false names, according to their Vietnam experience, office or
enlisted status, job category, and marital status. All the men interviewed

are white. Our veterans constitute a special, if not strategic, sample: they are likely to be better educated, more articulate, and more politically aware than other veterans. Again, our problem in this exploratory work is *discovering* just what sorts of concerns and dilemmas are constituent features of homecoming as status passage.

3. The university is, if not ideal, at least a place in which a lifestyle can be fashioned and considerable predictability achieved. And it is more than a place for simply making do in a situation of limited and limiting choice. An acknowledged commitment to the conveniences and work ways of the university strengthens role reacquisition. To deal with this question one needs, of course, a comprehensive sample of university and nonuniversity veterans.

References

Becker, H. (1960). Notes on the concept of commitment. *American Journal of Sociology, 66,* 32–40.

Becker, H. (1964). Personal change in adult life. *Sociometry, 27,* 40–53.

Becker, H., & Strauss, A. L. (1956). Careers, personality, an adult socialization. *American Journal of Sociology, 62,* 253–263.

Borus, J. F. (1975). The reentry transition of the Vietnam veteran. *Armed Forces and Society, 2,* 97–113.

Erikson, K. T. (1964). Notes on the sociology of deviance. In H. Becker (Ed.), *The other side* (pp. 9–21). New York: Free Press.

Glaser, B. G. & Strauss, A. L. (1971). *Status passage.* Chicago: Aldine.

Goffman, E. (1961a). *Encounters: Two studies in the sociology of interaction.* Indianapolis: Bobbs-Merrill.

Goffman, E. (1961b). The moral career of the mental patient. In E. Goffman, *Asylums* (pp. 127–169). New York: Anchor Books.

Helmer, J. (1974). *Bringing the war home: The American soldier in Vietnam and after.* New York: Free Press.

Hughes, E. C. (1945). Dilemmas and contradictions of status. *American Journal of Sociology, 50,* 353–359.

Hughes, E. C. (1958). *Men and their work.* Glencoe, IL: Free Press.

Irwin, J. (1970). *The felon.* Englewood Cliffs, NJ: Prentice-Hall.

Levitan, S. & Cleary, K. A. (1973). *Old wars remain unfinished.* Baltimore, MD: Johns Hopkins University Press.

Levy, C. J. (1974). *Spoils of war.* Boston: Houghton Mifflin.

Lifton, R. J. (1973). *Home from the war: Vietnam veterans, neither victims nor executioners.* New York: Simon & Schuster.

Moskos, C. (1970). *The American enlisted man.* New York: Russell Sage.

Ray, M. (1964). The cycle of abstinence and relapse among heroin addicts. In H. Becker (Ed.), *The other side* (pp. 163–177). New York: Free Press.

Schutz, A. (1964). The homecomer. In A. Brodersen (Ed.), *Collected papers, Volume II: Studies in social theory* (pp. 106–119). The Hague: M. Nijhoff.

Stouffer, S. A. et al. (1949). *The American soldier: Combat and its aftermath, Volume II.* Princeton, NJ: Princeton University Press.

Stone, G. P. (1962). Appearance and the self. In A. Rose (Ed.), *Human behavior and social processes* (pp. 86–113). Boston: Houghton Mifflin.

Strauss, A. L. (1959). *Mirrors and masks: The search for identity.* New York: Free Press.

Waldman, E. (1970, November). Vietnam veterans--transition to civilian life. U.S. Department of Labor, *Monthly Labor Review,* 21–29.

Waller, W. (1944). *The veteran comes back.* New York: Dryden.

Wiseman, J. (1970). *Stations of the lost: The treatment of skid row alcoholics.* Englewood Cliffs, NJ: Prentice-Hall.

Unit C

Business & Missionary Families and International Students

Business & Missionary Families and International Students

The chapters in Unit III focus on adaptation issues in diverse uprooting situations. Qualitative and quantitative differences abound between missionary families (or the missionary single), business families, and the international student. However, many similarities do exist; for example, sojourners of all three groups undergo culture shock and reverse culture shock. All three groups also strive to build genuine friendships, promote goodwill, and contribute to community welfare.

The mission purpose for each group is unique. Missionaries endeavor to gain converts for their religious faith. Businessmen attempt to sell a service or material product for monetary gain. International students endeavor to learn as much as possible.

The salaries and logistical support for multinational corporate families are generous in comparison to the monthly income and allowance funds of missionaries and interna-

tional students. With some exceptions, missionaries also generally commit themselves for longer periods of overseas service. Missionaries and some international students live "on the economy," often in contrast to corporate employees.

The reasonable challenge confronting the missionary and the sending organization is keeping the missionary whole and productive over an indeterminate period. In Chapter 13, Austin argues that reentry can be a growth process. He notes that key elements of the international cycle from recruitment to reentry must be considered within the framework of man's developmental process--missionary service does not occur in a vacuum. Themes of homecoming delineated are the examination of self-concept, value change and choice, realistic expectations, and a sense of loss. Renewed commitment to Christ and maintenance of a wholesome home environment form the bedrock of fruitful reentry.

The article by Kendall, Chapter 14, presents a candid case study of an expatriate business family assigned to London. In an absorbing analysis of the family's overseas stay, the fundamental problems are seen as: (1) leaving the expatriate social and cultural lifestyle; (2) educational continuity; (3) cash flow or disposable income; (4) home country housing; and (5) job shock. Sensible suggestions are made for alleviating each problem. One illuminating statement emphasized that multinational corporations (MNCs) should staff their personnel departments with personnel professionals who have lived overseas.

In Chapter 15, Howard characterizes the results of his interviews with the executives of 27 MNCs regarding repatriate integration. Formal and informal strategies used by MNCs to place returnees are cited. He offers a logical series of categories (e.g., job-related and family-related questions) to be used systematically in assisting the returnee. Cardinal principles are cited which should govern MNCs integration process.

Relocation, courtesy of The Company, is rehearsed in a tongue-in-cheek tone by Markey in Chapter 16. Prior to reentry, her family had lived in Rome, Paris, and Amsterdam for six years. The element of choice in America dumbfounded her--not to mention the items themselves! Eat generic or specialty foods? Use cash or credit? View TV or read magazines? Purchase a gray telephone or a bright red one? The dilemmas confronting a returnee are colorfully stated.

While the focus in Chapter 17 is on young nationals of Saudi Arabia who return home with a Ph.D., the content of Corey's article could well apply to thousands of international students. American educators and their foreign students see the reentering foreign student as a "bearer of technological and cultural light" from the United States. However, the cruel dilemma confronting young students is that they must "wear blinders to the cultural problems around them." Corruption and incompetence are the accepted mode of operation. Donning a mask of cultural conservatism often produces an intolerable tension. Thus for many, the "mask becomes the true face of the man." Corey calls upon American universities to take affirmative action to counter the effects of reentry shock.

13

Reentry Stress: the Pain of Coming Home

Clyde Austin

A substantial number of missionaries find the homecoming process to be more difficult than the initial adjustment to the field. Some ask, "Can we go home again?" or "What are the hazards of home shock?" A readjustment period of six to twelve months is normal. Reentry *can* be a "growth" process (Adler, 1981). Meintel (1971) sees reentry potential as "exhilarating," with opportunities for personal and intellectual growth. Indeed, traumatic experiences during reentry sometimes help to strengthen returnees.

The formidable challenge confronting the missionary and the sending organization is to keep our missionaries whole throughout the international cycle. Key elements of the cycle--recruitment, training, adjustment to the new assignment, continuing rigors of service, and reentry--are best established in the framework of man's developmental process. The missionary needs a definite understanding of missionary service as it continues through young adulthood, middle age, and old age. Clague (1980) accurately says, "Expatriation and repatriation should be examined as parts of an integrated whole--not as unrelated events in a person's life" (p. 11).

Conspicuous characters in the many-sided drama of reentry are missionary parents, their children, and individuals in the receiving society (*e.g.*,

From "Reentry Stress: The Pain of Coming Home" by C. N. Austin, 1983, *Evangelical Missions Quarterly*, *19*(4), pp. 278–287. Copyright 1983 by Evangelical Missions Information Service. Reprinted by permission.

church leaders, relatives, and friends). The drama intensifies as the homecoming date draws near. Parents often agonize. "Should we have reared our children overseas?" "Where do we fit in the USA church scene?" "Can I endure the shock of rediscovering self in a changed setting?" "How will I deal with the affluence of 'rivers of energy' "?

Self-concept

On the eve of reentry the question "Who am I?" may perplex a missionary. Meintel (1971) argues, "The most significant 'shocks' potential in strangerhood are those of self-discovery" (p. 47). In any major transition in life, to question self intensively is appropriate. Reentry is no exception. With a more accurate knowledge of oneself comes a relaxed acceptance of self (Smalley, 1963, p. 56).

A new identity emerges from the sojourn experience. One group of Peace Corps volunteers (Haan, 1974) underwent substantial change in self-definition. The women became more competent and assertive and the men more tender and emotional. For many teenagers, the Vietnam War drastically interrupted the processes of identity formation. The impact of the Vietnam War on the psychosocial identity of the teenage veteran was severe. Likewise, the major problem for the missionary teenager seems to be the management of social identity (Downie, 1976; Gleason, 1969; Herrmann, 1977; Shepard, 1976; and Werkman, 1980). Just as the American people did not comprehend and give a responsive welcome to the Vietnam veteran, many stateside Christians do not grasp the importance of a homecoming celebration and orientation for the returning missionary family.

Werkman (1980) reports, "The self-concepts of overseas teenagers appear to be less positive, and they seem to show less of a feeling of security and optimism about life in general" (p. 243). He points out that these results do not indicate that overseas-experienced adolescents are "less psychologically healthy," but rather that the sojourn does have an important effect on their values and attitudes. Useem (personal communication, November 9, 1981) adds the further word of caution that many overseas children are so protected that they experience "a *very* late adolescence." Whereas the normal period of adolescence is 14–18, overseas children may experience an adolescence which ranges from 18–28. Therefore, one might expect a later period of adolescent rebellion.

Value Change and Choice

Clashes in inner values may occur between homecomers and "receivers" in bewildering arenas: material possessions, family life, racial prejudice, national priorities in areas of ecology and politics, and Christian community conflicts. Sensitivity must prevail on both sides of what might be a considerable chasm in values if a "common pool of hurt" (Morrow, 1981, p. 19) is to be avoided.

Interviews with returning missionaries as well as formal studies (Bwatwa,

Ringenberg, Wolde, & Mishler, 1972; Moore, 1981) indicate that missionaries experience the USA as possessing "an embarrassment of riches." One missionary mother returning from the Far East said:

> Everybody looks rich to us. We stayed with good friends in a Western state who complained about the high cost of living. Yet, they are overweight; live like royalty. Many people talk about inflation and how they are cutting corners . . . but most are wasteful and keep on buying. Why is air conditioning kept so low? We freeze everywhere we go.

Perhaps few value conflicts hurt so much as those in the religious area. Far too many missionaries are tempted to assume a "holier-than-thou" attitude. Stateside Christians are characterized as "being more tolerant of sin" and "not as diligent in their service to God."

Expectations

When missionaries enter the mission field, they *expect* to have difficulty with language, religions of the host culture, attitudes of national Christians, nostalgia for the USA, and maintaining their own spiritual adjustment. Who would *ever* expect to feel like a stranger in his own country? Yet, overidealized expectations about "home" are a puzzling paradox.

The groundwork for this obstacle is often laid during the initial phases of culture shock. When difficulties with culture shock arise, expatriates tend to "glorify" institutions and traditions of their home country. However, when missionaries return, they do not *experience* the USA as they had remembered it. Sapir (1979) states, "It is often precisely the familiar that a wider perspective reveals as the curiously exceptional" (p. 1). The psychological discomfort resulting from this conflict can be harsh.

125

One major expectation of most returnees is that people will be interested in their experiences. An unusually capable missionary from Oceania relates:

> We were invited to a large family reunion shortly after our return. We discovered that most people were not interested in hearing the stories we were most anxious to tell. Oh, they listened about five minutes! Then they continued to talk about the Dallas Cowboys.

Another reports:

> One lady interrupted me to tell about their bus program. People want to know a little about the Philippines . . . not a lot. I must remember that. Answer questions briefly.

A returned missionary wife from South America laments:

> I wish that people had assumed less about us and helped us more. I went through this first year alone and I'm just now making some friends. It would have been nice to have someone to talk to about these things; someone you felt you could ask dumb questions like, "Is this a good price?" or "How do I change an air conditioning filter?"

In the area of personal grooming, a wife who has served many years in the Middle East observes:

> How I looked was a problem to me. Some women at church said, "Your hair is too short," some "too long." Someone said, "Everyone goes to a beauty shop." I didn't want to be pushed into a mold. Finally I said, "I'll do what I want."

A final therapeutic observation seems to be in order. This author is aware of a number of cases where the readjustment symptoms of severely troubled teenagers were relieved substantially by a return trip to the country of prior service. During the trip, these teenagers were guided lovingly through a reexamination of their over-idealized images of that country. Upon reentering the USA after this "journey of clarification," parents, therapists, and the children have more realistically addressed the mental health problems confronting the family. Church officials might object to the high cost of this procedure. However, if many other therapeutic approaches have been attempted unsuccessfully, such a trip might be the "missing piece" in the therapeutic "puzzle." More thought and prayer need to be given to this particular intervention.

A Sense of Loss

Another prevailing motif of reentry is a sense of loss. Moore (1981) discovered, in a study of 288 returned missionaries, that the second most difficult problem listed was "nostalgia and homesickness" for the mission field. Jansson (1975) graphically sketched what she calls a "sense of powerlessness" (p. 139). Useem (1981) affirmed, "The loss of an elite status is very difficult for parents." Zimmerman (1970) mourned, "What is most disturbing is a sense of loss. Where is the America I left four years ago? What has happened to Washington? The changes are so terrifying that it is hard to accept reality as real" (p. 38).

126

The sense of loss is pictured in an expressive manner by several representative missionaries:

> I am still not comfortable shopping here. It's not so much the variety, which some returned missionaries find daunting, but the lack of what I want. I can't stand canned things. I like to buy just fresh fruits and vegetables.

> I wish we could walk more. It's no wonder everyone has trouble with their weight here. So many of the streets don't even have sidewalks. Why is this such a motorized society?

> I'd forget to sweep the floor. It never occurred to me. I'd not cleaned house in the Middle East for eight years. It almost felt degrading to clean my home. I looked for a maid—couldn't find one.

> I miss taking time for people.

> In the summer of 1968, my father was involved in an automobile accident on his way home from a tent campaign in the northern hill country of Antonio. Unfortunately, the accident accelerated his kidney disease. We returned to the USA. Leaving that country was a traumatic experience, especially for a 13-year-old boy who was not fluent in English and was leaving everything he loved. By the age of 10, the only thing that distinguished me from a citizen of Antonio was my blue eyes and blonde hair. Adjusting to the American scene was extremely difficult; it was as if I had completely missed seven years of my life.

Other perplexing loss problems for the missionary parents are: (1) the big-fish-in-a-little-pond syndrome (One generally becomes a medium-sized fish in a bigger pond); (2) an underutilization of the skills and experiences gained on the field; (3) the loss of some degree of independence; and (4) a feeling of being in the old "rat race" again.

The Value of the Family

Prayerful preparation in all stages of transition helps to cushion the impact. A renewed commitment to Christ and the maintenance of a wholesome home atmosphere form the bedrock of a fruitful homecoming. In a dissertation of much practical importance, Sensenig (1980) stresses the invaluable role of the missionary father. Too often the father is a "phantom."

Herrmann (1979) further underscores the importance of the role of the family:

> *"MKs who have experienced these three elements of a basic sense of identity--belonging, worth, and competence--within their family, indicate having an easier time with identity formation in late adolescence and early adulthood. They are ready to adapt to new situations as they arise" (p. 5).*

Predeparture Preparation

When mother and father are at the helm of an adequate family communication process, several further steps are suggested as they contemplate reentry.

1. Begin preparation at least six to twelve months in advance.

2. Review reentry materials as a family.

3. Make a list of one's use of time overseas and then examine what needs to be changed or maintained on returning.

4. Develop a tentative USA family budget based on information from various stateside sources.

5. Examine possible difficulties you might encounter in family and friendships, as well as professional relationships in the areas of verbal and nonverbal behavior.

6. Use correspondence with friends, relatives, schools, and employers to communicate your future needs and learn what to expect.

7. Read USA magazines, journals and newspapers. Talk to recent on-the-field arrivals from the USA about current events. Ask for a "refresher course" on slang.

8. Be aware that you may experience depression, loneliness, fatigue, and illness as reentry symptoms of stress. You can be stressed either by happy or sad events. It will be normal for your family to go through a grief process.

9. Be alert to your own expectations and the expectations of others. Value conflicts are inevitable.

10. Be sensitive to a new discovery of self. Seek hobbies and community/church activities that fit new interests.

11. Reevaluate parenting procedures. Do not retreat from problems or other people. Monitor television offerings carefully. Our family didn't have a TV set overseas. When we returned, in a family vote, TV lost, 6–0. Bring back special belongings of children.

12. Begin an adequate vocational information program for the children.

127

Many nations do not permit children to work. Acquaint them now with the world of work in the States--part-time and full-time jobs. One of the missionaries in your team might become a vocational resource person for all of the missionary "cousins" in your group.

13. If possible, allow time for a gradual "decompression period" of two to four weeks on the homeward trip in order to relax and make adequate mental preparation for reentry.

14. Remember that reintegration will take time, possibly a year. Be resilient and keep a positive outlook.

15. Search for ways to meet others' needs (Philippians 2).

Patterns of Reentry Response

Asuncion-Lande (1980) suggests four "distinctive patterns of response" to reentry shock: excitement, re-establishment/frustration, sense of control, and re-adaptation (p. 4). The *initial phase* involves the joy of greeting relatives, friends, and former colleagues. Proud mothers and grandmothers prepare your favorite delicacies. In the *reestablishment phase*, you attempt to develop neighborhood friendship "roots," become reacquainted at church, and assist your children in adapting to school. Inevitably there will be conflict and frustration. The "honeymoon" is over. The family members may then strive to *control* friends or fellow workers in various conscious or unconscious ways to eliminate dissonant feelings they are experiencing. A sense of control lowers stress levels. The homecomer may question his decision to return. Finally, returnees look for ways to cope or *adapt*. Intercultural communication, verbal and nonverbal, plays an important role in readjustment.

Coping Strategies

Since there are "no absolute, universal consequences" of reentry (Segal, 1981, p. 13), returnees need a repertoire of coping strategies to meet different demands. Useem (1981) differentiates between "adjusting" and "coping." She says that although learning how to cope with American life is important, a child may not adjust. In some cases individuals may not be psychologically "at home" in the USA.

A refrain of reemphasis and caution is appropriate. Reentry stress *is* normal. However, reentrants *do* form a minority. As with other minority groups in our culture, certain prejudices or stereotypes are exhibited toward returning missionaries. Jansson (1975) has suggested that reentrants may acquire a "deviant identity." Returning teenagers are most susceptible to a heightened sense of not deviating from social norms. Werkman (1977) has stressed the principle that high school culture places a premium on excluding "unusual" people. Since established students are locked into groups or cliques, some returning children may be tempted by those teenagers living on the fringe of moral existence. According to Opubor (1974),

"In both the host and home cultures, the individual will be something of a deviant. The most edifying choice for the individual, and the goal of all constructive strategy, is how to make the individual a responsible deviant" (p. 29).

The Importance of Support Systems

A support group can serve as a forum for exchange of information and expression of feelings (Jansson, 1975; Werkman, 1980). Returned missionaries claim that the following individuals, groups, and/or activities were most helpful to them upon reentry, in descending order: spouse, friends, relatives, former missionaries, church members, college missions department personnel, reading materials, personal counseling, church leaders, debriefing with overseeing church personnel, psychological testing and evaluation, reorientation program, and family counseling (Moore, 1981, p. 45). It is important, but sad to note, that few churches sponsoring these missionaries provided personal and/or family counseling, psychological evaluation, or debriefing and reorientation programs. One missionary wrote the author after a program on reentry:

Your presentation last year was very timely in our lives. We were just returning from 16 years of mission work in Latin America. We were on a very bad guilt trip. We felt we were abnormal. We consulted a professional. You helped us put our lives in perspective.

After a counseling session, a young single lady declared:

After reflecting on what we discussed, I realized that you shed a lot of light on my confusion and you encouraged me. I guess I just wanted to hear you say I was 'normal' for feeling such things.

129

A Heritage of Tradition

One Christian professor (McMillon, 1982) has characterized the importance of tradition as follows:

Tradition is important to the life of a family because it reinforces and sustains ideas, values, and practices that are valuable and meaningful to them. . . . Paul encouraged the Thessalonians, (2 Thess. 2:15), and Corinthians, (1 Cor. 11:2), to maintain the 'traditions' delivered to them. . . . Every family needs its own traditions. They become a subtle reinforcement to the cohesiveness of the family as a unit (p. 18).

The benefits flowing from the traditions described by McMillon could be of inestimable value to the readjustment of a returning family in terms of: identity, roots, security, continuity, and celebration.

What About the Future?

To the best of the author's knowledge, no longitudinal study (before, during, after) has been conducted on missionary families. Further, there seems to be no comprehensive, in-depth study of serious mental illness among former missionary adults or children. Why do some families return with relatively few problems? Assumptions can be made, but no definitive research has been conducted. One missionary has wisely observed that a study should be made of families returned longer than a decade. He is convinced that only after a lengthy period of time can a family determine objectively what transpired in the first few years after reentry. Brislin (1981, p. 295) confirms the importance of later measures which show delayed effects. Special attention also needs to be given to the homecoming of singles. Loneliness has often been their unrelenting foe.

The home church or other sponsoring organization must be engaged in a continuous process of care, prayer, and inquiry on behalf of missionary families. The missionary family *must* be kept whole.

References

Adler, N. J. (1981). Re-entry: Managing cross-cultural transitions. *Group & Organization Studies, 6*(3), 341–356.

Asuncion-Lande, N. C. (1980). On re-entering one's culture. *NAFSA Newsletter, 31*(6), 142–143. Washington, DC: National Association for Foreign Student Affairs.

Brislin, R. W. (1981). *Cross-cultural encounters: Face-to-face interaction.* New York: Pergamon Press.

Bwatwa, J., Ringenberg, R., Wolde, N. & Mishler, J. (1972). *A study of the adjustment of missions and service personnel returning from overseas assignments* (Methods of Social Research, Sociology 412). Unpublished manuscript, Goshen College.

Clague, L., & Krupp, N. B. (1980, Spring). International personnel: The repatriation problem. *The Bridge,* pp. 11–13; 37. (Reprinted from *The Personnel Administrator,* 1978, April.)

Cleveland, E. T. (1979). *A program of orientation for "missionary kids" enrolled at Samford University* (Ministry Research Project). Unpublished doctoral dissertation, Southern Baptist Theological Seminary, Louisville.

Downie, R. D. (1976). Re-entry experiences and identity formation of third culture experienced dependent American youth: An exploratory study (Doctoral dissertation, Michigan State University, 1976). *Dissertation Abstracts International, 37,* 3493A. (University Microfilms No. 76-27,089)

Gleason, T. P. (1970). Social adjustment patterns and manifestations of worldmindedness of overseas-experienced American youth (Doctoral dissertation, Michigan State University, 1969). *Dissertation Abstracts International, 31,* 2494A. (University Microfilms No. 70-20,460)

Haan, N. (1974). Changes in young adults after Peace Corps experiences: Political-social views, moral reasoning and perceptions of self and parents. *Journal of Youth and Adolescence, 3*(3), 177–194.

Herrmann, C. B. (1977). Foundational factors of trust and autonomy influencing the identity-formation of the multicultural life-styled MK (Doctoral dissertation, Northwestern University, 1977). *Dissertation Abstracts International, 38,* 5373A. (University Microfilms No. 78-00,710)

Herrmann, C. B. (1979). MKs and their parents: The place of the family in building trust and autonomy. *Emissary, 10*(3).

Jansson, D. P. (1975). Return to society: Problematic features of the re-entry process. *Perspectives in Psychiatric Care, 13*(3), 136–142.

McMillon, L. (1982, December). Traditions: A way to enrich your family life. *The Christian Chronicle,* p. 18.

Meintel, D. (1971). Strangers, homecomers and ordinary men. *Anthropological Quarterly, 46*(1), 47–58.

130

Moore, L. A. (1982). A study of reverse culture shock in North American Church of Christ missionaries (Master's thesis, Abilene Christian University, 1981). *Masters Abstracts, 20,* 314. (University Microfilms No. 13-18,268)

Morrow, L. (1981, July 13). The forgotten warriors. *Time,* pp. 18–25.

Opubor, A. E. (1974, October). *Intercultural adaptation: Resocialization versus reacculturation?* Paper presented at the Reentry/Transition workshop at Wingspread, Racine, WI.

Sapir, E. (1979). In American Field Service, Program Development Department. *The AFS student study guide.* New York: AFS International/Intercultural Programs, Inc.

Segal, J. (1981, March). In Schaar, K. Hostage crisis in review: Psychology's continuing role. *APA Monitor,* pp. 1; 8–9; 13.

Sensenig, J. V. (1981). Perceptions of family and vocational responsibilities of missionary fathers: Educational implications (Doctoral dissertation, Michigan State University, 1980). *Dissertation Abstracts International, 41,* 3867A. (University Microfilms No. 81-06,482)

Shepard, F. G., Jr. (1977). An analysis of variables of self-perception and personal ambition in overseas-experienced American teenagers: Implications for curricular planning (Doctoral dissertation, Michigan State University, 1976). *Dissertation Abstracts International, 37,* 5735A. (University Microfilms No. 77-05,887)

Smalley, W. A. (1963). Culture shock, language shock, and the shock of self-discovery. *Practical Anthropology, 10,* 49–56.

Werkman, S. L. (1977). *Bringing up children overseas.* New York: Basic Books.

Werkman, S. L. (1980). Coming home: Adjustment of Americans to the United States after living abroad. In G. V. Coelho & P. I. Ahmed (Eds.), *Uprooting and development: Dilemmas of coping with modernization.* New York: Plenum Press.

Zimmerman, C. C. (1978). Washington is home. *Foreign Service Journal, 47* (2), 38–39; 45.

131

14

Repatriation: An Ending and a Beginning

D.W. Kendall

Something very interesting takes place when a manager and his or her family take a foreign assignment, live abroad, and then come home again. Most of these expatriates find it difficult to readjust to life in the U.S.--financially, culturally, or professionally. As a personnel manager counseling those going to and returning from overseas assignments, I have seen this reaction time and again, and would like to explore some of the reasons for it, and propose ways to ease the transition.

Managers who have lived abroad typically face certain facts of economic and political life upon their return.

For many multinational companies, the financial realities of the late 1970s and 1980s (examples would be the recession, costs of regulatory compliance, competitive pressures overseas due to differing views on profit margins by our Japanese and some European competitors) have put an end to the good old days when corporate expansions at home and abroad provided almost unlimited promotional opportunities. Then, most returning expatriates came back to a promotion, whereas now, particularly when more managers are being repatriated than sent abroad, most are lucky to come back laterally--and many come back to a lower-level job.

Likewise, it used to be true (say, before 1974) that a dollar salary alone provided for a very nice lifestyle abroad, and allowances could be saved--to be used when the expatriate returned--to buy the "big house on the hill." This has all changed now, since the dollar has weakened against major world currencies like the yen, the DM, and the Swiss franc. Now it takes most of an expatriate's salary and allowances to live abroad and his savings don't keep up with the price of real estate in the U.S. The following is a case study describing the experience of a U.S. family who spent five years abroad and then returned home.

A young, aspiring manager who had never really thought about an over-seas assignment (indeed, he had never really traveled abroad), was offered a position in Europe at the corporation's office in London. This man was 31 years old, had a wife and eight-year-old daughter, and had risen fairly rapidly from a nondescript job in the Midwest to a middle management position at the corporate headquarters in Philadelphia. Husband and wife were of conservative Midwestern working class stock, and had quite proudly integrated themselves into the suburban scene--nice house, big mortgage, car financed through the credit union, barbecue grill, stereo, and all the other trappings of Suburbia, U.S.A. Being fairly strapped financially, their pri-mary entertainment was visiting other suburban friends. Culturally they were, shall we say, underdeveloped.

134

Upon being offered the job in England, this fellow naively accepted on the spot. (He did give his wife a call from the office.) All the family mem-bers were excited about the prospects of living in England, although not one had any particular reason to know what it would be like. House and car were promptly sold, relatives were visited, furniture shipped (some stored), and the plane boarded for London.

The family decided to change their lifestyle dramatically, and, rather than take a house in Weybridge or Walton-on-Thames (the stockbroker belt, where you can almost duplicate the U.S. suburban scene), they found a small flat in central London. The daughter was enrolled in the international school. The neighborhood was mixed--a sort of emerging Greenwich Village--with some 60 percent foreigners and 40 percent financially comfortable Britishers. The wife joined the American Women's Club, the family joined the Ameri-can Church in London, and before they knew what was happening, they had quickly been embraced by the London overseas community. They lived so centrally that they didn't even have to have a car. Their allowances were generous enough that they could travel to the Continent three or four times per year via cheap package holiday plans. As a function of their position in the company, they frequently had to entertain visitors (or were entertained) at home or by going out to restaurants. They became interested in the theatre--the West End theatre district being only ten minutes from their flat. They started going to London's art galleries and museums and developed a keen interest in the arts. Their neighbors included Lee Remick, Alfred

Hyde-White, Paul McCartney, and Bernard Pomerance (author of *The Elephant Man*).

Each year they traveled back to the U.S. for home leave, and by careful conniving they could arrange a free stopover in Miami to relax on the beach at Key Biscayne. During their stay in Europe, they visited Russia, Sweden, Switzerland, Paris, Italy, Turkey, the Canary Islands, Greece, Amsterdam, and Spain, and their daughter took separate trips with the international school to Rome, Paris, and Geneva.

Professionally, this American expatriate manager took to his work. He liked the job, the people he worked with, the freedom of being away from the corporate bureaucracy, and the opportunities to do business in various countries in Europe. He developed a good deal of skill in the international aspects of his particular discipline, and became at a very young age a respected member of the European senior management team.

Mind you, overseas life was not just a piece of cake for this family. They lived in a flat in central London which was quite small by U.S. standards. There was no station wagon to haul home the groceries from the supermarket--indeed, there was no supermarket. Marketing was a daily chore, and everything was carried in. Also, they experienced the heat wave of 1976, and the power, garbage collectors, and bakery strikes of 1978. The point is, however, that they were happy to make the trade-off--for a small sacrifice of material ease, this down-home Midwestern family who had never had any interest in foreign travel, living abroad, or cultural pursuits, enjoyed five years of social and cultural feast.

135

The five years were two to three years more than the family had originally committed themselves to spend abroad. The daughter was entering high school and, by this time, had spent more of her school years outside the U.S. than inside. The parents became concerned about her missing out on a normal U.S. high school education, particularly the social aspects.

To make a long story short, this family moved back to the States, the husband back to a position with less clout in the head office, the family back to the suburbs. Gone were the museums down the street, the theatre ten minutes away, the celebrity neighbors, weekends to Paris, school trips to Switzerland. Gone, too, was the discretionary income peculiar to the expatriate situation; in the U.S. most managers invest heavily in their homes.

What the Problems Are
From this case, which from my experiences in repatriating people is typical, we can identify several problem areas which are common to most repatriation cases:

Leaving the Expatriate Social and Cultural Lifestyle.
What is left behind varies according to where the manager was stationed. In Europe it tends to be the life outside the home, the opportunities to enjoy

the arts, and to travel. In Asia and Latin America (particularly the more underdeveloped areas), what is missed is the poolside entertaining scene and the domestic help available for running the household. In all areas of the world, expatriates mind leaving a very special community that they feel genuinely a part of. Expatriates tend to cling to each other for support in a foreign country.

Educational Continuity Problems.
In "making the employee whole" (one of the worst terms in international compensation terminology), companies often provide schooling for the children of expatriate managers which is better than they had prior to transfer, or will have after they return. American schools overseas tend to be well staffed (with the companies footing the bill), classes are small, and the students come from well-educated families and are highly motivated.

Cash Flow or Disposable Income Problems.
It costs a lot of money to live abroad. Estimates of cost-of-living relationships for major cities relative to Washington (100) are: Buenos Aires, 144.8; Sydney, 127.3; Vienna, 165.9; London, 153.1; Paris, 157.4; Frankfurt, 174.8; Tokyo, 204.0; Singapore, 136.9.

136   Because of this difference, we pay the expatriate extra cost-of-living money, plus, of course, a foreign service allowance, and in some cases a hardship allowance. This means that the expatriate, just to live, is used to having and spending a lot of cash. This is a difficult pattern to break after coming back to the U.S., and is more difficult the longer the employee has been abroad.

U.S. or Home Country Housing Problems.
The financial impact of reentering the U.S. housing market is so significant to the repatriate that it's worth noting separately from the point above. Most expatriates rent because the price of homes abroad is extremely high. For example, a typical four-bedroom, Western-style home costs $300,000 in a London suburb, $500,000 in Paris, $1,000,000 in Tokyo, and $1,400,000 in Hong Kong. Furthermore, it is inadvisable for expatriates to bring capital into a foreign real estate market, due to devaluation risks.

Very often, managers sell their homes when they move abroad because of the difficulties of renting and overseeing them from a great distance. But there is no way for a manager to take his or her equity out of real estate for four or five years and earn nearly as much on any other type of investment. So, upon return, the employees encounter the financial and psychological setback of not being able to afford a house like they had before, even though their salary has risen over the period. Employees quickly begin to wonder if the whole thing was worth it.

Job Shock.
Working far from corporate headquarters, in a fairly autonomous situation, with mail communications in weeks rather than days, and telex and phone communications delayed by time zone differences, most expatriates have a degree of responsibility very much greater than they had prior to moving abroad. Even when they return to a significant promotion, people tend to feel that the headquarters bureaucracy net causes them to feel less responsible than before.

What To Do About Them
Now that we've identified these five areas, it is possible to suggest how a well-thought-out expatriation policy can help the corporation to eliminate, or at least minimize, the impact of these problems on the organization.

Social and Cultural Aspects of Expatriate Life.
This is one of the toughest parts of the repatriation problem to deal with, at least through policy, because these aspects are mostly perceptual and behavioral on the part of the expatriate family. Nevertheless, a well prepared personnel department in a multinational company will have a counseling capability which will at least sensitize the employee and the family to these issues prior to transfer abroad. It is my opinion that every personnel department for a multinational firm *must be staffed* with personnel professionals *who have lived abroad.* Travel doesn't count!

137

   It is most important to start the repatriation thinking process prior to expatriation and, through on-going contacts with the expatriate and his family, keep the thought process going while abroad. I visit expatriate families routinely while on trips overseas, and recently spent the weekend with one of our families in Japan. Through our discussions, the family was subtly reminded of the differences between life abroad and life back home. Counseling sessions during home leave also helps. Encouraging home leaves (not cash in lieu of, or other travel) helps to keep the employee in touch with life at home.

Educational Continuity.
This is another difficult problem. It is difficult for company policies to deal with the return to neighborhood public schools. At least one major company pays for private schools back in the U.S. for employees who serve four or more years abroad, the rationale being that once this pattern is set, it is hard to break. In my opinion, however, the costs of such a policy will prevent this from becoming a trend. Many corporations, however, do handle TCNs this way, particularly ones who have served in several countries and have put their children in the American system to assure continuity at all assignments. When these people return to their home countries, where language and educational systems are different, companies will

often pay for the children to finish their education at the local American school.

Cash Flow Problems.
There are several things which can be done here as a matter of policy which will help expatriates.
   Counseling Prior to the Move.
The employee should know how his or her compensation package is designed, what the elements are, and for what purpose each element is intended. Well-thought-out forms for keeping the expatriate advised of currency adjustments and other matters are also important.
   Counseling and information sharing which keep the expatriate and the family advised of price trends back home.
One of the biggest problems that employees encounter is to find when they come home that prices have gone up here too! This has the greatest effect when the expatriate has been living in a country where there is galloping inflation.
   Paying Allowances by Other Means Than the Monthly Check.
Up-front bonuses for foreign service premium, with the balance paid at the end of the assignment, make sense from both the cash flow standpoint and the tax equalization standpoint.

138

U.S. or Home Country Housing.
This is another tough issue. Basically, the first rule is that a person moving abroad temporarily (for less than ten years) should be encouraged (to the brink of threat!) to keep his U.S. house (or home country house). The biggest favor a company can do an expatriating employee in this regard, is to implement a policy of protecting the employee by rental guarantees and by having an outside company manage expatriate home rentals. This is quite common now among major multinationals, particularly for employees transferred abroad in the last two years. Companies who do not have such a program, or companies who adopted such a program recently and have expatriates returning who sold their houses prior to the implementation of such a program, can do little more than to extend interest-free or low-interest loans to employees to help ease them back into the appropriate housing situation.

Job Shock.
This is where the action is in terms of dealing with the problem through policy.
   Most importantly, and this cannot be stressed too strongly, a firm agreement must be reached prior to expatriation about the specific job assignment overseas, the term of the assignment, the over-base compensation package for the assignment, and the position, level, and

location to which the employee will return. This is best achieved through a contract!

A contract does three very valuable things: a) It keeps the employee thinking about his return date; b) It eliminates the anxiety the expatriate feels about what position, and under what circumstances, he or she will return--particularly as the return gets nearer; c) It keeps company management back home focused on the return date and forces human resources planning.

Managements, particularly American ones, tend to not like the idea of a contract of employment. One hears that a contract "connotes lack of trust," "limits flexibility," and "sounds too much like a union situation." There is almost unquestionable evidence, however, that industry, in order to attract the best people to work abroad, must move in the direction of contracts of employment, and, in my opinion, it's a good thing. Both parties will benefit from a more firm commitment to the success of the expatriate assignment.

Further, if other opportunities arise during the contract period, renegotiation should permit changes, assuming the changes are attractive to the employee and the company. Finally, if "contract periods" do result in management scrutinizing the planning process more closely at expatriation time, so much the better; many a career has gone on the rocks because talent has been sent overseas without enough thought about how to use that talent later, back home.

Many other things can be done to reduce job-oriented repatriation problems. Keeping the employee in touch with things back in the home office is important, and this can be done in several ways.

The "buddy system."

We all remember the buddy system from summer camp when we were kids. The same concept can keep the expatriate from getting lost. The idea is that a manager at the home location is appointed to look after the interests of the expatriate while he or she is abroad. The manager stays in touch with the employee, monitors the performance abroad, and counsels him or her on various matters when he or she visits headquarters on home leave or business. Toward the end of the expatriation period, the "buddy" takes a more active role, including representing the expatriate's interests when job candidacy is at issue. This manager is also sensitive to the "job shock" the employee may suffer when he or she gets back (ideally, the manager has had the same experience) and builds the knowledge of this phenomenon into the counseling sessions. This role, by the way, continues after repatriation until the resettlement is deemed complete.

Project Assignment.

The way many companies are organized, there is a fairly complete break, organizationally, when an employee is transferred abroad. Companies would be well advised to consider giving expatriate employees, where possible, some project assignments back in the headquarters location during their time abroad. These assignments could be timed to fit in with home leaves or other

139

business visits. The objective here is to keep the employee sensitized to the differences in environment which exist between the domestic organization and the more decentralized remote operations. This can go far to eliminate the shock upon returning.

If, in the future, we are going to have people who will want to go abroad and work for our corporations in overseas locations, we must design and administer policies which ensure that when the time comes to return home, the *family* is indeed returned and restored. From the company planning standpoint, repatriation should be seen as a beginning, not an ending. The company must have capable, internationally sensitive managers in both line and personnel positions at home and abroad, managers who are qualified to counsel, and, most importantly, capable of developing, administering, and fulfilling expatriation/repatriation commitments.

15

Integrating Returning Expatriates into the Domestic Organization

Cecil G. Howard

This research study was undertaken to determine how American multinational corporations integrate their returning overseas personnel into the domestic organization in the United States. In addition, it deals with some very pertinent aspects of the integration process. Members of management in 27 U.S. MNCs were personally interviewed by this author to gather relevant information on this subject. Topics considered significantly important to the repatriation as well as integration processes are discussed in the following section.

A position does not necessarily wait for a returning expatriate in most MNCs studied. If an expatriate goes abroad for a very short assignment, his domestic job might be saved. However, all MNCs make sincere attempts to find suitable jobs for their returning expatriates if overseas performance was satisfactory. Overseas expatriates, both managerial and technical, are generally aware of the possibility that a suitable job, or any job for that matter, may not be available to them on their return to the United States.

Normally, MNCs do not execute an employment contract with the outbound potential expatriate guaranteeing him a position on return. However, many MNCs sign an employment contract with expatriates in which is

Reprinted from the (January, 1979) issue of *Personnel Administrator*, copyright, (1979), The American Society for Personnel Administration, 606 North Washington Street, Alexandria, VA 22314, $30 per year.

outlined the terms and conditions of overseas employment. Job placement on return is done on an individual basis; there has to be a need or an opening for the homebound expatriate. If he is a long time employee and a good performer, some position will be found. He may be carried on the payroll for some time until a position becomes available. However, if his overseas performance was questionable or unsatisfactory or if he was recalled prematurely for some reason, he may not have a job on return. The weeding-out process for both the domestic employee and the overseas employee in many MNCs is the same. If unsatisfactory performance persists overseas, the incumbent will be notified accordingly. In a situation like this, management gives the expatriate sufficient time to look for a job elsewhere before employment is terminated. His employer might help him relocate with some other company in the U.S. or abroad, or he might be given some free time with salary to look for some other job in the U.S.

Strategies Employed by These MNCs to Integrate Their Expatriates.
A number of informal plans or methods are employed by these MNCs to integrate their expatriates on their return to the United States. Among those commonly used:

1. Putting the returnee in a "holding pattern" or on a "standby" basis until a suitable position is found or created for him. He usually receives a certain percentage of his overseas base salary and may be given some special assignment while he is in this holding status or may do nothing for the company. If he is a very capable individual, he may stay in this pattern indefinitely; otherwise the duration of this type of status is usually restricted.

2. Delaying expatriates' return until suitable positions can be found or created stateside.

3. Letting expatriates go if there is no high probability for a job.

4. Advertising the available job openings worldwide. When a domestic job opens up, all candidates, including overseas expatriates, are considered. If an overseas candidate is better qualified than those applying from stateside, he gets the job. An overseas expatriate is not in an out-of-sight and out-of-mind situation just because of his overseas location. He is not excluded from consideration for jobs elsewhere in his field of functional expertise.

5. Contacting other MNCs to explore job possibilities for its returnees.

6. Making use of external employment agencies to help place the returnee in another organization.

7. Sending the returnee's resume to all affiliates worldwide, including the U.S.

8. Force-fitting the returnee to a position, if the circumstances warrant.

How MNCs with Formalized Integration Plans Integrate Their Expatriates Into the Domestic Organization.

No employment contract guaranteeing the potential expatriate a job on return is signed in MNCs that formally plan their expatriates' return. There is generally an understanding between the expatriate and the company to this effect. This informal method of promising the potential returnee some economic security does not usually pose a serious problem to the parties, for all details of the expatriate's employment are included in his "career path" or "staff" plan. Management knows precisely where a particular employee will be in the organization and at what time. The staff plan is well laid out and job alternatives are clearly spelled out. It plans for people's professional careers and at the same time plans positional successions in the organization.

No one is sent on an overseas assignment unless management knows the specific objectives or goals of that assignment. All employees go to real jobs, know what the performance standards are and how the company expects that overseas experience to apply to a position that an expatriate holds on return. All this is explicitly spelled out in career path or staff planning.

Strategies Employed by These MNCs to Integrate Their Expatriates.

The following are the major strategies used by these MNCs to formally integrate their expatriates into the domestic organization:

143

1. Holding one individual responsible for the expatriate's return. In one company this strategy operates as follows: An individual in the overseas operating division plans an expatriate's eventual return to the United States and finds suitable employment. The expatriate knows exactly what position he will have on his return. If the request is for a premature return, the home-based organization will circulate the expatriate's resume among all the divisional managers. If a suitable job cannot be found for him, the expatriate will be "forced-fitted" to a position. In other words, the company will create a job or rotate a domestic employee to make his job available to the returnee. Management feels it has a moral obligation to the returning employee.

2. Putting the returnee in a "holding pattern" if a planned position for him is not readily available for some unavoidable reason(s). The individual in this status is clearly apprised about his future in the organization.

3. Making a firm commitment for a specific job on return.

4. Maintaining an adequate staff tracking system.

5. Selecting the right individual for the right job in the right location.

6. Advertising available job openings worldwide and sending resumes of returning expatriates to all operating divisions of the company.

7. Displacing a domestic employee to make room for the returnee.

8. Creating a new job for a returnee if he has the potential to be productive and extremely useful to the company.

9. Offering returnee's services to all major components in the organization.

10. Maintaining a formal sponsorship program. Under this program younger, rising employees are constantly watched by senior level managers and their careers are planned by the latter group.

11. Making the operating division originally releasing the expatriate for overseas assignment responsible for taking him back if he returns within the specified period of time.

Type of Assistance Given by All MNCs.

All multinational corporations provide some assistance to their returning overseas employees and their families. The type of assistance and its extent varies not only from company to company, but also from expatriate to expatriate in the same organization. However, all means used to assist an expatriate family can be grouped into the following categories:

Financial Support.

Offering a period of relocation time in which the expatriate is given support in terms of continuing pay and related fringe benefits.

Paying hotel living expenses until the expatriate family can find suitable permanent living accommodations.

Allowing the expatriate family to live on an expense account for a specified time period.

Logistical support.

Assisting the family in getting reestablished in the community.

Giving the expatriate time off from work to attend to personal and family affairs.

Arranging to have other company employees living in that same community to meet the expatriate family.

Arranging for the shipping of furniture and other household goods.

Giving the expatriate annual leave in advance on return.

Giving the expatriate family a check-off list to make integration easier.

Putting the family in touch with a real estate agent and paying for the agent's professional services.

Introducing the expatriate to his fellow employees.

Providing individual counseling, if needed.

Major Integration Problems Besetting MNCs.

American multinational corporations repatriating their overseas expatriates and their families back to the U.S. encounter a host of both operational and staffing problems. The nature of these problems and their complexity vary not only from firm to firm but also from returnee to returnee in the same organization. There is one problem, however, that causes some

144

concern to members of management in most multinational firms, including the ones which formally plan expatriates' return. The problem relates to this perplexing question: Where to place the returning overseas expatriate in the organization? As stated earlier, finding a suitable position for a returnee, particularly in firms without a formal career path or staff plan, becomes extremely problematic. Many times MNCs have to engage in complex staffing maneuvering to find a suitable position, or any position, for a returnee.

In addition to finding a suitable position for the returnee, management is normally faced with these questions:

Job-Related Questions.

How to assist the returnee in readjusting to the new organizational climate?

How should the company prepare the returnee for a new professional life in the domestic organization?

What kind of professional challenge to offer him?

How to keep him satisfied professionally?

How to offer him the professional challenge he has had overseas?

How will the returnee's overseas experience affect his stateside performance?

What if the returnee is professionally dissatisfied with his stateside position?

How should the company compensate the returnee for the loss of positional prestige?

How will his ability to operate independently affect his performance and others in the organization?

How might his lack of expertise in domestic operations affect his performance?

Might he have difficulty in conforming to the domestic organization's personnel policies and operating procedures?

How might he take the loss of positional autonomy he enjoyed overseas?

Monetary Questions.

How to compensate the returnee to offset the increased cost-of-living?

How to compensate the expatriate family for the monetary loss they generally suffer on return?

How will the inflation in the U.S. affect the expatriate family?

Family-Related Questions.

How to help the expatriate family readjust to a new life style in the U.S.?

How might the family react to a loss in their life style?

How to make the expatriate family happy?

How will the changing moral trends in the country affect the expatriate and his family?

145

What kind of housing accommodation will the family want and get?

Staffing Questions.
Where to place the expatriate in the organization.
How to take away the preferential treatment and attention which overseas assignments usually afford?
How to help him make a switch from an operating organization to a headquarters organization?
What should the company do in case the expatriate and his family want to return abroad?
How to acclimate the returnee into the managerial mentality and domestic environment in which the company operates.
Should his foreign vacant position be filled with another American or with a local national?

Logistical Questions.
How to get the expatriate's household goods on time?
How should the company get the expatriate in the U.S. on time for his domestic assignment?
How will the company take care of the minute details in repatriating the family?
How should effective communication with all concerned be maintained?
Might the company lose the expatriate to one of its competitors?

Types of Positions Given to Returning Expatriates.
A large percentage of the returning expatriates in the participating MNCs come back to comparable positions in the domestic organization. For example, if an expatriate is a controller abroad, he might get the same position in one of the domestic divisions of the company; but usually there has to be an opening in his functional specialty unless the company subscribes to the "force-fit" or "make-job" policy. In many cases the returnee accepting a comparable position in the parent company or one of its domestic affiliates loses the freedom, responsibility and authority he enjoyed in a comparable position overseas. Many MNCs use overseas assignments as a training ground for their promising and/or rising managers, but not as a stepping stone to a higher position back in the United States--the notion or belief commonly held in the management circle.

Evidently, there is no fixed pattern as to the type of position one might be offered on return. The type of position an expatriate is given on return is determined by a combination of factors, such as: 1) what type of position he held immediately before accepting an overseas assignment; 2) what kind of performance record he maintained in that domestic position; 3) what level assignment or position he held overseas; 4) how his performance was in that position; 5) why he is coming back; 6) the employment situation in the domestic organization; 7) the financial position of the domestic organization or the operating division to which the returnee might be assigned; and 8) what tangible contributions the returnee will make in the future to the betterment of the domestic organization.

Integrating returning expatriates into the domestic organization will be less problematic not only for multinational corporations but the returnees as well if the companies will take the integration process seriously and do something positive to make it work. The integration process will become much simpler and easy to administer if it is planned properly and based on the following cardinal principles:

1. *Selecting the right individual for the right position in the right location.* Assigning a domestic employee abroad whose qualifications to serve properly are inadequate or whose domestic performance has been unsatisfactory or mediocre will naturally create serious staffing problems on his return. On the other hand, an employee with a good performance track record at home will pose no problem and will be relatively easy to integrate into a suitable domestic position on return.

2. *Defining the purpose(s) of an overseas assignment.* An employee should be sent abroad with a specific purpose or goal in mind. Every overseas assignment should serve a specific goal(s) and should be clearly spelled out in terms of these questions: 1) Is the overseas assignment being used as a training ground for the potential expatriate? 2) Will the assignment be a stepping stone to some higher position in the domestic organization or abroad? 3) Will the expatriate fulfill a temporary staffing need abroad? 4) Is the company trying to get rid of an unwanted domestic employee? If the company management is attempting to accomplish the last purpose, it will of course encounter serious staffing and operational problems in properly placing him after he completes his assignment abroad. The first three situations are not likely to create any serious staffing problem.

3. *Developing career path or staff plans.* Proper staff planning is the key to the success of any integration process or program. If a career path or staffing plan is explicitly spelled out for an employee, integrating him into the domestic organization after his successful term overseas should not be difficult. Developing a career path or staffing plan is very simple and does not require sophisticated staffing expertise on the part of the staff planners.

4. *Formalizing integration plans or programs.* It is advisable that MNCs formalize their integration programs and place them under one key individual or department in the organization even if they have developed career path or staff plans for their employees, both domestic and foreign-based. Formalization of such programs minimizes staffing and procedural problems and injects operational smoothness in the system. Any multinational firm that repatriates a decent number of expatriates and their families in the U.S. should have the necessary expertise to develop and execute these programs. The program should be developed to satisfy the returnee's personal, positional and his professional needs. In addition, it must also conform to the organization's staffing plans and needs.

Any well-planned and well-managed expatriate integration program will eventually fail if it is not provided top management's total commitment in terms of adequate financing, qualified personnel and continued moral support. The benefits to be gained from such a program should be obvious to management and should never be underestimated.

16

The U.S.,
the Second Time Around

Judy L. Markey

The great escape was over. After living abroad for six years--Rome, Paris and Amsterdam--we were finally crawling into our own bed, in our own house, in Wilmette, Illinois, A-mer-ee-ka. Corporate machinations had taken our family from ancient pillar to baroque post, and once again we were relocating, courtesy of The Company. As the sequel to our exotic expatriate existence, we had chosen to plop ourselves down in about the most "Father Knows Best" house on the most "Father Knows Best" street imaginable. Were we sure about this? Was I about to turn into Jane Wyatt? Help.

Some of the boxes were unpacked, the rest--*domani* (an old Italian philosophy guaranteed to extend your life so you can grow to be old, if not Italian). We were beat and decided to do what we always do when moving to a new country (and America definitely qualified as a new one after six years away)--plunge right in.

Which meant: first, order a much-missed, deep-dish Chicago pizza, home delivery--a real nonexistent concept in the Old World. And then collapse on the bed and get initiated into this "Saturday Night Live" cult all our old friends seemed to belong to. Since we were tired of being foreigners, this seemed to be a painless way to re-enter.

"The Second Time Around," *The Bridge*, Winter 1980, pp. 19–20. Used with permission from Intercultural Press, Inc.

Wrong. Why are these people laughing? What is a *Rosa-dana-dana*? You're sure this is funny? We are definitely laughing to different drummers and my drummer is vintage '73. How can this be? I had faithfully read the show business section in *Time* magazine every week in a valiant effort to be culturally plugged in. Instead, I'm feeling genuinely obtuse and totally devoid of what used to be my sense of humor. No doubt this is due to jet lag. Maybe *domani*, things will be better.

Wrong again. *Domani* brings the Jewel. If you had grown accustomed to small, albeit seedy, specialty shops, where you can buy a little bit of this, but none of that because that's in the store down the street; if you had grown used to that, how do you think it feels to face those endless, sparkling, bountiful shelves at the Jewel? Everything from parsley to encyclopedias, from mouse traps to gefilte fish. Where to begin?

I'm used to going to about seven shops to get enough for soup and sandwiches. Italy had elevated specialization to a fine art: different shops for veal and pork, milk and cheese, salt and pepper. Salt was the trickiest. It was sold in tobacco shops, along with stamps (the post office being eternally closed or on strike) and Tampax. Kotex was sold elsewhere, of course.

But there I am at the Jewel, 45 minutes later, and still only halfway down Aisle 3. It is not just the element of choice dumbfounding me; the items themselves truly leave me stumped. Consider Wrapples. Pre-pressed sheets of quasi-caramel to wrap around apples. Or this indispensable item: two pieces of whole wheat bread enveloping a single slab of ham, all tastefully molded out of synthetic sponge. Does one weep with despair for aborted ingenuity, or roar with laughter at inventive obsolescence? Neither. But I buy the thing and mail it to a friend in Paris who is repatriating next fall. With that as a preview, she's bound to be psychologically better armed than I to cope with the abundance gone mad in these stores.

When I get to generic items such as peanuts, I am riveted. Who knows, they probably have generic football, and I am reassured that there is, despite this madness, a yearning for the basics; and that maybe, maybe things will really be all right. Generically speaking, of course.

Things are definitely all right at the checkout counter. What a pleasure not to have to supply my own oft-used shopping bags, and to find these obliging youths there for the sole purpose of packing my bags and wheeling all those ultrawrapped items to my car. 'Tis a luxury verging on decadence. Gone are the days when I gingerly balanced on my handlebags my string bag of brown eggs precariously wrapped in yesterday's *Le Monde*. God bless styrofoam, doublebagging, and packup personnel.

And the bill! A mere $88. A virtual steal. In Amsterdam a miniroll of cellophane tape went for $1.80, a six-ounce bottle of syrup for $2, and a pound of hom-boor-ghur for nearly $4. You can bet that $88 does not a foreign fridge fill. But $88 in America lays in a whole lot of supplies. Admittedly you do pay a price: You are forced to be congenial to the Have-a-nice-day sendoff. It's not that I want surliness--my lifetime quotient of that was filled in Paris--but a little distance and formality would be preferable to intrusive warmth and sensitivity.

That goes for the restaurants, too. People who used to be waiters and are now breathy talking menus bent on telling you their names are distracting. I want no personal information about this person. And his flowing recitation robs me of the great pleasure of weighty menu deliberation. In Italy, it's a slowly unwinding ritual. Order a pasta, savor it, see how you feel about a *secondo* --maybe yes, maybe no, maybe later. It's very civilized. No salad bars, no themes, no show biz. And it takes hours--long, lovely, well-spent hours.

Look at lunch here. Aside from it consisting of BLTs or PBJs and taking 4.7 minutes to consume, there is the dismal situation of my co-lunchee. There used to be occasional invitations from people of the opposite sex--often colleagues of my husband or co-workers of mine--elegantly attired, taking me to wonderful places and addressing me in slinky foreign languages. And it was very kosher (considering these men were of Italian and French descent). But thus far, the only males I've lunched with have been Phil Donahue and Bozo. Or is Bozo a lady? I don't even want to know.

Repatriation is tricky. And media is a big part of it. There is an unrelenting barrage. Not that they don't have TV and magazines over there, but they're in foreign languages. Thus the media does not serve to soothe you into a glazed stupor while the microwave is doing its thing. It requires concentration and motivation to watch TV, because you've got to be tuned in and translating.

Nixon's resignation in Italian was my linguistic *tour de force.* I had to really focus on that one. But then came the tough part--the psychological integration. Walter Cronkite wasn't there to lend the event an element of validity or perspective. American politics began to look even more surrealistic than usual.

There, with the nightly news, TV was a less than peripheral part of life. There just wasn't a whole lot to tempt you. For starters, daytime TV didn't exist. I went cold turkey off the soaps. Rough at first, but it's like quitting smoking: You feel so proud, so cleansed, (so smug). And there's the rub. Do I maintain my virtue and remain aloof, or plunge back into a *demimonde* I no longer know. The babes I left six years ago are now twice-divorced, jaded, and taking a full hour, no longer just half, to wend their tragic ways through my afternoons. I think I can live without them.

But not without "Sesame Street." Not ever again. I may have had a *jeune fille au pair* over there, but I guarantee that four hours a day Sesame Street does the job better--and you don't have to feed it or worry if it's going to get pregnant and quit.

I remember back when we were still in the States, my daughter was 3, and how the panic would set in during the Channel 11 auction. A week without Big Bird presented a terrible challenge. And splat! We were in Rome where their idea of creative children's programming was something like "Cubism in Yugoslavia Since the War." Usually followed by "Carrosello"--a whole evening's commercials bunched together so the programs wouldn't have to be interrupted. Of course, when my son first faced an American TV, he collapsed in sobs 10 minutes after the show began. The commercial came on and he thought "The Waltons" was *finito* --not to be seen again for another week.

The choices continue to stagger me. Not just the markets, or TV stations, but everything.

Telephones. I start to panic at the Phone Store when the Phone Person displays all those dazzling colors and thematic models. Life is so simple in the old country. You want a phone? It's gray and squat. That's all there is--you and Giscard d'Estaing, you and Princess Grace--that's it. Gray and squat. So, after much deliberation at the Phone Store, I finally choose from their myriad models. I choose a gray (they call it pewter) squat phone and feel instantly a bit more stable.

Then I am confronted with the Call Pack question. Do I have 120 units or 240 units worth of downtown friends? What exactly is a unit? It was so easy there. You called wherever you wanted--next door or Bulgaria--not to worry. Because when the bill came, it was not itemized. Not locally, not internationally, not ever. It was just a vast, staggering amount. And no questions asked, you paid it. You paid it with a check that was also gray.

Checks and cash--that was it when it came to payment alternatives. No charge accounts. That's another dilemma. I have no charge or credit cards. And after six years of dealing directly in money, I am loathe to open the Pandora's Box of credit. How long can one exist in Chicago without a Marshall Field card? It's becoming something of a point of honor with me--to see how long I can remain a nonentity in the world of plastic credit.

I made my Resolutions for Repatriation on the plane heading back to Chicago. I once had a friend who spent 20 years of her life in Shaker Heights, Ohio and six weeks in Grenoble, France. Upon returning home, she found great difficulty in recalling *"comment vous dites--ah oui,* milk," etc. Resolved therefore: Never to end a sentence with a gratuitous *n'est-ce pas.* Resolution No. 2: Never to talk about someone's "space." No. 3: To live the rest of my life as I've lived the first 36 years--without a food processor. And No. 4: Above all never, but never, buy a pair of Gloria Vanderbilt jeans.

But I don't think I can stick to all that. It probably is time to toss in the metro tickets, put away the passport, and replace my frayed map of the canals with the Chicago & North Western train schedule. It's so easy to be seduced by cushy old Chicago normalcy. I seem to be holding firm on resolutions 1, 2, and 3, but there was a terrific sale at Saks yesterday, and you know what? Those Vanderbilt jeans really do fit me better.

Anyway, is the Second City really so different from the Eternal City? Three major strikes in only two months--that would challenge even the Italians.

17

Cultural Shock
in Reverse

James R. Corey

When an American university confers a doctoral degree upon a student from an underdeveloped country, it often does so with the expectation that the student will return home and become an instrument of change, of progress in his native land. We educators see the foreign student as a bearer of technological and cultural light from America. We see his future as effecting technological development and putting an end to ignorance, superstition, and other kinds of cultural backwardness.

The student, too, believes in this idea. Anyone who has met and talked with many third-world students knows the zeal with which that dream is held. However, not many American educators have the opportunity to see exactly what becomes of the new Ph.D., to observe what happens to his dream when he tries to realize it at home.

From 1969 to 1977, I taught in a university program in one of the world's most conservative developing countries--Saudi Arabia. I witnessed the return from America of the first significantly large group of Saudi Ph.D.'s. Virtually all of them held the ideal that I described above: to move Saudi Arabia into industrial utopia and out of cultural backwardness.

So far each of these young men has been confronted with the same cruel

From "Cultural Shock in Reverse" by J. R. Corey, 1979, *The Chronicle of Higher Education*, April 9, p. 48. Copyright 1979 by *The Chronicle of Higher Education*. Reprinted with permission.

dilemma: If he wishes to assume a role in the prosperous and challenging area of technological development, he must give up any plans to tamper directly with the cultural life of the country. In other words, he must buy his future wealth and position at the price of wearing blinders to the cultural problems around him. It is a purchase that produces more and more personal tension, frustration, and bitterness as years go by.

The young Saudi Ph.D. returning home after a lengthy stay in the U.S. experiences something akin to reverse cultural shock. At 28 to 30 years of age, he has often spent up to 10 years--a third of his life--in America. When he steps off the plane in Jeddah or Riyadh or Dhahran, he re-enters an environment that is now foreign to him. Though Saudi Arabia has made progress toward modernity during the 10 years of his absence, it is only as an external mark on the landscape. At her cultural heart, she is as restrictive, as narrow, as apparently ignorant as she ever was when he was a youth.

Cultural traditions that he never questioned as a boy growing up in a squatty, brown village now dismay him by their barbarity and irrationality. He is shocked by the backwardness: His mother and sisters still cannot go out in the streets without covering themselves from head to foot in an ugly, black veil, or *abayah.* His sisters have no choice of whom or when they marry. He himself will marry a girl he has probably never spoken to nor seen. Women he knows will die because their men will not allow male doctors to examine and treat them.

156

Or consider what the young man faces in the business and legal sectors of the culture. The economic machinery of the country is almost without regulations; it is controlled by men's signatures. The question of what is possible in business is not answered by an examination of commercial codes and regulations, as would be the case in a developed country. Rather, the question of what is possible is directly proportional to a man's standing with those who control the economic machinery. Such a situation is ready-made for exploitation by the unscrupulous. In fact, that is precisely what the young returning Saudi sees: a business environment where paying off the men of influence is the accepted mode of operation, and a legal system that is inadequate to cope with the corruption.

In other areas the situation is just as bad. Deaths attributable to engineering incompetence occur daily. A girls' school collapsed recently, killing a score of youngsters. The highway-accident death rate in Saudi Arabia is appalling.

The problems of corruption and incompetence are the most devastating ills of a developing country, but the returning Ph.D. is almost powerless to do anything about them. He is paralyzed by time-honored cultural patterns. For example, direct criticism is culturally taboo, unless the criticizing is done by the "right" sort of person--but even then the critic may be as likely to suffer cultural ostracism as is the one criticized. A young Saudi who has been tainted by exposure to a foreign culture does not dare to criticize.

To be bothered by payoffs and influence-peddling is to be an exception in the culture. I recall, for example, trying to explain to a group of Saudi students why Vice-President Spiro Agnew was forced out of office. When I explained that Agnew, while governor of Maryland, was alleged to have accepted influence money from various contractors doing business with the state, my audience was unable to comprehend the offense. As one student put it, Why should a man want to be a governor except to use his position for personal financial gain?

As for criticism of incompetence, the critic will constantly confront the argument that the school collapsed or the car accident occurred because it was God's will that it should happen. Death, so the argument goes, is not something attributable to the engineer's or the builder's incompetence; death is the carrying out of God's plan.

Faced with those and similar cultural circumstances, the young idealist has few options. He can throw himself enthusiastically into a money-making area of the country's development, but to do so he must don a mask of cultural conservatism for the sake of the society around him. The mask will include wearing the correct national dress and disdaining foreign clothing styles, trimming his hair and moustache to the proper length and shape, marrying a local girl, speaking Arabic in public, and paying full lip service to the national religion.

157

But behind the mask he will live a quite different life. Within his own home, he will surround himself with the people and objects of his American life. His friends will be young and either foreigners or foreign-educated Arabs. He will speak English, his second language, almost as frequently as he will his native tongue. He will indulge his tastes for American food, drink, music, and reading material. Most importantly, he will escape from his own culture as often as possible. In fact, he will take as many business and vacation trips to the U.S. as he can possibly arrange.

This dual existence will not be without its adverse effects. I have often observed its results. It produces a tension which for some individuals is intolerable. Many cease to be able to perform productive work because their creative energies become paralyzed. Others discard whatever ideals they once had and become hedonists or alcoholics. A few live in self-imposed exile in the U.S. or elsewhere, waiting for a time when cultural changes will bring the country's technological and cultural advances abreast of each other.

But for most, the mask quickly becomes the true face of the man. Unable to cope for long with the tension of a dual existence, incapable of sustaining a "foreign" identity in his native land, the young Ph.D. simply reaccepts the culture. He allows himself to become an influence peddler and an incompetent. And when the next wave of young idealists arrives, they will find the first group standing in the way of their plan for social reform.

Saudi Arabia is, I am sure, not unique among the developing wealthy nations of the world. The same conditions apply throughout the Arabian peninsula--in Kuwait, Abu Dhabi, Dubai, Qatar, and the emirates of southern Arabia. They also exist in other emerging oil-rich countries--Libya, Algeria, Nigeria, and Iran, for example. It is those countries that are sending increasing numbers of graduate students to the U.S. Thus it may be possible for something to be done in the American universities to prepare these students to cope more effectively with reverse cultural shock.

I can suggest at least three steps.

First, foreign graduate students should not be encouraged to stay on in the U.S. for extended periods. They should return to their home countries for summer vacations at four-year intervals, at a minimum. Two-year intervals would be even better, given the rapid pace of industrial change in their home countries. Currently, it is common for foreign students to spend eight or ten or even more years in the U.S., taking courses the year round. Many universities even urge this pattern on the students, in an effort to help them overcome language problems and course deficiencies from their previous educational backgrounds.

158

Such students are the ones who experience the profoundest shock upon returning home. Certainly, the present level of airline service around the world should make it easy for nearly all of them to go home for the summer every few years and see their country's culture first-hand.

Second, professors themselves could do more to help such students cope with their frustrating futures. Too often graduate courses are offered in such a way as to imply that their content has no relevance to particular cultural, geographical, political, or economic contexts. Subjects are presented as though they are to be practiced in an ideal world, uninfluenced by outside factors. Fields like money and banking or highway design or public health--or a hundred others--do not respond to absolute laws, although they are often taught as if they do.

In fact, the usefulness of such courses to the student is directly proportional to the student's understanding of how *relative* their content is. The foreign student needs to be encouraged to go beyond the American applications of his subjects. He needs to think about money and banking under conditions where all banking interest is considered usury, about highway engineering where drifting sand and wandering camels are the main menaces to moving traffic, about public health where camel's urine is still believed to be the only disinfectant that really works. The student needs to be encouraged to see his courses in the context of his native environment, not just in terms of American applications.

Finally, the foreign student needs to realize that American solutions to political problems like corruption and incompetence will not necessarily work when he gets home. I know several students who have spent a few years in jail because they apparently forgot that they left American-style freedom behind when they flew east from Kennedy Airport.

Reverse cultural shock is a real problem for many foreign students. It is time for American universities to undertake measures to counteract its effects. Any diminishing of the effects of reverse cultural shock will, in the end, benefit all the parties involved.

Unit D

Reentry of Third-Culture Children and Their Parents

Third-Culture Kids

So You are Going Home

Closure and Commencement

Practical Guidelines in the Positive Adjustment of Missionary Children

Reentry of Third Culture Children and Their Parents

In a discussion with overseas families, perhaps no topic is more emotionally volatile than the sojourner's children. In lectures or workshops on reentry, I have observed that some parents believe automatically that I am talking about their children. Parents, as you read this unit, strive for objectivity. Don't be on the defensive! Do be open to new ideas which enlarge understanding of your children.

I have reviewed more than seventeen significant studies of MKs conducted during the years 1934–1984. The primary reentry problem of MKs is social adjustment. In their college work, though, they attain higher grade point averages than the children of any other repatriate group. Would it not be instructive to know how well all TCKs are adjusting, in all facets of life, ten to twenty years after college graduation? Equally regrettable is the fact that few efforts have been made to study those TCKs who never enter college or who are college dropouts.

I am convicted that the world's leadership should come in large part from the TCKs in our international schools. We must explore creative avenues of guidance so that we tap the undoubted potential of our TCKs. Their developmental plans must be just as carefully outlined as the career paths of corporate expatriates. Pre-field and on-the-field training of TCKs must be inseparably linked to home leave training, post-return orientation seminars, and invigorating seasoning during the college years.

Useem and Downie, in Chapter 18, give us a sensitive view of the TCK. Although TCKs have been reared overseas, they are not "integral parts of those countries." When they return to the USA, they have a "marginal" social identity; they stand "in the middle." They do not fully identify with either the USA or the foreign country where they lived.

The fathers of the children are generally highly educated or highly skilled. The families have moved usually because of the fathers' employment. Hence, the parents' overseas employers or sponsors are critical in determining their geographical location, the kind of school they will attend, their friends, and the languages they will learn.

163

The family unit is often more cohesive in the overseas setting. Fathers take a more active role in children's lives. The family and the school form the twin underpinnings of continuity for TCKs. After college graduation, they continue to look for their "rootedness" in international occupations. Their life pattern exemplifies "coping" rather than "adjusting."

Merritt, in Chapter 19, insists that if MKs recognize that they will feel like foreigners upon reentry, their ability to deal with alienation and rejection will be enhanced. "The danger that MKs face is the danger that God's people always face: they are tempted to imitate either Elijah or Jonah, rather than Jesus."

When this article was written, Leila was a senior at Coronado High School in Lubbock, Texas. She has lived in Kenya, Africa, most of her life--from 1969 to 1981. Her parents, Hilton and Avanell Merritt, were missionaries there. While her remarks are painfully candid, everyone interested in missions will find the implications of her words sobering.

In Chapter 20 in a charming, conversational journal-entry form, Hunter, a missionary husband and father, tenderly sketches details of a love affair with London which began during a visit twenty-five years ago. In the eleven years time he has lived in London, two daughters and a son were born, and his wife has become bi-cultural. Now they must say goodbye--the parents and son (age 11) say goodbye to London and two daughters, (ages 20 and 18), who will remain in England to pursue their education. "It is time

164

to go home. But where is home?" Husband and wife say farewell to Hampstead Heath and Parliament Hill, the ancient East End, and West End with its theatre district. They say goodbye to loyal friends and their spiritual community with a sense of impending loss and loneliness. Their grief and anger are overshadowed by the warmth of God's love.

Their commencement in Colorado is marked by the joy of seeing old friends and family, affluence, a more circum- scribed world view, "plastic" money, "talking" cash registers, and aspen rather than plane trees. "Home will always be defined a little more broadly now."

Harrell, in Chapter 21, summarizes the data gathered from in-depth interviews with 15 MK teenagers. Her goal was to develop guidelines for the successful cross-cultural adjust- ment of young people. General needs identified as a result of these exchanges were a positive self-image, trust-bond relationships, educational preparation, smooth adjustment from one culture to another, and bi-cultural experience. Constructive guidelines are set forth pertinent to the general needs. In each need area, she records student comments which cogently support the stated guidelines.

18

Third-Culture Kids

Ruth Hill Useem and Richard D. Downie

"The first day, the teacher stood me up in front of the class and said I was from Singapore. The kids at that school were tough. They started calling me Chinaman and harassing me. I didn't like being called that. I thought it was something bad to be. I did well in school, though. The teachers liked me, and the school was easy. The schools I went to overseas were tougher."

"When I was 16, I came from Japan to a small town in Indiana. I remember the first time I was out on a date--all we did was drive around to McDonald's and different places. The whole night! I never really got involved much in the school life. A lot of the kids were not planning on going to college, and so we didn't have much in common to talk about. I think I was pretty strange for them, too."

"I think part of the problem when I came to the States was I looked American but I did things that were not quite American. I had fun trying to be an American. It was an act in a way."

No, these are not the observations of new immigrants or foreign visitors. These are the reactions of American third-culture kids (TCKs) who have come "home" after living abroad as dependents of parents who are employed overseas. Although they have grown up *in* foreign countries, they are not

From "Third-Culture Kids" by R. H. Useem and R. D. Downie, 1976, *Today's Education*, September/October, pp. 103–105. Copyright 1976 by the National Education Association. Reprinted by permission.

integral parts *of* those countries. When they come to their country of citizenship (some for the first time), they do not feel at home because they do not know the lingo or expectations of others--especially those of their own age.

Where they feel most like themselves is in that interstitial culture, the third culture, which is created, shared, and carried by persons who are relating societies, or sections thereof, to each other.

Although some Americans were living outside the United States before World War II, the great burgeoning in numbers of Americans moving overseas began after the War. Now, there are approximately 300,000 school-age American children overseas. Their fathers are missionaries; visiting professors and teachers; representatives of the U.S. government (e.g., employees of the Department of Defense, the Department of State, etc.); employees of international and multinational corporations and financial institutions (e.g., Exxon, First National City Bank, Bell Helicopter); and American employees of international organizations such as the World Health Organization and UNICEF. These fathers are usually highly educated or highly skilled people who are forging the networks that intertwine and interrelate the peoples of the world. (The mothers may be employed overseas, but in most cases, the families have moved because of the fathers' employment.)

To be sure, Americans are not the only ones involved in third cultures. For example, Japanese businessmen work and live in the United States and in Southeast Asia, and diplomats from all countries represent their governments in posts all over the world. Their dependent children can be found in university communities, in the United Nations International School in New York, in the capitals and large cities of the world, and in some of the same overseas schools as American children. In this article, we shall limit our discussion to American TCKs.

The parents' sponsor in the overseas area is crucial in determining the specific part of the third culture in which the TCKs live, the kind of school they attend, the host nationals and third country nationals they will know, and the languages they will learn. These children even have labels that reflect their parents' sponsors--"Army brats," "MKs" (missionary kids), "biz kids," and most recently "oil kids."

Overseas, one of the first questions a TCK asks a new arrival is "What does your father do?" or "Who is your father with?" The answer helps to place young people socially. If, after returning stateside, a TCK asks such a question of a young person who has been reared here, the latter's reaction may be one of puzzlement or resentment. Unlike that of TCKs, the social life of young people reared here is not directly influenced by the father's employer.

TCKs are attached to the third culture through their parents' employers, who hold parents responsible for the behavior of their offspring. (If a dependent grossly misbehaves, he or she may be sent home, and the employer may reassign the father or terminate his employment.) Therefore, fathers take an active role in their children's lives and in making family decisions.

In one study of third-culture families, only 6 of 150 TCKs reported that their mothers always or usually made final decisions about family matters. (It should be remembered that almost all overseas American families have both parents present.) Fifty-three percent of Department of Defense dependents claimed that only their fathers made final decisions; 41 percent of children of missionaries said their fathers had the final say in family decisions; and the others involved in the study, including 75 percent of children of those representing the federal government, reported that both parents, and occasionally the children themselves, were involved in decision making.

Most children and youth overseas do not resent strict parental controls, because all of them attached to the same sponsor come under similar rules and, hence, there is community reinforcement. Besides, the overwhelming majority of TCKs (close to 90 percent) like, respect, and feel emotionally attached to their parents.

There are many reasons for this. The high mobility of third-culture families, who usually move every one, two, or four years, seems to have the effect of bringing individual family members closer together. They share the common experience of moving into unfamiliar territory and offer each other mutual support in the face of change and strangeness. Parents are often the only people with whom TCKs have a continuing relationship as they move from one location to another.

American families overseas spend more time together (unless the children are in boarding school) than do their stateside counterparts--and the time together is often not taken up with mundane aspects of living. Mothers are home managers rather than housewives, because they usually have servants to clean up the spilled milk, make the beds, cook the meals, and chauffeur the children. As one overseas mother said, "It's amazing how pleasant conversations with children can be when you are not frantically trying to get the supper on, answer the telephone, and nag the children to pick up their clothes."

The family provides one form of continuity for TCKs. The schools offer another.

There is a remarkable similarity among the approximately 600 schools attended by American children overseas. There are also great differences.

These include variations in the size of the student body (from 10 or 12 up to 6,000 or so); differences in sponsorship (e.g., Department of Defense schools, schools assisted by the Department of State, private and entrepreneurial schools, those sponsored by corporations, and those run by Catholic orders and Protestant churches); and widely different make-ups of student bodies (e.g., from Americans only to Americans in the minority).

All of these schools place a heavy emphasis upon academic performance, and the secondary schools are college-prep oriented. The curriculum resembles that of stateside schools with the same orientation, but the overseas schools usually offer enrichment courses in the local language and culture. Books and materials (which often don't arrive or come late) are generally imported from the United States.

The avowed purpose of most American-sponsored overseas schools has been to prepare American pupils for entering the mainstream of American society; stateside schools and colleges, to the extent to which they notice TCKs at all, have been concerned with their "problems of adjustment" to their peers. Neither the overseas nor the stateside schools have seen the TCKs as people who, as adults, will be following in their parents' footsteps and fulfilling mediating roles in the increasingly conflictive but interdependent global system. Nor do the schools see that solving some "problems of adjustment" offers TCKs valuable experience that can help prepare them for their future roles--which will probably be international.

One reason the schools lack appreciation for the great potentialities of these young people is that few educators have studied TCKs. In a bibliography on third-culture education that we compiled at the Institute for International Studies in Education, only 10 of the 50 dissertations listed concern TCKs--how they feel and perform, what they value, what they aspire to, and how they view the world and themselves in relation to it.

(Given the rather thin reeds on which to rest generalizations about these youth, and given the rapidity with which third cultures and national cultures change, we warn the readers that what we are reporting here is suggestive rather than definitive.)

One study of 150 college-enrolled TCKs of varying sponsorship and residence abroad (but all of whom had spent a minimum of one teen year overseas) produced a dramatic finding: not one preferred to pursue a career exclusively in the United States. One-fourth named a specific place overseas where they would like to work (usually the location where they had lived during their teen years); 29 percent expressed interest in following an overseas-based occupation but wanted to move from country to country; 25 percent wanted to be headquartered in the United States with periodic one- or two-year assignments abroad; and 12 percent wanted to be employed in the United States but to have opportunity for overseas job-related travel.

In order to qualify for careers in the third culture, these young people recognize that they must be well-educated and/or highly skilled. (There are few unskilled or even semiskilled third-culture occupations.) Thus they aspire, even when in secondary school, to attain college degrees, and many anticipate getting professional and advanced degrees or mastering highly specialized skills.

One important reason that TCKs want to work in an international occupation, whether pursued entirely or partially abroad, is that they feel most "at home" in third-culture networks. Only 7 percent report feeling "at home" with their peers in the United States, while 74 percent say they feel most comfortable with people who are internationally oriented and who have lived abroad.

Yet such preferences do not imply that a person is rootless or has made a "poor adjustment." As one TCK with Asian experience says, "I guess I could live anywhere and be comfortable. I have always liked to think I get along with all different people. I don't feel bothered by a lack of roots, and I don't think I have a lot of problems because of that."

To be sure, some TCKs have severe emotional problems that cannot be resolved without outside help--and some problems not even then. But the rate is probably not greater among these foreign-experienced youth than it is among the general American population of the same age.

The reported experiences of these youth suggest that they cope rather than adjust, and as one student of multicultural persons describes them, they become both "a part of" and "apart from" whatever situation they are in. A TCK with Asian and African experience explains, "I find myself sitting back and objectively observing Americans and American society, occasionally smiling and occasionally shaking my head. I get along comfortably with both, but then again, there is a bit of me that remains apart."

Most third-culture kids are more familiar with foreign languages than are their stateside counterparts. One researcher reports that 92 percent of the TCKs she studied learn one or more foreign languages, mostly languages used in many parts of the world, such as Spanish, German, and French. Twenty-six percent claim knowledge of languages other than, or in addition to these, such as Yoruba, Hausa, Urdu, Kijita, Swahili, Amharic, Kalagan, Marathi, Kisukuma, Chinese, and Quiche. (In U.S. public secondary schools, less than .5 percent learn languages other than French, Spanish, German, and Latin.)

171

TCKs learn some languages in schools abroad and some in their homes or in the marketplaces of a foreign land. One-third of these youngsters are children of cross-cultural marriages and/or foreign-born parents, and they use a language other than English at home or when visiting relatives. Some pick up languages from the servants in the home or from playmates in the neighborhood.

Although most third-culture kids lose their proficiency in the foreign language when they return to an all-English-speaking environment, many pursue languages they have already learned, and some become literate in the languages they can speak. Few have emotional blockages about learning a new language--particularly if they perceive it as useful for the career they want to pursue in the future.

What can stateside teachers do to assist these youth when they return to the United States? Perhaps the best answer is for teachers to challenge them academically, both because this gives them continuity with their past and because this helps prepare them for the futures they desire.

Teachers should also try not to make these students' uniqueness a problem for them in school. Each TCK wants to be treated as an individual, not stereotyped as the "new student from Kuwait."

One TCK who lived in the Far East sums up her feelings about her experiences upon returning to the United States in this way: "I was made to feel like an odd person, a creature from another place, and I wasn't. I speak English, and I understand everything Americans say. My teacher and the people in the town where I was living didn't really see *me* --they just saw the difference."

References

Soddy, K. (Ed.). (1961). *Identity: Mental health and value systems.* Philadelphia: J. B. Lippincott.

U. S. Bureau of the Census. 1970 Census of population. (1973). *Americans living abroad.* Subject Report PC (2)-10A. Washington, DC: U. S. Government Printing Office.

Useem, J., Donoghue, J. D., & Useem, R. H. (1963, Fall). Men in the middle of the third culture: The roles of American and non-Western peoples in cross-cultural administration. *Human Organization, 22,* 169–79.

Useem, R. H. (1973). Third culture factors in educational change. In C. S. Brembeck & W. H. Hill (Eds.), *Cultural challenges to education.* Lexington, MA: D. C. Heath.

Useem, R. H. (Ed.). (1975). *Third culture children: An annotated bibliography.* East Lansing: Institute for International Studies in Education, Michigan State University.

19

So You Are
Going Home

Leila Merritt

So you are going home. Great! Isn't that exciting?

Well, I was excited . . . though I was sad to leave the mission field. Therein, you see, was my problem. I was not going home. My parents were going home, but I was not. After all, Kenya was my home.

Upon arriving in the States, an incredible number of people hugged me and said, "Aren't you glad you're back? I bet it's a relief to be home." Truthfully, I felt like an American on the mission field, but in America I felt like a foreigner because I had been raised in a Christian family and had lived in a foreign country.

If MKs, or missionary kids, can see this before they reach the United States, they will be able to deal with the alienation and rejection without feeling guilty. The danger that MKs face is the danger that God's people always face: they are tempted to imitate either Elijah or Jonah, rather than Jesus.

The Elijah Complex
If you follow Elijah, you become bitter and afraid, unable to see God's hand in anything. After the great victory that Elijah won on Mount Carmel, he was elated, right? Wrong. Didn't he praise God for His power and thank

From "So You Are Going Home" by L. Merritt, 1983, *Strategy*. October/December, pp. 1–3. Copyright 1983 by Abilene Christian University. Reprinted by permission.

Him for the opportunity to serve Him? No, he did not. God cared for his needs in a special way. Wasn't Elijah thrilled? No, he was not. He said, "God, with all I've done for you, all I've given up for you, look what you have done for me. You sent me to people who are trying to kill me. None of them care about you, your word or your prophet. They're trying to get rid of me. I'm the only one left, and they're trying to kill me."

This can happen to the MK. You have had a sense of service and have seen exciting growth in God's kingdom. You come "home," and God takes care of your physical needs in astounding ways. But you realize that America is not paradise. Instead of trusting God for your emotional needs, you think: "God, the work to which you called my parents is causing me an awful lot of trouble. The lessons I learned overseas make me more mature than these kids. Now they're trying to make me as narrow and shallow and immature as they are. They really couldn't care less about anyone outside this country, and they don't even want to hear about how I've seen you work overseas. I'm the only one who really knows what's going on."

This has been a particular problem for me. As I was taking World History, and the teacher was discussing African revolutionaries, the person sitting next to me said, "Kinyaahtaah? That's a weird name." A weird name, huh? What about yours? Just because every third person in Lubbock is not named Kenyatta does not make it a weird name. I did not say it quite like that, but I thought, "Hopeless provincial."

174

At the bus stop, someone asked me where I was from. When I said, "Kenya," he wrinkled his nose and said, "Kinyaa, Texas--never heard of it."

Before I attended my first football game, my dear father went up to the security officer and said, "This is my little girl, and she's never been to a football game before--she's been in Africa. Take good care of her." I was so embarrassed! The policeman raised his flashlight at me and said, "Do you speak English?" I was tempted to say, "Ula goola pishu gila," but I restrained myself.

Can you see, when feelings of alienation set in, how easy it is to feel superior and lonely? This, then, is the problem. Some real differences exist between the missionary kid and the American teen. We, as MKs, need to retain the qualities we developed overseas, yet we must not believe we are superior.

The solution for us is the same as it was for Elijah. Be realistic. God told Elijah that He had seven thousand in Israel who had not worshipped Baal. Should the MK really think that he or she is the only person in America who knows that different peoples use different names, that there is such a thing as propriety, that the world does not revolve around Lubbock? I felt that way. But was I the only teenager who had ever come back from the mission field? Of course not . . . though none of the others seemed to be in Lubbock. Some Americans know what is going on. The MK can find friends in the States as long as he or she does not feel superior to them. Please don't let the blindness of those about you distort your own vision of God and of others.

Where are those seven thousand? We have no record that Elijah ever saw them. I have not seen seven thousand. One or two . . . maybe . . . but not seven thousand. The relationship of missionary kids with God has to be strong enough to sustain them. The MK must believe that God will take care of him or her in the same way that He cared for Elijah.

The Jonah Syndrome
If the MK follows Jonah, he worships a worthless idol--conformity.

Jonah was similar in a lot of ways to missionary kids. The word of God came to Jonah and sent him to a city of foreigners. Did Jonah want to spend his life and energy with people that were not his own? Apparently not. He paid a fare to get on a boat full of foreigners in order to run away from God. While on the boat, he pretended to be just like the foreigners he wished to avoid. It was no use. A storm finally forced him to admit who he was.

We fail to realize how easy it is to get ourselves in the same type of situation. I did. Just like Jonah, I started out with the word of God. I knew more about God and His word than most 15-year-olds. But when the pressure came, I really did not want to appear as one of God's people in a foreign land. So I paid my fare to get on the boat of "being American." The fare cost a small amount of my personal peace, a larger amount of self-respect, and nearly everything in my relationship with God. Are you willing to pay that price? I was.

I got on a boat with people who had nothing in common with me and pretended to be one of them. I began by pretending that I liked their music and hairstyles; I eventually pretended that their values were mine. I enjoyed it for a while--my friends thought I was really a neat person--but a storm arose. Just as the sailor asked Jonah who his God was, my friends asked me where I stood. Eventually I could avoid the question no longer. I had to admit that I, like Jonah, "worshipped the God of heaven" (Jonah 1:9). Once I had admitted it, the sailors threw me into the sea--my friends deserted me. They were not mean. They simply were not equipped to handle the situation. Once I had admitted my beliefs, the worst was over. The tragedy occurs when people will not admit to whom they belong. They think, "It'll get better . . . it'll get better." It *will not* get better until you admit who you are. It did not for Jonah . . . it did not for me . . . it will not for you.

Jonah used God's way of escape. That is the only way to escape conforming to the world. First, he admitted what he had done. Second, he accepted the consequences. Third, he threw himself on God's mercy. After I admitted what I had done, I accepted the consequences . . . impatiently. I was ready for His mercy. But, from inside a fish, it is hard to see divine mercy. So I attempted to find my way out. It went something like this: "Okay,

God, here I am. But I'll get out of this fish all by myself. If I got myself in, I can get myself out."

What was I going to do? Dance on his belly until he threw up? That was not too good. He might spit me up at the bottom of the sea, and I cannot swim. Maybe I could grab his left tonsil, climb up the back of his tongue, and sit in his mouth until he yawns. Then I could jump out. Excellent! But I still cannot swim. It seemed so futile. I did not even know if fish have tonsils. I was not sure if they ever yawned.

My plan for escaping the world was no better than the one I had for escaping the fish. I initially decided to attach myself to the girl in study hall who looked lonely. I thought she could fulfill my emotional needs. But she chewed tobacco. Then I decided to chase a good-looking boy, thinking that would take care of my problems. And it might have--until he dumped me for the tobacco chewer. Finally, I decided to throw myself into talking to people who have problems. Surely that would make me feel good. It did . . . temporarily.

None of these schemes really worked. Both Jonah and I had to throw ourselves on God's mercy. We got ourselves in, but God had to get us out. Jonah 2:8 says, "Those who cling to worthless idols forfeit the grace that could be theirs." Jonah clung to the worthless idol of being independent of God. I clung to the worthless idol of being independent of God. I clung to the worthless idol of being an American. It did not work.

176

The Jesus Mentality

Our third alternative is to be like Jesus. Who could have had more culture shock than Jesus? He gave up being the Ruler of Heaven to become the son of conquered peasants. He had been a spirit; now He had a body. Surely He must have looked at people and said, "Made in *our* image? You've got to be kidding."

Jesus fed the five thousand, and they were extremely grateful. In fact, they were going to make Him king until He told them that they merely wanted the free lunches He could provide. So they left Him. Do you think it might have crossed His mind that they were shallow? Do you think that when the Jews said that they did not need freedom from sin because they were Abraham's descendants that Jesus might have questioned the width of their world view? When they accused Him of casting out demons by Satan, do you think He knew that their hearts were impure? Jesus knows what it is like to be rejected by His own (John 1:11).

First, He knew the principles of His actions. Without ever giving up His claim to being the Messiah, He participated in Jewish customs. He did not officiously reorganize the temple, the Roman Empire and the world. In the same way, I can do "American" things without giving up my special relationship with God. I am not too holy to attend football games. I am not too perfect to enjoy American humor. I am not too mature to have fun with others. As long as I remain true to my God, I can be involved with Americans.

Second, He refused to let public opinion change Him. When the Pharisees demonstrated their hypocrisy by asking why He ate with sinners, Jesus did not make excuses. He said, "I come to sinners." He kept doing what was right. He had healthy defiance. I must not be so afraid of what Americans think, so desperate for companionship, that I will subordinate God's will to that of others. If I let my desire for acceptance dictate who I am, I have fallen into Jonah's trap.

Third, Jesus remembered His purpose. It would have been easy for Him to get so busy raising the dead, healing the sick, and training His disciples that He forgot the crucifixion. All of those things were good, but they were not His destiny. Jesus was able to retain His integrity because He remembered His purpose. I must not get so wrapped up in re-entry shock that I forget what I am doing. To be like Jesus, I must know my principles, have some healthy defiance, and remember my purpose.

20

Closure and Commencement: The Stress of Finding Home

Victor L. Hunter

Today I must say goodbye. Goodbyes are important. Without a meaning-ful goodbye, an effective closure, there cannot be a creative hello, a new beginning and hopeful commencement. I have always found it important to mark the times and seasons, the significant events in my life and my family's life, with ritual and symbol. Such marking somehow reaches beyond the commonplace and ordinary and has the power to reach those recesses of one's being which, though not easily accessible to conscious thought, nonetheless exercise a remarkable power in one's life.

I knew instinctively where I must go to end one journey in order to begin another. I crossed the footbridge into Hampstead Heath and began the climb up Parliament Hill. By conservative estimate I had done this some five thou-sand times. It represented all with which I was familiar. Hampstead Heath was the place where I came to walk, to think, to sort things out as I would wander through its lanes and meadows or sit by its ponds. It was a place of quiet and beauty located in the center of the hustle and bustle of life in London. As I reached the top of Parliament Hill, virtually the highest eleva-tion in London, I turned and surveyed the expanse of city below me. There to the left was St. Paul's Cathedral, to the right the Post Office Tower. In between were the buildings, the train stations, the narrow streets, the

From "Closure and Commencement: The Stress of Finding Home" by V. L. Hunter, 1985. Written expressly for this volume. Copyright 1985 by the ACU Press.

churches, and the parks that I had come to know through many years. I was looking at history, both social and personal. I lifted my eyes beyond the city to the vast stretches of the Kent Downs which formed a backdrop to the Thames Valley. As a seagull, driven inland by the winds over the choppy Atlantic coast, screeched overhead, I searched that distant horizon for a meeting point between my past and future.

I first walked the streets of London as a young college student a quarter of a century ago. It was the beginning of a love affair with a city, a country, and a culture that has thrived into its silver jubilee. Since that time I have lived with my family in this city for eleven years. Two daughters were born here and received all their secondary education in its schools. They have forgotten how to speak "American." My son has attended only a British school, and this for the past six years. My wife feels virtually like a "native" and is often mistaken for one.

But our life as a family in this city has now been brought to a halt through circumstances beyond our control. It is time to go home. But where is home? What follows is a journal account of some of my feelings and thoughts as I have gone through the stress of finding home. Here is no systematic thought or theoretical approach, but simply the account of head and heart of one man and his family who have faced closure and commencement.

180 **Journal Entry**

It is now clear that we must return to the United States. We means my wife, my eleven year old son, and myself. My two daughters, at the ages of 18 and 20, have decided to stay in Great Britain. They will pursue their own careers here--one in training as a registered nurse, one studying theology at St. Andrews University.

Tonight I feel an emptiness, a void, the ache of hollowness. I have experienced the strength of this feeling only once before--at the death of my grandmother, with whom I was very close. Is this then a new kind of death? I suspect so. Over hushed tones we talked with the members of the theological community with whom we have lived and worked for the past six years. We all knew that our lives would be forever changed. Simply put, there are people, places, experiences, and events ranking among the highest values of our hearts that are going to be lost. It felt like a death had occurred tonight. We cried together.

Journal Entry

I must remember that we are all experiencing this event from different perspectives and different levels of maturity. This came home dramatically to me today in a conversation with my daughters, H and C. Neither are they going home, i.e., returning to a place and culture they have known before, nor are they staying home--in the familiar surroundings and with the people they know and love. In a very real sense, their home is leaving them. They will be living in the same culture but with many familiar underpinnings removed. They must find a new way of life in a familiar culture. For them there is a gigantic shifting of ground.

H is undergoing these changes while working on a cancer ward at the hospital. She is under pressure to learn and not make mistakes. She has seen death personally and close up--maybe twenty people over the past ten weeks, some her own age.

C, on the other hand, is in the midst of her A-Level examinations. The marks she receives on them will be the only marks that count for these past two years of study and will determine whether she goes on to university. If she receives the required grades, she will make her way alone to St. Andrews University, the old medieval, walled, university town anchored on the rugged and bleak east coast of Scotland. She is under tremendous pressure for an eighteen-year old. Success on her examinations will mean fulfillment and achievement--but also certain separation from us and from all her friends in London. It is a success she wants very much, but one tinged with loss and separation.

As H and C are undergoing the stress of new beginnings and new careers, a time when they naturally want the solidity and security of their home, their home is disappearing before their very eyes. I was surprised (foolishly) at the level of grief and anger in H and C in today's conversation. Perhaps it was because my own grief and anger was at such a delicate stage that I was unable (unwilling?) to let them express theirs. Until today, that is. Today they made known their genuine grief over the "loss" of their family and the "loss" of the community of which we have all been a part. Grief also over reducing a Christian ministry and social service program they felt deeply committed to and desired to have continue. They feel angry at me for "folding my tent" and going back to America, for not "fixing things" so they could go on unchanged. They fear that Mom and Dad will go back and become middle-class Americans and will lose our commitments and international vision and will simply adopt uncritically the American value system and view of the world.

181

Journal Entry

The hidden fears have begun to come out at night. In the dark and lonely hours of sleep the ego relinquishes its control, and the subconscious is left free to roam the valleys of the mind and heart. H's dreams have become preoccupied with death. I was also awakened last night by L's crying. The cry and the groan must have been invented to express feelings too deep for human words. They are an integral part of human communication. Tears are the out-going tide to carry loss from our lives.

Journal Entry

I feel as if life has turned into an emotional roller coaster. Our family is experiencing a tremendous warmth and closeness--lots of laughter, family meals, times with friends. As departure time draws closer the sweetness of these moments heightens. They are then often followed by a sense of impending loss and loneliness. I find myself trying to engineer psychological "upness." Depression in me or other members of my family angers me. It is foolish of me to attempt to organize life away from grief. Tonight we planned a special dinner. We all looked forward to it with great anticipation. Each member of the family was to cook a particularly loved family dish. H and C promised their delicious French *profiteroles* for dessert. But when something went wrong in the delicate preparations and they were a total flop, tears and anger followed. Then I became angry that the failure of *profiteroles* should cause such stress and upset on an evening that we were supposed to enjoy together. Tension in the family was so thick you could slice it. Of course, the failure of the *profiteroles* had nothing to do with the realities we were experiencing, and we all acknowledged that before the evening was over.

Journal Entry

182

H has had the wisdom to seek out an independent professional counselor with whom to discuss her grief, anger and depression over our leaving and the events surrounding it. I applaud her wisdom.

Journal Entry

We have begun to break down the house. Each member of the family has many details to attend to. It will be a three-way split, and each has to get organized for the future. But everything that is happening under the pressure of time suggests the feeling of utter chaos--externally and internally. I have become an inveterate maker of lists, my gesture toward order. I even find myself making lists of lists, what I call my index to chaos. I find that any attempt to place order on chaos is a creative act.

Journal Entry

The language of farewells has its own set of nouns and verbs. The nouns are persons, places, events. The verbs are intransitive and belong to the category of being--for to say goodbye or to grieve always touches the verb "to be." That is, they are related to who we are as persons, to our existence, to those realities and relationships that at the deepest level make us who we are. I have found myself in recent weeks prefacing many activities--whether in places we go or with people we are seeing--with the words, "Well, this is the last time. . . . " I think it drives my family a little crazy.

Journal Entry
I believe it is important to help each family member stay within "shouting distance" of each other in terms of the way each person, at that particular level of maturity, is internalizing the process of the closure of one aspect of our life together and the commencement of another. This was brought home to me by two experiences relating to my eleven-year old son. I had assumed he understood that we were going back to America and what that would mean. And he was always excited by the prospect, looking forward to it with great relish. America meant to him holidays, family reunions, travel, excitement. His view of America was that of the vacationer, drawn from his only experience of the country--our brief holidays "back home."

Recently he came to me and said he wanted to have a party for three close school friends. "What kind of party?" I asked. "A goodbye party," he replied. He had begun to internalize the reality of "going home." It meant separation from his closest friends of six years. He wanted to give each a gift and he knew what he wanted to give. He wanted each of them (and himself) to have a T-shirt with THE FEARSOME FOUR printed on the front. On the back would be each of their names. It appeared that he wanted to wear his connection with the past into the future. Perhaps on a more sophisticated psychological level, he did not want the future to obliterate the past or to go into the future without affirming the camaraderie of the past.

The second experience which made me aware of his process of internalizing the closure has been his overall relationship to his older sisters. He is now spending enormous amounts of time with them. And they have intuitively understood his needs for this as well as their own. This perception has given them some incredibly special times together.

183

Journal Entry
We went to an end of school function tonight. As we walked home along Fleet Road, C and I turned to each other and simultaneously began to cry. No words were spoken. None were needed. Only touch.

Journal Entry
I find that sending and receiving letters has become very important. Friends and family have been communicating about life in the United States, sending grocery cash register receipts, newspapers, etc. It has begun to put me back in touch with stateside realities. I have also found it cathartic to communicate with family and friends about our experiences in London, especially during this transition period. This process seems to me to be a bridge-building endeavor between the two cultures as well as between our past and our future.

Journal Entry

This has been perhaps our most important week together in the process of closure. It has been the "week of days." L's day with H and C was a day at Kew Gardens walking and picnicking and enjoying the beauty of England. I do not know what transpired. They were events that belong only to the terrain which mother and daughters can walk. H and C each had a day with their brother. Again, the experiences of those days belong only to their hearts. I can but be grateful they have had them. And then there were my days with H and C.

H, C, and I lunched together in a garden pub. We then walked the old street markets and explored dusty used book shops. We took in a late afternoon movie. We then dined together at a restaurant of their choice. It had been a day of laughter, reminiscence, relaxation, and enjoyment. In over three hours at dinner father and daughters left no stone unturned in conversation as we talked about life in general and our lives in particular. We said and acknowledged things never said before. We talked of careers, values, faith, family, sexuality, hopes, disappointments, fears, joys. We ended the night by strolling arm in arm along the Thames and casting pennies into the ancient river under the pale lights of Waterloo Bridge as we made our hopes and wishes known for the future. Father and daughters were friends in a new way. It was a night of passage into deeper adult relationships. In saying goodbye to each other and to our current "home," we were able to greet and affirm the new future in hope and anticipation. We affirmed the new journeys yet to be taken, as individuals and as a family.

L and I also had our day together. It was primarily a day to say goodbye to a city we loved in order that we might be free to anticipate the future. We had lived and loved and learned in this city for over a decade. It provided a way of life we enjoyed. Here we had raised our children to adulthood. So we simply walked the streets for ten hours--from the ancient East End with its unchanging and narrow cobbled streets to the blare of the West End and the neon blaze of the theatre district. Each place had its corner in our memory which we acknowledged with gratitude. We ended where we had begun so many years before--in the first restaurant in which we had dined together. Sad to be leaving, yes. But we felt the circle had somehow been completed.

Journal Entry

We leave for the United States in a few hours. The house is now quiet, its darkened, middle-of-the-night, empty rooms only occasionally catching the glow from the street lamps beyond the trees in the front garden. There is nothing quite as final or lonely as an echo in an empty house. But tonight I hear other echoes--echoes of the warmth and laughter of all the years in this place with my family.

This day has felt like a $33\frac{1}{3}$ rpm record of these past few months played

184

at 78 rpm. So much has been packed into its hours. C received her A-Level examination results, and there was much rejoicing at her success. H was given highest marks for her second term of nursing. Again, great joy. A steady flow of friends called at the house to say goodbye. My literary agent telephoned to say that my novel had just sold in England. The editor of the publishing house came by to meet me before I leave for America.

Finally, our family closed the door on all others to spend the last few hours together. Throughout these weeks and months we have sincerely said our goodbyes and placed an honest closure on this segment of our life together. We spent tonight in giving gifts and exchanging letters. The girls gave L and me a batik of our house, done by a local London artist. They gave our son a framed collage of all the significant places and events of his time in London. Each of them gave us letters, a final seal of our relationship, which contained their thoughts and feelings too deep for the verbal telling. I gave each of the children the dedication page out of a theology book I have dedicated to them. But mostly we just sat together and talked of journeys already taken and journeys yet to be.

As I sit alone now in this darkened room, the last few hours of my time in this house and this city slipping away toward dawn, I feel fundamentally at peace. I believe that genuine closure has taken place. Am I sad? Yes. It is not a sadness of depression or desperation, but simply the sadness of something ending that has been so good. The consummation of a dream is its own death. It is, thus, the paradoxical sadness of fulfillment and joy.

Tomorrow a new journey begins. I want to begin it in anticipation and in openness. I want to be neither forgetful of the past nor frozen in it. And I am a bit afraid. I want to walk rather slowly, knowing that I will find both more and less than I expect as I try to find home once again.

Journal Entry

The United States of America. First impressions and feelings upon re-entry fairly well run the gamut. Friendliness. The banality of its advertising. The joy of seeing old friends and family. Inevitable comparison between American and British friends. Overwhelming abundance and prosperity. A more circumscribed world view. The delicious taste of a Hershey. New prospects for the future. Funny money. A stranger in my own home town. Out of touch in many conversations. I remind myself continually to keep my eyes open and my mouth shut. Not an easy task.

Journal Entry

I got lost in a supermarket today. I had to get a grid map to find my way out. How many acres did this store cover? Then I was greeted by a talking cash register. I have decided only to do big shopping lists. How can one go to a supermarket and expect to find only three items?

185

Journal Entry

I notice that my wife, my son, and I are doing everything together. I take it we are in something of a psychological huddle and will eventually take our own, more independent places in the game plan. However, the psychological huddle may be very necessary at the moment.

Journal Entry

My son's friends in London were named Ian, Peter, and Christopher. He came home today and told me he had met some new friends--Clint, Dax, and Shane. L and I thought this extremely funny--reverse culture shock in the names of your son's friends.

Journal Entry

We left behind the chaos of breaking down our house. We have entered the chaos of trying to get started again. Will order ever really be a part of our lives again? Disorder is getting very frustrating to live with.

Journal Entry

I have been out of "charge account land" so long that I can't get credit. The more you owe here the better your credit. I must learn how to overspend again.

Journal Entry

The supermarket was easier today.

Journal Entry

The small church with which I am working has given us a wonderfully warm reception. There is an authentic sense of community, of caring, and of saying "welcome home." Intuitively, along with their welcoming reception, they have given us two important "gifts"--space and pace. By space I mean they have welcomed us but have given us room and privacy to find ourselves without "hovering" to "see how we are doing." By pace I mean they have not rushed us into involvement faster than we are prepared to move. This experience has caused me to see that space and pace are important elements in handling re-entry stress.

Journal Entry

I find people fascinated with the fact that we have lived abroad for eleven years--fascinated for about thirty seconds. Others are genuinely interested. I do not talk about it much. It is an experience I have decided cannot be explained easily. My "favorite" conversations are with people who say, "I was in London once. The people are really rude, aren't they." "Some are, many aren't," I respond. I leave it at that.

I find myself in a strange position. For years I bit my tongue at negative

European generalizations about Americans. Now I bite my tongue at negative American generalizations about the English. I feel torn between two
worlds.

Journal Entry
We have had trouble finding a violin teacher for our son. In London, his
talents were greatly admired. We now live in a much smaller community,
one in which the arts are not particularly valued. There is a small strings
group in our son's school. Only girls play violin. He went to the strings
class today. He came home feeling an oddity and explained to his mother
that he was too advanced to play at school. Anyway, boys don't play violin.
These were not statements of pride, but of embarrassment. Little things tend
to get to us while we are more prepared for the larger stresses of readjustment.
I found L crying tonight. She said, "I want to go home." "We are home,
dear," I replied. "Then why doesn't it feel like it."

Journal Entry
Today we had a wonderful time with members of our family who visited
our new home in the mountains. We picnicked. We showed them our house
and our land. It really has begun to feel like home. We are embracing it
and our rural community. We are making new friends. Some order is beginning to appear in our chaos. We try not to rush it, but it is difficult.

187

Journal Entry
The supermarket was easier yet again today. It really does make shopping
easier. But I do miss the conversations with the butcher, the green grocer,
and the baker. I talked back to the cash register today. I think the grocery
store has become a symbol.

Journal Entry
I have decided that everyone in America has an answering machine on their
telephone. I am getting tired of leaving messages and talking to machines.

Journal Entry
There are all kinds of provincialism. I used to laugh when a British friend
would say, "Kansas? Isn't that out by California." Today, I was treated to
an American version of provincialism. Somehow it seemed more offensive.
My son and I were standing in the checkout line at, you guessed it, the
supermarket. The cash register was droning away prices in its canned voice.
Then we overheard the conversation behind us.
Man: "That proves *Time* magazine is a communist front."
Woman: "What do you mean?"
Man: (pointing to a picture of Gorbachev on the cover of *Time*) "They
put Gorbachev on the cover of their magazine."

Woman: "Who's Gorbachev?"

My son and I stared at each other and then broke into laughter as he whispered, "Don't say anything, Dad." I didn't.

Journal Entry

L and I have begun to spend quite a bit of time together simply getting acquainted with the area--driving through the region, exploring stores, going to the library, visiting museums, dining out, talking with "natives"--in short, discovering a new sense of place and belonging. We have begun to discover the importance of giving as much attention to re-entering this culture as we did in entering a foreign one. And to cultivating as much patience with our frustrations.

We are also learning to watch our blindside. About the time we feel the transition is behind us, something happens to create a new "homesickness." Tonight it was nothing more than our biological time-clock. We were feeling quite blue for no explicable reason. Then we realized we had been back in the States the same length of time we usually were on visits before returning to London. But this time we are not returning. Although we miss London, we do not pine for it. While we would like to "go back," we also want to "go on." We're getting nearer home.

188

Journal Entry

A letter arrived today from my youngest daughter in England. I note part of its contents in this journal simply to reflect the experience of loss in any transition. This is an eighteen-year old's view, but it speaks a wisdom beyond her years. I have learned that in experiences of transition, parents had best listen to their children rather than to impose upon them how they "ought" to feel. C wrote:

> I feel kind of lost at the moment. I miss our house and I miss you all and I miss the J----s and the way things used to be. It still isn't real. None of it is real and none of it is fair. I feel scattered around and I don't feel whole. I want to be twelve again and relive the whole thing. It was too good to be true, wasn't it? It's like someone very close to me has died and I won't ever get over the mourning. It is too soon to face a new relationship--whilst I still mourn the loss of the old.

Journal Entry

I resolve neither to heal the wounds too quickly nor to prolong the mourning into neurotic suffering. Such is my resolve. It may take more wisdom than I have. Yet today as I drove along Colorado 73, I felt near home. Yes, home. Literally, for this is where I now reside. Emotionally, for I have begun to "live" here. Psychologically, for I feel it is where I want to be. But home will always be defined a little more broadly now. This home can house memories of other times and places without being haunted by them. This home will have many rooms and I will be free to live in *all* of them. I need not despise one to enjoy another, and I need not be ashamed of missing one while living in another.

There will still be times of sadness and much that I will miss. But I do not want to miss the present by missing the past or miss the "here" for missing the "there."

As I said, this mountain highway felt like home today. The valley ranches nestled up against the mountain forest. As I looked beyond the valley and up the scree to the snowcovered peaks of the high country, I saw that meeting point of past and future I had searched for on Hampstead Heath so many months ago. For here, too, is a good place to walk, to think, to sort things out as I wander along these lanes and meadows or sit by these ponds. There are no London plane trees on this high westward heath, but there are aspen aplenty. Both are beautiful, but it's important not to confuse them or attempt to make them what they are not. This is an important part of being home.

21

Practical Guidelines in the Positive Adjustment of Missionary Children

Betty Harrell

Experience in a missionary environment has led me to believe that there are positive factors involved which may contribute toward a valuable heritage for children. A bi-cultural experience, if positively approached, has tremendous potential for American young people--in enlarging their world view as they have opportunity to be part of a helping relationship where mutual needs are met and in realizing the unique contributions of differing peoples from other languages and cultures. It has been my observation that a positive experience is not always the result to such an exposure. Some missionary young people (MKs) have been deeply hurt and reflect this in their family relationships. Even though negative reactions result in only a minority of situations, they are important for study in the light of our goal to provide maximum aid in meeting the needs of each individual child.

Hypothesis
Since not all Summer Institute of Linguistics (SIL) young people derive a successful experience in a cross-cultural setting, guidelines which are developed and communicated to parents and school personnel, can aid in achieving maximum cooperation in building a positive adjustment for young people. Needs have been observed in the following areas:

From *Practical Guidelines in the Positive Adjustment of Missionary Children* by B. J. Harrell. Unpublished master's thesis, University of Oklahoma, 1977. Adapted by permission.

1. to be a vital part of the family decision to go abroad.
2. to be a contributing member of the SIL team.
3. to be "accepted" in the total environment.
4. to be part of an enlarged school program.
5. to be more active in the national community life.
6. to have opportunity for greater preparation for return to U.S.

The purpose of this study, therefore, is to establish some definite guidelines geared toward inciting greater participation by family and school in building positive adjustment by teenagers in the cross-cultural setting. Such guidelines must be general enough to be implemented in any mission school, regardless of geographical location, where children of the SIL are educated. It has been illustrated in many situations that parents will more effectively continue their work if their children and young people are happy because their needs are being met.

Data gathering was conducted during the summer session (1976) of the University of Oklahoma SIL training program where fifteen young people, presently or recently MK teenagers, were interviewed in-depth concerning their reactions to missionary life. These interviews followed a preliminary questionnaire which was designed to build rapport and elicit attitudes pertinent to developing guidelines. The results of the questionnaire led to the following generalizations:

192
1. The home is the greatest single supportive factor in the positive adjustment of young people in a cross-cultural experience.

2. Educational opportunities on the field are excellent, often superior to those in the United States, for a variety of reasons.

3. Young people enjoy knowing other cultures in an individual way and feel a cross-cultural experience compensates for what is left behind in the U.S.

It became apparent during the interviews that it was necessary to first identify basic needs before the data could be organized and interpreted to illustrate practical ways of meeting those needs. The data received illustrated that SIL students would be receptive to the implementation of the following recommendations and guidelines. The responses are organized into the general need areas: self-image, trust-bond relationships, educational preparation, motivation, adjustment and bi-cultural experience.

The Need for a Positive Self-Image
1. Each individual must have acceptance for who he or she is as a person. Parents and teachers reinforce this positive self-concept when they do not compare children with each other. This involves the "vision" of what one can become, the unique contribution of each individual now and the lack of pressure to produce or "be" what someone else expects. Each young person must be valued for what he is in himself.

2. Each child needs to know that he is more important to his parents

than the work which has brought the family to a foreign culture. This is transmitted non-verbally through attitudes, as well as in words. When a child really knows this, numerous adjustments can be made because there is an inner security.

3. The young person needs to sense he has been part of the family decision to go to the "field." The family is made up of team members who are doing the Lord's work together. Each must sense a responsibility as a contributing part, sharing the needs, achievements, frustrations, problems and joys together.

4. A healthy self-concept encourages independence, responsibility, good rapport with adults and the ability to adjust to change--yet a willingness to submit to authority because it is not a threat. Positive reinforcement helps to cope with insecurity.

5. The extended family concept of the mission field aids in the realization that people care about each other, that problems can be shared and that interpersonal relationships are important. Families and teachers must not be too busy to really listen and keep the lines of communication open.

6. Close family ties with fewer social pressures and material acquisitions aid in positive attitude building. There is more individual attention and time spent together as a family than in many U.S. home situations where there is a tendency to pull families apart into peer groups. There is a need for greater sensitivity into what the young people are really thinking and that their thoughts are considered important. They often want to share with adults but sense barriers. Large problems are often family-based.

7. Young people need self-expression without the fear of losing the security of an "image." They want to really talk to adults without recrimination if they say something "out of line." They want to lower the "mask" and be honest--yet be loved and accepted.

Comments Concerning the Need for Positive Self-Image Drawn Directly from Interviews

"My father cares more about the work than he does about me."

"I was able to help build one of the bases. I felt I was useful and not just a thing . . . I was part of my family's work."

"My family has taught me to believe in myself. I was taught being different was okay."

"There are huge 'families' on the base. Everybody cares about me. In the U.S., nobody really cares."

The Need for Trust-Bond Relationships

1. Children and young people need a stable and positive home environment. It came through loud and clear that if the family attitude is positive and the atmosphere secure, other negative factors can be faced successfully. If parents are negative and the home one of conflict, positive

193

factors on the outside do not always compensate. Children need a safe environment where they are accepted and loved for themselves, a place where they can air their feelings and know they are trusted. The attitude of the parents is the key to adjustment. Even when families must be separated, a trust-bond relationship can be established and the children made to feel top-priority. When parents are too absorbed in work or the job is number one in importance, the children know it and the lines of communication are broken. Love builds trust.

2. Young people need to know they can trust those in whom they have confided. They want to be encouraged, not always told. They want adults to admit when they have made mistakes rather than pretending to be right always. They respect adults who have the courage to ask forgiveness. Small group sharing sessions as well as one-to-one relationships are essential to young people. There is a need to reach out to others, knowing that what is shared will be kept as a sacred trust.

3. The attitudes of teachers in the school are quickly analyzed by young people. They know how deep the interest, how sincere the conversation, how genuine the concern. It is a unique privilege for a teacher to have the opportunity to touch young lives, especially in a close environment where it is possible to be more than a teacher. It is an awesome responsibility to reach out to each student as an individual with special needs, interests and abilities.

4. The relationship between family members is a factor so important that it is impossible to measure its effects upon a child. Children recognize conflict and inflicted hurts. Positive or negative attitudes permeate everything that is said or done in a home environment. Children know when parents really give of themselves, their time and their concern. They know when they can communicate without threat. They recognize acceptance, encouragement and trust. There is an indescribable bond, woven through years of love that can keep the family unit intact through the most difficult experiences.

Comments Concerning Trust-Bond Relationships

"I was away from my parents for half of the year. I never resented it because I always knew they loved me."

"I know there is an important job for my father to do but he has to be gone so much. People above him don't seem to realize that we need him too."

"I had a teacher who promised she wouldn't tell but she did."

"My parents kept in touch in so many neat ways--tapes, notes, ham radio."

"I have seen my father neglect my mother. He felt he made the sacrifice for the Lord but I wonder if the Lord wanted that. The spark of love is gone from our home now."

Need for Educational Preparation

1. The school must enlarge its curriculum to include more preparation and usable skills for return to the U.S. culture. The young person needs vocational training to help him fit into the job market as well as mini-courses for U.S. social survival.

2. The responses from the young people in this study illustrated that the academic curriculum for college-bound students is excellent with isolated exceptions. In some cases, the choice of electives is small due to the lack of trained teachers in certain subject areas. The small size of the classes and the personalized teaching put most of the students "ahead" when they return to U.S. schools. There is a need for more counseling of high school students who are investigating a college or a vocation. Information sessions and career days should be enlarged. More consideration must also be given to current events, the arts, the improvement of the science areas and practical electives.

3. Greater use of the environment and international setting should be emphasized through language learning activities. This is not only a great cultural privilege for the young people but a time to build lasting friendships. School sponsored functions with the national community have been encouraged in some areas, especially through sports and music. More activities actually planned by the young people themselves can be a great incentive to learn from the environment, see and become absorbed in the culture, thus enlarging their total educational experience.

195

4. The unique base setting is an excellent opportunity to encourage creativity among the students. It is a natural environment for "do it yourself" skills and tribal exposure. As tribal visits are correlated into the total school program, flexibility can encourage rather than discourage the use of these opportunities to learn. Base work projects should be included in the curriculum so that all have the time to really become involved in the total team program. High school could also be more effective in helping the student to develop his unique life style, stressing interpersonal skills. The school should be flexible enough to allow new ideas. Students should be included more in the actual planning with more opportunity to follow individual interests at varying rates of speed. The challenge should be kept high without coasting levels for those who have almost completed requirements. MKs want and need challenge.

5. The high caliber of teaching was noted by the students. Persons who desire to work in this setting are by and large creative and highly motivated. Parents and teachers work closely together for the good of the student. Teachers are considered "aunts" and "uncles" as well as staff, encouraging a good rapport in the community. When a poorly adjusted teacher finds himself in this close situation, it makes for conflict which is difficult to cover. Students react by either ignoring them or giving superficial adherence. The high turnover in teachers each year is a problem for the administration but

is taken in stride by the students. Because of the tremendous influence exerted by the teacher, he must be chosen with care.

6. The difficulty of securing library books and equipment poses a problem for the base school. Wycliffe Associates (WA) have been extremely helpful in meeting this ever-present need.

7. The place of Bible in the school curriculum should be given priority since this is the core of the SIL curriculum. It should be carefully planned and taught by well-trained teachers. Students often feel it is the first subject to go in a curriculum change, that it is sometimes taught by just anyone who is free and that it lacks the challenge of the other academic subjects.

8. The caliber of student on the field is very good and needs academic challenge. As the staff is available, more elective school courses should be introduced. Stress on achievement is a plus to motivation as are correspondence courses to supplement the possible local curriculum. In such a situation, it is possible to allow the individual to stretch his capacity academically. There is a need to provide help for the "special education" student who has difficulty in competing with his classmates. Education is a tool to prepare the leadership of tomorrow. It must not be a neglected aspect of world missions.

Comments Concerning School Preparation

196 "My education was superior except in the sciences and current events."

"I wish we could have more independent courses which someone on the base could monitor."

"The Bible classes were a let-down. It seemed more like Bible stories than meaty study . . . wish they would stress practical applications. Kids don't buy just "we believe" anymore. They want to study attitudes and reasons."

"The library is always a problem. The periodicals are late and books are in poor condition. There is little variety and most is out of date."

"We want to learn more skills and how to hold down practical jobs."

"We should do more with foreign languages, especially the language of the country."

"I wish they'd help us know how to cope with the drug and sex problems in the U.S."

"Teachers should be carefully chosen because they influence everything so much."

"I wish we had a counselor in school. I saw one boy completely change . . . withdrawn and moody. If only someone could have helped him in the beginning."

"There were so many things we didn't know anything about . . . like politics, recent changes in society, current issues."

Need for Motivation
The necessity of numerous moves and changes often leads to a lack of motivation in the young people. The family and the school must work together to challenge them to look beyond the present and plan for the future.

Comments Concerning Motivation
"Why make friends when I always have to leave them?"
"Why reach out? I don't even know where to begin."
"I resent leaving my good friends. I should make new ones but it all seems so hard."
"Being neutral is safer."
"I'm afraid of the future."

The Need for Smooth Adjustment from One Culture to Another
1. Changing from one culture to another brings "shock," insecurity and unhappiness. There is a need for more adequate orientation to the differences on the missionary base and what is expected. This shock is especially acute on the return to the U.S. culture because of societal change. The school must take a more active part in orientation activities with the old kids planning and participating. There can be a "big brother" and "big sister" program, small group sharing, "aunt" and "uncle" responsibilities on the part of the staff and a real gathering-in of the new person. Because of the service orientation which motivates the SIL work, MKs learn independence and often mature very young. There is so much responsibility that they may feel guilty about the fun in "play." The young people are important as people in spite of the pressure to get the job done.

2. The return to the U.S. is often a greater adjustment problem than going to a new culture. Many times it happens following graduation from high school when the young person is in the throes of many radical changes. It involves leaving the family for the first time, being separated from childhood friends and small base activities, and being asked to adjust to college routine in a huge environment where organizational life is automated. He is economically insecure without funds to buy what everyone else owns; he is psychologically deprived when his acquaintances go home for the weekend and socially insecure when rapid changes have made the U.S. culture seem alien. SIL is initiating "foster" U.S. parents with the "home" taking the responsibility for definite invitations. There are activities for "kids" on week-ends in some areas and caring families are simply "opening" their homes when they are needed. There are "call me" holidays, ham radio contacts with parents on the field and newsletters about what "everybody is doing." These programs and activities are tremendous and meeting the needs of many MKs. They should be extended to other areas of the country, possibly through WA, Regional Directors or Member Relations. A suggested project for WA would be a summer airplane excursion to take the "kids" home to

197

their families on the field. In some cases, parents have found it advantageous to plan the furlough year for this first critical separation time.

3. The base school should enlarge its preparation for U.S. re-entry by continuation and expansion of subjects during the high school years geared to skill building designed to meet real problems. Children need to know U.S. dress styles, hair length and how to use a telephone. They need to understand U.S. currency and how to balance a checkbook. They need usable vocational training. They should be taught current events and what is going on in the States. These skills will help them over the rough period of feeling a "cultural misfit," the sense of confusion and frustration and the realization that "this just isn't home."

4. There must be parental awareness in the area of adjustment. Many parents do not prepare their children because they themselves feel unprepared. Training sessions are needed for families as they return to the U.S. to the same extent that they are needed in preparation prior to the mission field. Small group sharing can be effective for parental training as can open-ended case studies. Human relations seminars as begun at Norman SIL are excellent helps because they do not constitute a threat to the parents. The positive attitude of mutual learning filters down to the children.

5. There is a feeling of dehumanization for the individual in the change from a small, caring community to a large, impersonal one. If one is prepared for this drastic change, it is possible to cope with the painful loneliness which results. Young people find it difficult to share "precious memories" with those who can't understand or don't wish to take the time. The Christian community must be educated to their responsibility in bridging this gap. The Regional Directors could be very effective in this area as they allocate speakers to various locations. WA could also assume leadership in helping to promote awareness of needs. Missionary young people want to be treated like normal people, not put on a pedestal as having made a special sacrifice. The literature arm of SIL could work with WA in this educational training. The home office could also aid families as they return to the U.S. in meeting some of these deeper needs. MKs can be made aware of the privileges they have experienced and the unique opportunity they have to share with people who have not been able to go.

6. Return to the States is often a time of confusion, doubt and disillusionment for a young person. They know the "right things to say" but are suddenly faced with tremendous spiritual challenges. Many find this a time of growth spiritually because it is not possible to "sit on the fence." They must learn to tolerate the feelings and beliefs of others and yet have a personal position to share. They see hypocrisy, unconcern and manipulation as well as faithful dedication in the Christian world. They become lost in the "sea of bigness," constant change and speed of relationships. They are overwhelmed with choices and faced with "too much too fast." The world shouts, "Do, taste, experience, buy, absorb, read, feel, be--and do it quickly."

It may appear to be a life of excess, tension and rejection which can result in deep-down hurts and withdrawal. Some young people believe that only MKs can really understand MKs. This is an area where former MKs can have a tremendous ministry. There is a need for a concerted effort on their part to find the lonely ones and aid in their adjustment. This could be coordinated through the Huntington Beach office as files are kept of MKs.

7. Many missionary young people feel "special" on the field and find it difficult to adjust to being just another "nothing" in the U.S. Parents, school and close friends can be instrumental in talking through these feelings before the problem arises. Interpersonal relationships are again needed. The impression of superficiality brings hurt to those who have known meaningful experiences. A polite nod in response to pictures of Indian friends leave the feeling that the U.S. is an uncaring society--too busy with "things" to care about "people." People who do understand must help out young people in this area.

8. The lack of freedom and the threat of physical danger is an adjustment to teenagers returning to the U.S. The U.S. "rat race" with pressures to conform is another attempt to limit freedom for which the young people must be prepared to cope. Having grown up in a close community where it is relatively safe and secure, teenagers must be helped to develop the inner security and wisdom that will carry them through. Some feel confused and find difficulty coping with contemporary sexual mores and temporarily lose purpose and direction. The home and school are the two major areas of preparation. MKs are isolated from the outside world on a base. It is a unique haven and in many ways unrealistic. This must be communicated through the years before the rude awakening. When the family is supportive, children can face many problems--adjustments, moving, leaving friends and even deep hurts--and grow stronger for the experiences.

Comments Concerning Adjustment
"Nobody is interested in the neat things I've done or the wonderful places I've been. They don't even know where it is. It makes me sad."

"I don't know any of the people who are famous. Everything has changed here."

"I'm the best soccer player on the team."

"Kids in the U.S. tell us that we're really important. They wish they could go where we've been."

"I had a terrible problem of relating and being accepted here. I feel part of three cultures. I am accepted at home for what I am."

"People seemed to care more about buying things than getting close to people."

"I have trouble making up my mind. There are too many choices."

"I feel like an ant among ants."

Need for Bi-Cultural Experience

1. It is a positive factor when the family as a whole can participate in the national community life. The attitudes toward the nationals carry over from the adults to the children and are reflected in their desire to make the most of the bi-cultural experience. It is a privilege for young people to have the opportunity to know people from different language backgrounds and realize their unique contributions. This exposure often results in maturity and freedom of thought, as well as the keener appreciation of individual worth. World travel is valuable in helping the person to break out of his ethnocentric framework and form non-prejudiced and empathetic judgements. There are tremendous advantages to cross-cultural living. Young people in a mission setting can not only better understand but actually "feel" with others.

2. A bi-cultural experience is a valuable dimension in the total educational experience of a teenager. They are not content to merely speak a few words of the language but desire to go deeper. Few of the young people were afraid of the possible problems, medical or social, which some adults fear. In some situations, they felt contacts should be supervised because of the differences in cultural norms.

Comments Concerning Bi-Cultural Experience

200   "I want to go back because it is more home than anywhere."

"No American can understand all me. I feel a real common bond with the nationals and am more comfortable there."

"I cried hard when I had to leave my friends."

"There is security and less pressure in the tribe."

"I'm not so one-sided when I understand people who think differently than I do."

"Our parents and the school isolated us from the culture."

Evaluation of Study Time in Norman

This study was a tremendous experience for me, though frightening and overwhelming at times. I often felt that I was on to something very significant and was afraid of missing the full intent of what was being shared so sincerely. The young people went out of their way to be helpful and seemed to appreciate my interest in being there. They were candidly honest and shared deeply in some areas. I came away feeling that I was involved in a beautiful experience and had made some lasting friendships. I am not convinced that the Norman sample is truly representative of all SIL missionary young people because they are the ones who have returned, either with their parents or alone to begin their own training. However, I feel it has opened some tremendously interesting insights from which I can learn, both as a parent and as a teacher. I am anxious to implement what I have learned and desperately want it to count in a positive way toward the team effort of enlarging the educational opportunities for our MKs, especially through the difficult teenage years. We are engaged in helping a wonderful group of teenagers and I trust we will learn from past mistakes and enlarge on the successes. It is an exciting prospect to work together toward goals with such potential. While the school program can aid in an easier adjustment, both to the new culture and the old, **the home is the vital key** to a positive experience for our young people.

Personally, I desire a new awareness of young people's needs so that I may become a better mother, teacher and counselor. As I become more personally involved in the national community of my host country, I hope to encourage my students to do the same. I seek more interaction with the nationals and a deeper appreciation for them.

The challenge is for us to continue the team effort to better meet the needs of our MKs, learning from each other the most effective methods and means to reach the goal, a positive bi-cultural experience for all of our MKs.

Unit E

How to Make Reentry Work: Guidelines for Reentry

Return, Readjustment, and Reminiscence

Can They go Home Again?

Rules for Re-entry

Common Unexpected Situations and Special Concerns

How to Make Reentry
Work: Guidelines for Reentry

A major transition can be an exciting period of renewal in a person's life. It can also be a humbling experience. When I greeted an acquaintance shortly after the end of our family's 18-month stay in South America, the essence of his reply was, "Oh, you've been gone?" Third culture adults (TCAs) and TCKs are eager to share their bi-cultural heritage with fellow citizens. They don't want to be treated as "strangers at home." Third culture people (TCPs) increasingly see themselves as valuable human resources, and they should be treated as such. The following articles are offered with the hope that the ideas presented will facilitate cross-cultural migration.

Some earlier articles which offer stimulating segments on reentry preparation are Werkman (Chapter 1), Freedman (Chapter 2), Austin (Chapter 13) and Howard (Chapter 15). In formulating a reentry program these chapters as well as those in Unit E and the Appendixes should prove to be useful.

Guither and Thompson, in Chapter 22, provide a pragmatic discussion of reentry divided into three areas: (1) preparing for return, (2) adjusting to life at home, and (3) lasting effects and impressions. This chapter-length discussion, one of the few to be found in the literature, was chosen to give the reader a coordinated and authentic overview of the homecoming process. Confronted with the authors' refreshing candor, the TCP can map realistic reentry strategies.

In one of the pioneering articles in the reentry literature, Brislin and Van Buren, in Chapter 23, lay the groundwork for successful reorientation programs for international students. The seminars involved East-West grantees about to reenter their home environments after a two-year stay in Hawaii. Janis' concept, "the work of worry," formed the theoretical basis for the seminars. East-West grantees, just prior to reentry, were asked to work out potential difficulties in their minds.

The first session of the seminar "deals with family and personal aspects of returning home." The following session contrasts short-term and long-term adjustments. The third part focuses on job selection and interpersonal relationships. The fourth session--what the authors call the "non-Western perspective"--is planned solely by the participants. Concepts from social psychology form the basis for a session on attribution and non-verbal behavior. The final session underscores the importance of maintaining cross-cultural relations. The authors conclude with vital comments on program evaluation and overall program administration.

Since it is not unusual for repatriates to change jobs, Irish's rules in Chapter 24 are important. Ten immensely practical rules for a job search are given. The job search might require four months to two years. Ample time should be taken to "research the self" *before* searching for a job. Among his commendable ideas are saving ample money, using the past as a "stepping stone," and "networking"--"using other people to help you think through what to do next."

In Chapter 25, staff members of the Training Department of International Resources, Campus Crusade for Christ, enlighten reentrants on how to confront "Common Unexpected Situations." Forty-five specific incidents are concisely presented followed by the probable reaction of the individual. Sensible suggestions are made about how to deal with each incident. A concluding section treats two special concerns: (1) parents returning with children, and (2) children returning home alone for schooling. Suggestions are made for dealing with either circumstance.

22

Return, Readjustment, and Reminiscence

Harold D. Guither and William N. Thompson

Most American families who have lived overseas for a year or more look forward to their return with great anticipation. They can hardly wait to reach their homeland flowing with pure milk and safe, unboiled water, with dependable electricity and automatic long distance telephone service and where everyone speaks English.

In the isolation of a foreign post, however, some people develop feelings of self-importance and greater than justified expectations about how people will greet and accept them when they arrive home. Their joyful anticipation may quickly wilt into disappointment, frustration, and antagonism as they experience a "reverse culture shock."

People back home have continued to live their lives about the same as usual. The fact that you were gone has not really affected them and they will usually have only a casual or passing interest in your experiences. Being prepared for this indifference may be just as important as preparing to live overseas. "We were very disappointed to come back and realize the smallness of most Americans and their lack of interest in foreign affairs, especially in this age when the world is so small," one wife related. Another returning wife remarked, "We have much more interest in international work and

From *Mission Overseas: A Handbook for U.S. Families in Developing Countries* (pp. 149–162) by H. D. Guither and W. N. Thompson, 1969, Urbana: University of Illinois Press. Copyright 1969 by the Board of Trustees of the University of Illinois Press. Reprinted by permission.

problems, but very few people are really interested in someone else's foreign assignment."

Not all families experience indifference, however. Many are asked to tell about their experiences, advise others, show slides, and display costumes, handicrafts, and souvenirs that they have brought back with them.

Preparing for Return

Making plans for return should begin before you leave the U.S. if your overseas assignment is for one to two years. If you are on a longer assignment, some plans will begin from six to twelve months before you depart from your overseas post. The main planning considerations should include: (1) the husband's job upon return; (2) where the family will live; (3) school plans for children; (4) vacation and travel en route home; (5) shipping personal effects and household goods before departure. Many of the above considerations will depend upon the departure date which may hinge upon completion of the overseas work and arrival of a replacement in some situations.

Husband's Job

Many families know that the husband will return to work for his employer at some U.S. location. This decision may have been made before departure. For others, the end of the overseas assignment will mean locating a new position. Men in this situation have successfully located new jobs or several prospective opportunities through correspondence. So, when they arrived in the U.S., interviews were arranged and final decisions could be made without great delay.

A Place to Live

When the location of the husband's job is known, a place to live becomes the important question. Families who own a house that they can move into probably have the easiest resettlement experience. If you must find a house or apartment, real estate dealers, rental agencies, friends and employers living in the town or city where you are going can assist if you let them know your needs several months before you arrive.

Schools

Arrangements for children to attend public elementary or high schools can usually be arranged upon arrival. If you have children who will be entering college, then you should start from six to nine months before you return to file applications and provide the necessary high school records. School authorities at the overseas high school should assist by providing the necessary transcripts. You should write to the office of admissions at the college or university where your son or daughter wants to enroll.

The Return Trip

Going home can be one of the most enjoyable parts of a foreign assignment. However, you should plan it carefully. The job overseas will be completed. You will have experienced hectic days and nights in the rush and whirl of last-minute activities preparing for departure. How fast you must return, of course, may depend upon job requirements and school schedules at home. However, two weeks to a month on the return trip should be considered a reasonable length of time to relax, enjoy yourself, and prepare for returning to your home community.

If you follow a direct air or ship route home, you will usually have to pay nothing extra for stopovers along the way. Your major additional expense will be for hotels, meals, and sightseeing at these stopover points. Many families will never have similar opportunities to see these places again at such a reasonable cost.

Travel plans for return, including airline, steamship, and hotel reservations can be arranged through travel agencies in your host country. By the time you prepare to return to the U.S., your foreign travel experiences should have given you many ideas about what you would most like to see, what others have told you about, and how to get reasonably priced hotels that provide adequate service for your needs.

Shipping Personal Property

In the final weeks before your departure you will need to arrange the shipping of personal effects and household goods that you can't carry with you on the return trip. Many families simplify this job by selling much of the property that they can replace in the U.S. However, host government and U.S. government regulations may restrict how much you can sell or to whom you can sell. Check with the U.S. Embassy on these matters.

There will be certain items that you will want to ship home. Finding reliable and capable shipping agents will be more difficult than in your home town. You may need to supervise packing very closely to make sure that fragile items are packed properly. Or you may have to get the materials and pack your own goods.

If you have both air and sea freight shipping allowances, then you should decide which goods you want to arrive first. You should also insure against loss during shipment through an insurance company that has claim representatives in the United States.

Final Departure

In planning your departure allow enough time to pay respects to host country officials. You should also allow some time for host nationals to show their gratitude and appreciation in their customary ways. "The host nationals shower many farewell parties and ceremonies upon Americans about to leave. We had 26 in the last 21 days before departure," one university professor reported. "This was not anticipated and took time allocated to the orderly withdrawal and homebound preparations."

Adjusting to Life at Home

Men, women, and children all undergo adjustments to living in the U.S. again after living overseas. For some the "reverse culture shock" will be more severe than for others. A popular story (but sometimes almost true) that makes the rounds among people who go back overseas after a home leave illustrates the indifference and preoccupation among many people.

A person went on home leave after two years overseas and met an acquaintance on a main street in his home town. The local citizen recognized his absent friend, appeared puzzled, but showed no feeling of pleasure upon seeing this man who had been absent overseas. After some hesitation he commented, "I haven't seen you for some time, have you been away?"

We asked a philosophical university professor who had helped build a new university in East Africa if he felt people realized all of the efforts he and his colleagues had put forth in this project. He quickly responded, in effect, "People are not interested in all your wonderful experiences, but they will always be ready to tell you when their daughter is going to have a new baby."

210

One of the frustrations comes from a feeling of status gained abroad (often imagined) that is either lost or not recognized when a family returns home. One wife expressed this feeling when she intimated, "My husband was a professor, and that means something abroad. When we came home we both felt keenly that loss of status."

Cleveland (1960) summed up the situation most concisely when he concluded, "Home loses some of its sweetness because the people there do not seem to share the overseas American's interest in life abroad" (p. 24).

Return to the Servantless House

Women face adjustments differently from other family members after living overseas and operating a household with servants. About two out of five university staff wives admitted that return to the stateside "no-servant" pattern required some adjustment.

Some face a bit of "culture shock" getting back into the pattern where equipment instead of people provide service. Others reluctantly return to doing dishes, ironing, and cleaning, jobs they had turned over to servants for several years.

Some realize how dependent they had become upon domestic help. "I particularly had a hard time making up my mind what to buy at the grocery stores, the choices were almost too much!" one wife recalled. "Getting a meal together seemed quite a chore, I hadn't done it for so long."

Children also realize that things have changed. "My children couldn't figure out why Mommy was no longer just Mommy," one mother related. "Now she was chief cook, cleaner, and doing ironing and normal household chores."

Entertaining patterns undergo drastic changes. "I avoided big company dinners for awhile," one homemaker reported, "but finally got into the swing again." "Entertaining is more difficult," another related; "I'd forgotten how to do it gracefully with no help." Many wives overcome the help problem by making their entertaining simpler.

Homemakers have sometimes had to undergo a physical and mental reorientation. They had to work harder physically and give up some of the leisure time to which they had become accustomed. "I was considerably more disorganized than I remembered before we left," one homemaker recalled. "Adjustment was mainly physical," another related; "I immediately lost 20 pounds."

Some had an unusual craving for certain foods they did not have overseas. One woman reported that she couldn't stop munching potato chips. Another craved chocolate graham crackers. Gaining weight soon became a problem.

Others had to adjust to new work routines. "Returning to no servants meant a large house and yard to care for," one wife related; "six people had to be fed, clothed and chauffeured back and forth to school. There was little time for personal freedom."

Just as men require time to readjust to their work at home, homemakers also need time to make the readjustment. "It took about one year to get back into the habit of doing my own work," one wife confided. "I seemed to have slowed down physically and needed time to get back in the swing of things," another remarked. 211

Many women feel they had no problems making the adjustment. "I actually looked forward to doing things for myself once more," one homemaker declared. "Return to conveniences and privacy was a blessing," another commented.

Many women appreciate servants overseas but they appreciate modern household equipment even more. "I have found that machines can really replace people," one homemaker emphasized. "I would always prefer machines to lighten household tasks," another remarked.

Sometimes the readjustment to a servantless house requires a family conference and special cooperative efforts. One mother related, "When we moved in I had a little talk with my son and daughter and told them that I hadn't done housework by myself for almost nine years and if we all pulled together it wouldn't be any trouble for any of us. They keep their own rooms, pick up their own messes, and I think I am in a more pleasing situation than my friends who do not have this cooperation."

Although some women do miss their servants, most would never exchange the house overseas for the one they have at home. "Coming back to hot and cold constantly running water more than made up for lack of a houseboy and baby nurse," one wife concluded. Another summed up the feelings of many when she remarked, "There is no place like home in the good old U.S.A."

Returning to the Job
While the family adjusts to living at home, accepts begrudgingly the passive interest of friends and neighbors in their overseas experience, and enjoys the often-taken-for-granted privileges of stateside living, the husband faces his own occupational reorientation. A sympathetic and understanding family can be most helpful during his first trying months on the job.

When a man prepares for an overseas assignment, he should recognize that he will come back with broader interests in international problems, with more sympathies for foreign students and visitors to our country, and sometimes with less interest in some of the jobs he did before he went overseas. The job he leaves at home may be taken over by someone who will do it differently. Only a few can return and take over the same job they left and do it in the same way as they did it before.

The men who make the most successful re-entry into U.S. employment have managed to integrate their overseas work with their professional interests before and after the overseas assignment. The overseas assignment should contribute to a man's career growth and development. Unfortunately, for many it has disrupted their careers and provided no opportunity to weave their experiences into their work upon return.

212

If overseas work is going to be an asset rather than a liability, the man and his administrators must plan and specify his role overseas before he leaves the U.S. Assignments can be designed which make it possible to use a man's professional talents, let him contribute to the overseas project, and return to the U.S. where he can help with the project or other related international work in the university, the government agency, or the private business which employs him.

Interviews with government and university staff members who have served overseas reveal that many do not feel that they have an adequate opportunity to report and discuss their professional experiences, observations, and recommendations. Disappointments, frustrations, and lack of recognition create a resentment within some of these men so that they seek other jobs or return to overseas assignments.

Most men returning to work after an overseas assignment do not realize that they will need some time to reorient themselves to living and working in the U.S. environment. Some can make this readjustment in a few months while others may require a year or more. Administrators of returned university faculty members usually estimated a longer reorientation time than the man himself. During this reorientation and adjustment period it should be possible to determine to what extent a person's overseas experience has changed his interests as well as his abilities to handle specific jobs upon his return.

The teacher, professor, or research scientist who teaches and does research overseas and who returns to continue teaching and research may readjust and progress in his field with little obstruction. But for others, their research was interrupted and their teaching was at lower levels. When they come back, they may find themselves two or more years behind their colleagues who remained at home. The teacher or professor who becomes an administrator overseas may come back into a vacuum, and without help may flounder for months or years before he finds a useful, satisfying place for his talents.

Technical specialists and advisors in government or business projects may fall behind in their fields after several years abroad. Medical doctors who render invaluable service overseas may also sense a need for more exposure to the latest knowledge in their fields. Engineers often take more new ideas and technology abroad than they can bring back from a less developed country.

The scientist and professional person may return to study, engage in research, or enter into a newly developing field of interest. In time he will find his place of service, but he will often need sympathetic assistance and encouragement from his administrators and employers.

Some men return from overseas with specialized knowledge and experience that opens doors to a new career. Doctors may return with special knowledge of tropical diseases they have never seen in this country. Veterinarians see tropical diseases and nutritional problems of animals that may rarely occur in temperate climates. Agronomists gain knowledge of tropical soils and crops that may contribute to teaching and research programs on U.S. university campuses. The economist or sociologist has had the opportunity to work in a special "laboratory"--the developing country itself--to observe and gather information that was not possible at home. For some men, the work experience in a developing country provides the needed background for administrative positions with government, universities, and businesses engaged in overseas operations.

Not all men, however, can shift into an international career upon their return. Those who do may have to change employers, relocate, and make greater adjustments than if they remained where they were before going overseas. Each man must decide for himself the costs and benefits of relocation. A man's age and the number of years before retirement naturally enter into his decisions.

Men who return from overseas readily recognize the professional risks of going overseas. However, many did not realize the risks involved before they left. If they had, some would undoubtedly have hesitated or decided not to go. As a result of their experiences, however, many would consider another overseas assignment but would be more selective and study the situation very carefully before accepting. Most would be willing to go back to the same country where they worked because they have developed a sympathetic understanding of the people and their problems. Many would also like to work in a different country to gain a broader perspective of international problems in their field of interest. For most men, the personal gains have outweighed any professional losses. And some have gained professionally as well.

Lasting Effects and Impressions
As time passes and the family resettles into a stateside living routine, some of the trivial happenings and frustrations of overseas living are forgotten. But no family can break away from American life, live in a foreign culture, and return without undergoing some lasting changes.

Community Activities
Almost every family that returns to the home community has some opportunity to tell about life overseas, present slide talks, and display souvenirs and native goods. However, the overseas experience stimulates some to participate actively in other community activity.

University faculty members and their wives develop greater interest in foreign students and their welfare. They entertain foreign students in their homes, participate in foreign student group activities, and may serve as faculty sponsors. "I'm chairman of the lending center on the university campus," one wife related. "This center loans warm coats, household items, and baby furniture to foreign students and their families."

Those who have lived overseas maintain a greater interest in international affairs. They participate in discussion and study groups and attend more travel lectures and seminars related to foreign service. Some promote and support their church foreign mission programs more actively. "My church women's society now makes bandages and hospital gowns for the mission hospital," one wife reported.

Seeing problems overseas may also stimulate some to participate in community affairs with a domestic emphasis. "I have worked with the anti-poverty group and Planned Parenthood Association," one wife reported. "We have become more closely identified with the civil rights program," another commented.

Personal Habits and Interests
Living overseas also affects a person's interests and living habits. Those who have lived as foreigners in another country sympathetically and enthusiastically offer friendship and assistance to foreign visitors. A few have provided room and board to foreign students. Friendships with others who have lived and worked overseas seem to grow more readily than with those who have never been outside the U.S.

New hobbies evolve out of some foreign assignments. Reading articles

214

about the host countries, collecting records of native music, collecting stamps or coins, and cooking local dishes are only a few examples.

Political and personal points of view reflect overseas experiences. "We are no longer isolationists," one wife declared. "We have a greater awareness of needs for civic and community service, greater interest in national and international affairs, and sympathy for foreigners on our soil," one wife related.

Both children and adults unconsciously develop a tolerance for other people that they never had before. "We have a new tolerance for all people and a feeling of pride in being accepted as friends in new surroundings," one wife reported. "The exposure to a new culture was fascinating and enlightening, another related: "I feel that it helped greatly to make our children tolerant and more understanding of the problems of minority groups."

Those who want to continue to live and think as they always have should probably not consider a foreign assignment. "Our foreign experience has made it impossible to return to our former rut, so we will be seeking new horizons of service," one wife observed.

Effects Upon Careers of Children

If children are in junior or senior high school when they live overseas, their impressions may influence later study and career choices. Some students take more interest in foreign language study. Others study political science, international law, international business, economics, anthropology, or diplomacy, partly because of interests developed out of their overseas exposure.

Interest in helping people overseas grows into career decisions for some young people. "Our daughter developed a strong feeling for people of other origins," one mother reported. "She joined the Peace Corps." "Our oldest son went into film and television with a desire to make documentary educational films for the uneducated masses," another reported. "He realized this type of thing is their salvation, a quick way to start their education." Others have taken teaching jobs overseas.

The desire to travel and learn more about foreign countries continues for others. "Our middle son joined the Navy to go traveling again," one mother related. "All three older children are planning to return to Europe and other countries either for further education or future work," another reported.

Foreign experience may also influence domestic career choices. "Our daughter is now a most successful social worker, due in part, I feel, to her understanding of the people during our overseas assignment," one mother pointed out. "Our son, who received his M.D., is interested in tropical medicine," another reported.

Undoubtedly, young people develop a broader perspective when they live abroad. During their impressionable years, overseas living cannot help but influence to some extent their career choices.

Doing Things Differently Next Time

As families look back upon their overseas assignments, most of them would not greatly change the ways that they lived or carried on their assignments. But with their experience they have gained insights about how they could have made their experience an even more enjoyable one. The regrets expressed by wives of university staff members will apply to most Americans going on overseas assignments in developing countries. In summary, they suggest:

Learn more of the language. By knowing the native language they feel they could have developed deeper friendships with native people, avoided communication difficulties with servants, and acquired a better understanding of the country and its culture.

Mix more with local people. Language at times proved a barrier. The whirl of American social activities sometimes took time away from opportunities to get better acquainted with local people. Some wives overcame the language problem by teaching English to local women.

Perform more volunteer and charitable services. Some wives regret that they did not try to teach local women housekeeping and cooking skills, or help in hospitals or with charitable projects. One wife expressed the feelings of many when she commented, "It is too bad not to be fitted to do anything constructive in a society where there was such want and need."

See more of the country. The opportunity to travel and learn about a country when you are living there far surpasses what a tourist can ever accomplish. Many families do travel extensively in their host country. A few wish they had not delayed and had traveled more. Those without cars often wished they had bought one or taken one along.

216

For Most--a Worthwhile Experience

Like many of life's experiences, an overseas assignment has both its pleasant and unpleasant features. A few families look back with unfavorable feelings and are apprehensive for others who are considering an assignment. These feelings are usually based upon some unpleasant experience for a family member. "Professionally, it was two years wasted for my husband and two very difficult years for our youngest daughter," one wife related. "My husband missed contacts with others in his field, a good library, and was generally out of touch with his profession," another remarked.

However, despite problems, frustrations, and disappointments, nearly all families look back with pleasure and satisfaction upon their overseas assignments. In their recollections, many include a note or two of caution, however. "Our five years abroad were the most enriching of our lives," one wife recalled fondly. "I would not suggest that anyone without a spirit of adventure or who insists on push-button control living, women especially, go to a primitive country." "It was not an easy six years, but no six years in the States would have given our family so many interesting experiences, so many friends, or this kind of opportunity to give help and accept help," another related. "The job of sorting through the family's entire possessions, worrying about the number of pounds each person could take, deciding what to take, throw out, and store. . . . I'd hate to have to do it again," one wife confided, "but I would if I had the chance."

Most families treasure their new knowledge and new friendships more than anything else. "We extended our horizons greatly, grew more tolerant of other cultures, developed more awareness of ancient history, and enjoyed the travels that were part of the whole program," one woman remarked.

Some also gain insights into strange cultures and Americans overseas at the same time. "It gave us an understanding that cannot be obtained any other way," one wife observed, "a perspective you cannot get without being in a city where you do not understand the language, where there are no American newspapers or magazines, and the people smile and say 'yes' and you do not know whether they mean 'yes' or 'no.' There were some wonderful Americans there, along with some not so wonderful. We have kept up with a great many. It is a special kind of friendship like no other."

When the overseas experience also adds a new member to the family, it takes on a special meaning. "I loved being in a new and different environment, meeting new people, learning to appreciate a different culture, experiencing new foods, learning to be grateful for abundance," one homemaker recalled. "The fact that we are adopting a wonderful little boy that we brought back is enough to make it worth it without all the other benefits."

217

Many feel like one wife who concluded, "In spite of the many frustrations at times, I wouldn't give up this experience for a million dollars, and hope to go again someday."

Most families go overseas to help the people of a developing country. Some of the lasting benefits of their experiences, however, accrue to our own country. Americans who have lived overseas bring back an intense appreciation of and loyalty toward their country.

After a person travels around the world he looks at his country with a more critical eye and an open mind and appreciates many things much more. "I thoroughly believe it would do all Americans good to live in a foreign country for a year or two to see how the rest of the world lives and thinks," one commented. "It makes one more open-minded and proud of our heritage."

The position of local women in the developing countries prompts many American women to sympathize with them. "It made me appreciate my own country and I thanked God almost every day that I was born an American woman," one remarked.

Americans who had given part of their lives in service to others overseas return feeling enriched with priceless experiences. Their overseas assignment has become the focal point of their lives.

They gain knowledge of how the other people of this world live. Many will be better citizens of our own country. They have a better knowledge of other cultures, religions, and geography. They realize how very fortunate they are to live in this country where we can say and do what we think is best. They widen their horizons and those of their children. They have learned that the material things of this world are not all that count for good living.

References
Cleveland, H., Mangone, G. J., & Adams, J. C. (1960). *The overseas Americans.* New York: McGraw-Hill.

23

Can They
Go Home Again?

Richard W. Brislin and H. Van Buren IV

Benjamin Franklin once (1784) related an experience he had with people moving from one culture to another:

> At the treaty of Lancaster, in Pennsylvania, anno 1744, between the Government of Virginia and the Six Nations, the commissioners from Virginia acquainted the Indians by a speech, that there was at Williamsburg a college with a fund for educating Indian youth; and that if the chiefs of the Six Nations would send down half a dozen of their sons to that college, the government would take care that they be well provided for, and instructed in all the learning of the white people.

The Indians' spokesman replied:

> ... We are convinced ... that you mean to do us good by your proposal and we thank you heartily. But you, who are wise, must know that different nations have different conceptions of things; and you will not therefore take it amiss, if our ideas of this kind of education happen not to be the same with yours. We have had some experience of it; several of our young people were formerly brought up at the colleges of northern provinces; they were instructed in all your sciences; but, when they came back to us, they were bad runners, ignorant of every means of living in the woods, unable to bear either cold or hunger, knew neither how to build a cabin, take a deer, nor kill an enemy, spoke our language imperfectly, were therefore neither fit for hunters, warriors, nor counsellors; they were totally good for nothing.
>
> We are however not the less obligated by your kind offer, though we decline accepting it; and, to show our grateful sense of it, if the gentlemen of Virginia will send us a dozen of their sons, we will take care of their education, instruct them in all we know, and make men of them.

From "Can They Go Home Again" by R. W. Brislin and H. Van Buren IV, 1974, *International Educational and Cultural Exchange*, 9(4), pp. 19–24. Reprinted by permission.

Cleveland et al. (1960, p. 25) tell of an experience shared by many people who live temporarily outside the United States and then go back to their home towns. They quote one of their interviewees:

> *In my home town there are probably many people who still don't realize that the world is round. I remember when we got home from Moscow people asked me how it was there, but before I could open my mouth, they would begin telling me how Uncle Charlie had broken his arm. They profess interest in things abroad, but they really aren't interested.*

These stories are a good introduction to the experiences of East-West Center grantees as well as to our program designed to lessen their potential difficulties. The East-West Center is an international educational institution located on the main campus of the University of Hawaii. Over 1,000 participants each year come from the United States and 40 countries and territories from Asia and the Pacific area. There are three types of participants (degree students, professional development students, and fellows), but this presentation is concerned mostly with degree students.

These participants almost always have the equivalent of a bachelor's degree from a school in their home countries, and they come to the East-West Center both to participate in its programs and to earn master's (sometimes Ph.D.) degrees at the University of Hawaii. The participants, then, are away from their homes for an average of 2 years. Certainly there are advantages to the rich experience of living and working with many types of people one meets at the Center, but it is not all a bed of Plumeria petals.

When a person lives in a culture other than his own for a significant length of time, his attitudes and outlook change (Bochner, 1973; Useem and Useem, 1955, 1968; Cleveland et al., 1960). Many aspects of his home country will also have changed, for instance, the attitudes of his friends and family and the physical elements of the environment that he remembers. An interesting and important fact that has emerged from research in recent years (Bochner) is that a person who is most successful at adjusting to a new culture is often the worst at readjusting to his old culture.

Perhaps the explanation is that a person who adjusts readily is one who can accept new ideas, meet and talk intelligently with people from many countries, and be happy with the stimulation that he finds every day. This same person may readjust poorly when he goes home since his new ideas conflict with tradition. He can find no internationally minded people, and he finds no stimulation in the country he already knows so well. Training to prepare people for such *reverse* culture shock problems has been uncommon. For these reasons, we have been involved in research on reorientation cross-cultural seminars, and we sometimes call it our "Can you go home again?" program.

The seminars involve East-West Center grantees who are about to return home after a 2-year stay in Hawaii. The seminars include U.S. participants since few of them will return to home towns in which they will have daily contact with friends from Asia and the Pacific. Actually, we have found that the readjustment-to-home can be most severe for U.S. participants because they do not expect any problems. Instead, they maintain that "I'm not going back to another country!" We argue that in many ways they *are* going from one culture (the State of Hawaii and the East-West Center) to another (somewhere on the mainland U.S.A.).

We are now building a file of specific, critical incidents that students encounter back home, such as jealousy on the part of colleagues, friends' indifference to their intercultural experience (we call this the "Uncle Charlie" syndrome, referring to the anecdote related previously), and return to close supervision by parents as opposed to their relative independence at the East-West Center. These critical incidents are based on letters and reports from participants who have returned home. Many will be given as examples throughout this presentation.

We do not suggest that students will have these problems, but rather we present these and other conflicts as potential problems and encourage students to think them through. The assumption is that if students work through these issues before going home and prepare for potential conflicts, they will have fewer problems after they actually return home. During these seminars at the East-West Center, of course, the students have social support from staff and friends which they might not find at home.

Worrying Helps

The theoretical basis for the seminar is that of Janis (1958; see also the summary presentation by Elms, 1972), who wrote about preparation for stressful events. Using the concept, "the work of worrying," he argued that worrying about potentially stressful events is helpful. Such work can force the person to learn as much as possible about the event, to prepare for its negative effects so as not to be surprised by them, and to envisage what he might do if any of the negative effects indeed occur.

The principle has widespread application, and Janis (1958) made one specific recommendation for its use with surgical patients. He suggested that if patients were told basic facts about their upcoming operations and were able to work through in their minds exactly how they might feel, they might be less affected by post-operational pain. The goal is to have people *not taken by surprise* when they feel the inevitable post-operational pain.

Egbert et al. (1964) found in a study that such "worry-prepared" patients felt less emotional stress, were given less pain-killing medication, and were released from the hospital an average of 3 days sooner than control patients who did not undergo such preparation.

Based on this work, we have asked East-West Center grantees, just before they return home, to work out potential difficulties in their minds. We present them with stories like that told by Ben Franklin to stimulate thinking. We also talk about the beneficial aspects of such thinking by explaining the medical research by Janis and Egbert and by sharing humorous stories with them.

We suggest only that the possibility of such problems exists. The charge has been made that we tell people what *will* happen, and that this is paternalistic. Our response is simple: we don't.

Content of the Program
We have held four reorientation seminars at the East-West Center (May 1972, December 1972, May 1973, December 1973), all run over a 2-day period. Improvements, based on staff and participant feedback from the earlier seminars, have been incorporated into the later ones. The following summary describes the content of the May 1973 seminar. Each session is begun by a "kickoff" speaker who brings up different issues to stimulate thinking, and then participants have open discussion. Kickoff speakers always present specific difficulties *they* and others have faced, and we include these here since they both give an idea of a session's content and the issues brought up in free discussion. The participants do almost all the talking for 75–80 percent of any given session.

Friends and Relations
The first session of the seminar deals with family and personal aspects of returning home. Emphasis is on relations with one's mother, father, siblings, and friends. At every seminar, at least one person was about to return home (Asia) and be faced with an arranged marriage, and these people had been dating freely in Hawaii. At the last seminar, the kick-off speaker was an American who told about his own stress in returning from Japan to Akron, Ohio. If speakers relate their own experiences (as they have done at every seminar), participants see that the readjustment is a normal process and that they are not "kooks" if they are faced with a problem.

222

The following is from a former participant's letter, and it is typical of the examples given by the speakers:

> One of the most difficult things to adjust to was living at home with my family. The forced independence being away from home became something I grew accustomed to; living in a dorm or apartment, not having to tell my where-abouts all the time [etc.]. Things such as these which were considered of positive survival value (independence) are not acceptable at one's own home. Even among friends, I felt there was more need to conform. It was hard to change from home-living to apartment-living abroad, but it is perhaps even harder to change back again.

Some participant comments during discussion of the general topic of relations with friends and family are as follows:

> I think the expectations, mine and my friends and relatives, might have undergone a change. There will be an initial period of adjustment when failure to meet up to the expectations might result in frustration and tension.

> I am afraid to go back to my old self. It is so easy to return to your old shell and adjust yourself to other people's expectations. The hardest thing is to keep and develop what I have learned here.

> Be aware of "too" Westernized behavior and attitudes picked up in U.S.A. which might offend relatives and friends back home.

Short-Term Adjustments

The emphasis in this session is on the issues that would be problematic over a *short* period of time as contrasted to a longer period of time. We recommend that a person not be overwhelmed by short-term problems and should not feel that "I'm making a poor readjustment" if small problems are immediately troublesome.

For instance, adjusting to the custom concerning which sex walks through doors first is a short-term problem, advancing on the job is a long-term issue. Another recommendation is for participants who want to change their old culture. We suggest that they try to change smaller, more manageable aspects rather than the culture as a whole. From a letter:

> Now that I am back, I realize how difficult it will be for me to use my East-West Center studies to change the curriculum in my department. I want to put the "new math" into my school . . .
> But before I can even plan any new curriculum, I must convince my principal and the staff of the school that this is a worthwhile change. There is strong resistance, especially from older teachers . . .
> I believe it may take me two years before I can convince the staff to let me try my new ideas. But I think it is very important that I not give up, but keep trying . . .

Professional Relations

The third part focuses on the problems involved in returning to a job and professional colleagues.

Speakers have given especially vivid examples. A staff member from Japan has reported that Japanese often *hide* the fact that they have an American college degree since it is not so useful in job advancement as an in-country degree. A staff member from the Philippines emphasized that she is especially careful about interpersonal relations there, because such relations are much more sensitive and can interfere with work to a greater degree than in the United States. The following is a letter that we use, and was written by a person whose colleague had received an East-West Center grant. Incidentally, this is the first author's favorite discussion starter.

> Please pardon me for writing suddenly to you to ask a favor of you. My name is . . . I am a teacher of English at Senior High School in Kyoto, Japan. I am 39 years old, so I'm not qualified to the admission to your university. However I want to study English at your university by all means. Is it quite impossible for you to lift the age limit from 35 to about 45? You might think that it is troublesome to teach a 40-year-old student, but I hope you'll teach a student who is very eager to study though he may be rather old.
> To tell the truth, one of my fellow teachers is going to enter your university. He and I live in the same small town, and I am his superior at our school. In this situation, it is impossible for me to continue staying at the present school, he will be greatly respected as an English teacher by all the teachers and students at our school and the inhabitants of our small town. On the other hand it is easy to guess what will happen to me. I have been worried for the past several months.

From participant discussions:

I might look forward to a different job where I can put into use the knowledge that I gained here. I might find that this cannot be done in my present job.

The employment problem is the major problem. I am worried about the prospect of going home and doing nothing.

Feelings of frustration on the job for not being able to do what I think I can do due to insufficient funds, facilities, etc.

Communication with current happenings in my academic field will be cut off.

Non-Western Perspective

This session on the non-Western perspective did not exist at our first seminar (May 1972). Its addition is an example of our desire to improve based on evaluative feedback. After the first seminar, an Asian participant wrote on her evaluation form that it was clear that the seminar had been "structured by American scholars" and that the staff should be more aware of the Asian psychology.

This comment struck us as quite reasonable, and so we asked the Asian students at later seminars to design their own session. We asked a Japanese female graduate student in psychology, who had read all the evaluation forms from the first seminar, to provide as much direction as necessary. At one of the later seminars, the participants decided to have an open discussion of what others back home will *expect* of the returnees. While, as American outsiders to this session, we would have to say that the group seemed quiet and that the ideas expressed seemed repetitious of those brought out in other sessions, the participants rated it highly. We realize the value of a session designed by the group as a whole, so we will retain such a session for future seminars.

Playing the Role

In one session participants were asked to prepare short skits, acting out what might happen after they return home. Participants were given the option of writing a script or simply writing down a few ideas that they would develop as the role play or skits continued. The skits were videotaped and played back to the staff and participants immediately on a TV monitor. The videotaping increases the impact (Bailey and Sowder, 1970), and adds to the popularity of the session since everyone enjoys seeing himself on television. The tapes are available for examination by visitors to the East-West Center.

In the seminars, almost all participants have chosen to be somewhat humorous in their skits, reinforcing our recommendation to keep a light heart concerning readjustment. All roles such as "father," "mother," and "boss" are played by participants. Some of the skits went as follows:

1. A returning son shows slides of the East-West Center to his parents,

224

and they comment on the scanty clothing of the girls and talk about an arranged marriage for their son.

2. A returnee comes home to a party arranged by her family, relatives, and old friends. She is shocked to see how *they* have changed because they are wearing the latest fashions, doing the latest dances, and using the most current slang.

3. A Pacific Islander returns home and is faced with an ultimatum from his father: either he cuts his hair or he leaves the house.

4. Former participants are at a party with people who know little or nothing about Asia and the East-West Center. The chatter is filled with embarrassing pauses, non sequiturs, ridiculous generalizations about Asians, and so forth. Finally, the participants and the other people break a previously arranged engagement with, "Well, I just remembered we have to do something else."

5. A female participant is being interviewed for a job by the boss of a small company. It becomes clear during the interview that the boss is interested in typing speed, not experiences with living and working with people from 40 countries; job experience, not ability to translate into Thai; and shorthand, not abstract knowledge of generative grammatical theory's generalizations to English language teaching.

Nonverbal Behavior   225

The session on attribution and nonverbal behavior draws material from the social psychological literature. We explain general notions of attribution theory (Jones et al., 1971), especially two major findings: (1) People judge actions of others as due to traits, but that they are more likely to judge the same actions in themselves as due to situational pressures; (2) People use extremely limited and sometimes faulty information in making trait inferences about others.

This leads to a question for discussion: Will people back home make trait judgments based on the behavior that they see in returnees, even though this information is limited? Will the trait inferences be negative (uppitty, too-Americanized, snobbish, know-it-all, etc.)? Our approach is similar to the culture assimilator work of Fiedler et al. (1971), who also use specific and critical incidents of this type to generate understanding of the attribution process.

The emphasis on attributions made by others leads into nonverbal behavior since participants have often learned gestures common to other nationalities. We show a videotape that we have made on American gestures, and then ask, "Are you bringing any back, and will there be problems because of it?" For instance, Americans scratch the side of their head when thinking about the answer to a difficult question, and Japanese scratch the top of their heads. The question for discussion: What will people think if they see a Japanese returnee making the quick American version of this nonverbal behavior? We have already presented the principle that there will be a trait inference from this inadequate piece of data, so the important point is that there *will* be an inference. Other examples center around the greater amount of bodily movement involved in American as contrasted with Asian gestures, the differing distances people use in ordinary conversation across different cultures (Summer, 1969), and the fact of returnee-as-oddity and thus the subject of much discussion by people back home.

Keeping in Touch
Finally, we have a session on maintaining cross-cultural relations. This session has the largest number of specific recommendations and is most unique to the special nature of the East-West Center. It is led by the alumni officer who tells about what East-West Center publications the participants will continue to receive, different associations organized by former participants in various countries, the alumni directory, occupations now held by former participants, names of volunteers in various countries who will help the new returnee join the alumni organizations, and so forth.

Generally, recommendations deal with maintaining ties with people in the different countries and how to meet others with similar international orientations. We always schedule this session last because it is uplifting, positive, and a relief after the analysis of potential negative aspects of returning home.

226

Rating the Program
A treatment of the reorientation seminar's evaluation is especially difficult because one of the authors (Brislin, 1973) has published perhaps the most severe criticisms of cross-cultural training evaluation in general. In those publications, he recommended the following among many others: (1) gathering behavioral measures related to recommended program outcome, such as the types of interpersonal interactions occurring *outside* of program hours; (2) comparing people who have gone through a seminar with those who have not; (3) gathering data long after a program ends, since the goal of the seminar is to affect future behavior; (4) being evaluated by people not associated with the original program.

We recognize that these standards are desirable and, therefore, are least satisfied with the evaluation aspect of the reorientation seminars. Our efforts will continue and will include follow-ups of seminar participants long after they have returned home (number 3, above), by people not associated with the original seminars (number 4, above). To date, we have three major sources of information, mostly aimed at showing "how we are doing." The data gathered tell (1) if participants are enthusiastic or if they are bored, (2) if they are learning anything, and (3) their suggestions for future programs.

Measures of both single session and total program acceptance are determined by standard attitude scales, specifically semantic-differential adjectives.

After each session, participants completed a questionnaire containing these seven-point scales: useful-useless; boring-interesting; unimportant-important; bad-good; intelligent-unintelligent; unstimulating-stimulating. The participants also completed scales measuring their feelings about having learned anything new, their thinking about the future, and their insights into themselves as returnees. This method is admittedly not innovative or exciting, but it gives us valuable information and "keeps us on our toes" because we gather it for every program.

In the table we use examples from two programs, and show how the evaluation design extends into the future. Note that ratings of the sessions have been maintained or have increased across the two programs, and that the same ratings will be gathered in the future. One session from the first seminar was rated so low that it was deleted from the next seminar. The second program's ratings are very high, perhaps because we took many of the first-program's participant comments into account, as mentioned below. Complacency is a luxury we cannot enjoy.

The measure of learning is simply the participants' answers to this question, completed before and after the program: "What problems do you think you might have after you return to your country? These might be any type of problem such as personal, family, job-related, and so forth."

The results from answers to this question are likewise encouraging. The average number of answers (summarized for all programs to date) increased from one before the seminar to four after the seminar. This shows that participants are indeed learning and are becoming more cognitively complex in their thinking about the future.

227

Evaluation Data from Participants in Various Seminars for Four Sessions

	NAME OF SESSION			
Various Seminars	Role Relations	Short/ Long-term Adjustments	Role Playing & Videotaping	Maintaining Cultural Ties
Seminar 1 (5/72) (N=22)	22.8	34.8	34.6	33.9
Seminar 2 (12/72) (N=12)	deleted	34.6	38.3	36.1
Future Seminars	will not be used	Design includes gathering feedback from future seminar participants		

N-Number of participants
Note: Cell entries are averages for responses to 6 seven-point evaluative scales (see text). A perfect score would be 42.

One reason that the ratings improved from earlier to later sessions is probably because of the excellent participant comments for the first (especially) and second programs. For instance, during the first seminar, we tried a session devoted to role relations in marriage and in the family; but it was not completely successful; and so we did not have such a seminar again (see table). The participants' answers in response to the open question, "Do you have any other comments?", tell why.

Not well enough focused.

Too short. No substantial development in the discussion.

Not enough time given for explanation of the sociological terms involved.

We presented another comment that led to improvement earlier in describing the genesis of the "Non-Western Perspective" session. As a final example, one participant felt that students would be able to contribute more if they knew in advance what the seminar was about. Following up, we prepared reading material and circulated information to potential participants before the next program, letting them know when we were available to talk with them about the upcoming seminar.

Place and Planning Important

228 The physical setting of the reorientation seminar is very important. If we have learned anything from our experience with the programs, it is that the seminar must be held at a good distance from the East-West Center, preferably at a camp or retreat over 20 miles away. Without this removal from the Center, the situational pressures of invitations from nonreturnee friends, need to go to the drugstore for a tube of toothpaste, and competition from television take their toll on session attendance. Consequently, when the faithful see that attendance at sessions has decreased, their morale declines. Our recommendation is that seminars be held away from a familiar environment that has a well-established schedule attached to it.

In general, the planning, administering, follow-up, and evaluation of transportation, housing, food, and service are a very important job. These details can often make or break participants' favorable response to a program. We recommend one person be assigned the responsibility for all the mechanics of a program so that the details do not interfere with the program. Allow time for planning and carrying out these comparatively insignificant and annoying details lest you find yourself in the position of man who, for want of a nail, loses the battle.

It would be easy to argue, using exactly the data presented in this paper, that we are causing returnees needless worry. Critics could point to the respondent who gave only one potential problem prior to the seminar but seven after, and they could say that ethical concerns come into question.

Our response is that the worry will be beneficial for many returnees if problems actually do arise.

Even if problems *do not* occur, the returnees who participate in the seminar will learn what *does* happen to a large number of people. One of the implicit assumptions of the East-West Center is that Asian, Pacific, and U.S. grantees will learn about the nature of people who have a multicultural orientation. One aspect of such people, of course, is the nature of the issues faced when they move from their "home" culture to another and back.

Because of our seminar, participants have an opportunity (for the most part, their only formal opportunity) to learn about this process. This point became clear to us when a participant congratulated us on the seminar and said, "I've learned so much. I never dreamed that there were all these things that can happen when people move from culture to culture."

References

Bailey, K., & Sowder, W. (1970). Audiotape and videotape self-confrontation in psychotherapy. *Psychological Bulletin, 74*, 127–137.

Bochner, S. (1973). The mediating man and cultural diversity. In R. Brislin (Ed.), *Topics in culture learning* (pp. 23–37). Honolulu: East-West Culture Learning Institute.

Brislin, R. (1973). The content and evaluation of cross-cultural training programs. In D. Hoopes (Ed.), *Readings in intercultural communication: Vol. III* (pp. 79–122). Pittsburgh: Regional Council for International Education.

Cleveland, H., Mangone, G. J. & Adams, J. C. (1960). *The overseas Americans.* New York: McGraw-Hill.

Egbert, L., et al. (1964). Reduction of postoperative pain by encouragement and instruction. *New England Journal of Medicine, 270,* 825–827.

Elms, A. (1972). *Social psychology and social relevance.* Boston: Little, Brown.

Fiedler, F., Mitchell, T., & Triandis, H. (1971). The culture assimilator: An approach to cross-cultural training. *Journal of Applied Psychology, 55,* 95–102.

Franklin, B. (1844). Remarks concerning the savages of North America, pamphlet. In *The works of Benjamin Franklin, Vol. II.* Boston: Tappan and Dennet.

Janis, I. (1958). *Psychological stress.* New York: Wiley.

Jones, E., et al. (1971). *Attribution: Perceiving the causes of behavior.* Morristown, NJ: General Learning Press.

Sommer, R. (1969). *Personal space.* New York: Prentice-Hall.

Useem, J., & Useem, R. (1955). *The Western-educated man in India.* New York: Dryden Press.

Useem, J., & Useem, R. (1968). American-educated Indians and Americans in India: A comparison of two modernizing roles. *Journal of Social Issues, 24* (4), 143–158.

24

Rules for Re-entry

Dick Irish

Coming home and starting over--something most overseas Foreign Service employees must face when they leave the diplomatic profession. It is a time of both new stresses and new opportunities. Though the person ending a Foreign Service career has some special problems not faced by colleagues in other fields, in most respects he or she is not much different from other career changers. Job-search experts have adopted several useful rules for changing careers. Many of them can be adapted for the former Foreign Service employee. Let's look at some of the rules that can help make for a successful re-entry:

Rule One: Take Time

The shock of re-entry often clouds good judgment. The anxiety to get on with it and be "responsible" can result in poor decision-making. But time is needed to re-adapt to the curious customs of the North Americans. So, forget looking for work for a few months; the point of coming home is to start feeling at home.

Since the pressure to find a job is usually greater than the desire to protect your larger interests, it can be a big mistake to take the first job offered.

From "Rules for Re-entry" by D. Irish, 1983, *The Foreign Service Journal*, January, pp. 22–25. Reprinted by permission.

One former special assistant to an ambassador, for example, jumped into a seemingly attractive job on Capitol Hill only to spend the next two years extricating himself from a tricky political situation. Another ex-Foreign Service officer (FSO) accepted a job in the Rocky Mountains without an interview or an elementary check-out of the employer. A word to the wise: Caveat employee.

Budget time for the job search. In these tough times it usually takes at least four months for career changers with demonstrated job-search skills to find work. For others, unskilled in job-search techniques, it can take more than two years. All the more reason for a returning overseas American to take time off to research the self before searching for a job.

Rule Two: Spend Money

Nothing benefits a professional job campaign as much as the willingness to spend money on it. It takes money to find a job--plane tickets, a printed résumé, temporary living quarters, etc. Re-entry is expensive.

The same applies to the overseas American who comes home and invests in a small business. Many forget to do at least six months of intensive research leading to a business plan before making the plunge--with predictable results. So, whether you are looking for a job or researching a business opportunity, budget enough money to live comfortably for one year after returning home, plus four to five thousand dollars to finance the job search itself. Savings are for emergencies, and unemployment is a legitimate crisis. Moreover, candidates who spend money on themselves feel better, impress employers, and have a competitive edge on other unemployed professionals who seem poor and miserable.

232

Rule Three: Stop Feeling Sorry for Yourself

Self-pity is self-destructive to the job searcher. It's one step away from self-contempt. And a candidate who feels bad about him or herself is bad news in a job interview.

Much of this self-pity comes from a belief that one is a victim. A disappointing assignment, an ungrateful boss, or being caught in political crossfire aborts many careers. There is a strong tendency to blame others for our problems. One ex-Peace Corps representative, for example, went into deep shock after being fired. Six months later the anger and disappointment still infected his approach to possible employers. As he discovered, a sour disposition will spoil an otherwise effective job campaign.

Another reason the jobless blahs overtake returning overseas Americans comes from the belief that the employee is who he or she last worked for. Thus, to many diplomats abroad, leaving the Service means losing their identities. One ex-FSO was so devastated by separating from the Service he was unable to think of himself as anything but a defrocked diplomat. Identity in the job search has nothing to do with organizations. Identity has to do with *accomplishments* and *functions,* many of which should carry over to the next job.

A part of the problem stems from thinking an organization *took care of us.* Thus, in leaving the Foreign Service, we feel helpless to take care of ourselves. But the confusion is in our minds--not our stars. Feeling dependent on organizations to take care of us prevents us from taking care of ourselves (i.e., finding another job!). Thus, a "self-directed" job search--in which we focus on ourselves--is a good way to vanquish self-pity, feelings of victimization, and inappropriate dependency.

Rule Four: Break Up and Start Over
To banish self-pity and get on with the job search one must break with the past. Clinicians call it separation anxiety. Feeling abandoned by a past employer need not mean being helpless in finding a new one. But nobody starts over (in a marriage, a relationship, or a new career) who hasn't turned from the past and faced the future.

The way to turn your back on the past is to get angry. Focus on what was unattractive in your overseas job: unchallenging work, excessive travel, a blocked career path, and so forth. Get mad about it and be glad to be rid of it. The point is to get angry at something other than yourself. Otherwise, anger--turned inward--is bound to cause depression. And depressed job candidates are depressing to employers. An even better solution is to use the past as a stepping stone--a lesson learned--and go on to the next level of the learning pyramid.

233

Starting over means translating overseas experiences into marketable domestic qualifications. Re-entering Americans can apply their international expertise to a host of stateside crafts, trades, and professions. One FSO is now a sugar broker for a soft drink firm; an international development expert now manages a hospital; and a former Peace Corps staff member currently raises money for a non-profit international organization. Thinking overseas experience is useful sets the stage for re-entry success.

Rule Five: Get Excited
The trick in looking for work is to get excited by the search itself. Dreading the idea makes re-entry more difficult than it need be. Treating the job search as an adventure helps to finesse a tight labor market. All the more reason to spend money on yourself, take an occasional three-day pass to the beach, and have fun making the career change. One exiting FSO so feared the job search, he spent the next five years gaining a law degree, then an MBA, before finally looking for work. Further schooling simply postponed the inevitable while undermining his self-confidence. Part of his problem was thinking his leaving the Foreign Service was a punishment; his stint in graduate school was his penance. But it became a kind of purgatory.

While important, the job search can be taken too seriously. Feeling it's a life or death matter shields the career changer from the pleasure of it. Take a *playful* attitude to finding a job. Solemn job seekers are nowhere near as attractive as enthusiastic job candidates. Concentrate on the exciting future rather than the interesting past.

Rule Six: Focus on Function

Effective career changers focus not just on *position* but on *function*--i.e., whatever they do as well or better than anyone else. That might be giving speeches, writing reports, selling ideas, mediating conflicts, or many other skills. Moreover, no matter what their former rank, title, or status in the Service, returning overseas Americans will function best at what they like. Thus, figuring out what you *can do* is one step away from knowing what you *want to do*. Unfortunately, career changers often overlook their natural talents and therefore don't connect with a job that would make them happy.

Remember function when preparing your résumé. Focus on functional skills--organization, report writing, conflict mediation, agricultural and business skills, and a thousand others--that translate into domestic jobs. If an FSO gathered and analyzed information in Ghana, why can't he do risk-analysis for an American bank? If an AID agricultural officer specialized in wet-rice farming in Southeast Asia, why can't she study similar techniques in South Carolina? If a PCV organized credit unions in Bolivia, why can't he manage credit unions here at home?

234

This means reprogramming your résumé and interview presentation away from past organizational associations (you are what you *did*, remember, not for whom you did it), job titles, and rank. Otherwise résumés are simply tedious recitations of "duties and responsibilities"--the boiler plate of boring job descriptions. The answer is to focus on accomplishments and results abroad and how they translate into needs here. Translation of functional accomplishments means, however, junking foreign policy and development jargon and instead expressing overseas experiences in plain English.

Rule Seven: Write Your Résumé

Preparing your résumé will increase your confidence and excitement while helping you translate your overseas skills into new, marketable functions. Take at least two weeks to jot down every job and function you've ever performed. You will be surprised at their diversity and the talents required to do them. Undiscovered skills will emerge, and a pattern of your unique combination of interests and abilities will begin to be revealed. You may then begin to apply these abilities to the areas of work that appeal to you the most.

Now write your résumé. Use books from the library on format. Be very businesslike . . . neither shy nor clever. Your next employer wants an objective view of who you are--and only you have all the information. Use active verbs--managed, directed, produced, created, supervised. Use numbers. Name specific achievements--"wrote 50-page monthly report" . . . "arranged 125 embassy dinners per year" . . . "personally contacted 35 people regularly to poll commercial response." If the résumé needs polishing, an executive search firm or friend with a professional flair may be able to help.

Don't be discouraged if you have to send out large numbers of résumés. One rule of thumb is to expect responses from only three percent of your mailing, and that from these job interviews, only one actual job offer may result. Finally, concentrate on writing good job letters. It is an art that can be developed by studying one of the many good books on job hunting.

Rule Eight: Know Where You Want To Live
Another reason six months or so might be necessary in moving back into the mainstream is the importance of where you live to career prospects and overall success. Knowing where you want to live can shape what it is you want to do--and vice versa. Your job skills may help you determine the area where they can best be used (i.e., computer technology: Boston, New York, Dallas, West Coast, Raleigh). Many former Foreign Service employees become so accustomed to uprooting every few years they feel unnatural settling down. Having moved five times and taken three jobs in two years, one ex-FSO confuses motion with movement when it's only running in place. She still hasn't made the transition.

235

Her reverse culture shock is well known. While Foreign Service personnel are often posted to Washington, the capital is merely a port of entry, not necessarily Mainstreet, U.S.A. Learning about which parts of the country reflect your interests, values, and job direction should precede looking for work. Feeling at home in the Shenandoah Valley can take as long as becoming accustomed to Sri Lanka.

Rule Nine: Network
Networking is curiosity made visible. And curiosity coupled with imagination is the chief quality needed to make the leap to a new career. Since most re-entering Americans don't know what they want to do and hesitate to admit it, the transition is often troubled. A good idea when coming home is to talk with former colleagues who have made the transition. Networking means using other people to help you think through what to do next.

Networking also means revealing your need for help by talking to a wide variety of employers and enlisting their support. One ex-AID official got a job-lead on the tennis court of a country club. Another former FSO was interviewed on the New York shuttle. And a third found work through his father's best friend.

All the more reason to spend several months not looking for a job so much as interviewing for information: networking. That means bouncing ideas off employers and finding out about jobs that may not be advertised--or may not yet exist. The knack of networking is taking employers off the hook by not asking for a job so much as advice. It means winning an ally in the job search, letting *this* person connect you with *that* one. It means doing an investigation about yourself and the world of work. It's really no different than what diplomats do on foreign assignment: talking to key host-country nationals, developing an information network, learning the language (the jargon of a new trade), and eventually getting on top of a job. Well, the job of re-entry is *to find* a job. That entails using people to help you locate hidden skills and hidden jobs.

Rule Ten: Be Flexible But Set Goals

Many overseas Americans feel embarrassed at not knowing what they want to do when they come home, so give yourself a break and don't try to make the transition too quickly. For the best and brightest, thinking through the first few steps can be extremely difficult. The career options available, the perplexity of self analysis, and the patience necessary to change vocational direction--plus reverse culture shock--are all challenging. When it works out well, whatever returning Americans choose to do at home seems in retrospect as if it were *meant* to be. The invariable response of successful career changers is to wonder why they waited so long to do it. The truth is that time is needed to weigh options, calculate risks, take into account talent (i.e., functional skills), and research the self via networking.

236

Also, take a playful attitude in the job search. Figuring out what to do is a result of letting go, feeling good about the self, and allowing the unconscious to do its job. Ideas surface on the periphery of the mind. Often, wacky job objectives are the most realistic in terms of functional talent. The frame of mind best suited to thinking through new career steps is marked by openness, curiosity, imagination, and knowing the world is mad. A sense of humor helps.

The ex-Peace Corps staffer managing a tomato farm in southwest Virginia, the ex-FSO leasing Lear jets to foreign governments, and the former AID mission chief directing a Planned Parenthood program in Pennsylvania are recent examples of overseas Americans who have made imaginative leaps into other careers. All three were confident of making the transition and deeply interested in *something*--farming, aviation, family planning. The self-directed job search is centered in the *self*. "What is it you want to do?" is still the toughest question asked in an interview. Returning overseas Americans need to answer that question before beginning to look.

Setting goals is tough: friends, family, and colleagues are often no help. They may put down aspiration on the grounds that a radical career change is unrealistic. Also, many career changers want other peoples' approval when what's really needed is *self*-approval. That often means saying no to what other people say you should do.

Another clue to knowing what you want to do is sensing you have the skills, say, to be a sportswriter even though you lack a journalism degree or newspaper experience. But the two most important predictors of success on the job aren't education and experience. Rather, they are motivation and ability. All the more reason returning overseas Americans need to convey their abilities and desires before representing education and experience to domestic employers.

Finally, while re-entry is often painful, it's a chance for personal and professional renewal. The price of re-entry is often paid in the coin of anxiety and guilt. That's part of the stress of re-entry and the career change. Fortunately, like other personal crises, re-entry is an opportunity for growth. The profusion of opportunity in America makes that price well worth paying.

25

Common Unexpected Situations and Special Concerns

Campus Crusade for Christ, Training Department of International Resources

Common Unexpected Situations

Frequently, returning staff are surprised or caught off guard by situations which they are not anticipating. The following examples illustrate some of the more commonly occuring situations. Along with these examples, some *possible* responses or reactions plus some suggestions are given to help deal with specific incidences encountered.

Staff Returning Home	Response/Reaction	Suggestions
Did not expect to arrive feeling so physically and emotionally drained.	Tiredness, lethargy	Schedule in several transition days of rest and relaxation between departure and home arrival. Do not overschedule your time upon return.
Did not expect to feel so "foreign" upon return.	Confusion, disorientation	Reduce feeling of "foreignness" by making yourself aware of changes at home

From *A Guide to Reentry: Field Test Copy* (Sections IV and V, pp. 10–21) by Training Department of International Resources, Campus Crusade for Christ, 1980. San Bernadino, CA: Campus Crusade for Christ. Adapted by permission.

Staff Returning Home	*Response/Reaction*	*Suggestions*
		and within yourself before returning.
Did not expect a "let down" feeling after arrival.	Disappointment, unfulfillment	Be prepared for a possible "let down"--realize that you probably have been operating on an "emotional high" prior to return and shortly after.
Did not expect to feel so unsettled: living out of a suitcase, traveling constantly to see supporters and friends, having no place to call home.	Frustration, irritability, tiredness	Mentally prepare yourself (and family) prior to leaving. Ask God to make it a time of challenge, ministry and personal growth. Try to establish a semi-permanent base from which you can operate while at home.
Did not expect transportation would be such a difficulty.	Isolated feeling, frustration	Arrange ahead to have transportation available to you during furlough. Accept the fact that you may *not* be able to get around as conveniently or freely as you might wish.
Did not expect readjustment to take so long (more than a few days.)	Discouragement	Readjustment *can be expected* to take some time--more for some than for others. This is only natural.
Did not expect an extended recovery period from illness contracted while abroad.	Discouragement, resentment toward God	Anticipate a medical exam upon arriving home from the field. Do not be surprised or feel guilty if rest or other treatment is prescribed.

240

Staff Returning Home	Response/Reaction	Suggestions
Did not expect to be a "3rd culture person" upon return--not able to reidentify fully with one's own culture.	Unsettled feeling, confused	Realize that you *have* absorbed some of the host culture, and that you never will be able to return fully to the past way of life. See this as a positive benefit.
Did not expect so many adjustments in returning from a simple to a more complex life-style.	Anxiety, frustration	It is not easy to be transferred suddenly from one type of culture to another. Expect to take some time to readjust. Focus on the "best" parts of each culture--not the negative aspects.
Did not expect it to be as difficult fitting back into the flow of things at home or at work.	Insecurity, anxiety	Do not expect to adjust right away--especially if you have been away any length of time. Getting readjusted takes time. Relax and enjoy the challenge.
Expected things to be pretty much the same back home.	Unsettled feeling, insecurity	Actively look for changes instead of allowing them to take you by surprise.
Did not expect changes in social custom, etiquette, dress, styles, music, morals, etc.	Insecurity; disappointment	Keep informed of national and local news. Have your parents or friend send you current newspaper and magazines prior to departure.
Did not expect to be so out of touch with current issues at home (political, economic, educational, etc.)	Embarrassment, feeling "out of it"	Again, it only takes a little foresight to plan ahead a bit of reading to bring you up to date.

241

Staff Returning Home	*Response/Reaction*	*Suggestions*
Did not expect changes in cost of living; inflation's effect on housing, food, clothing, auto, etc.	Discouragement	Plan out a tentative budget prior to return based on cost of living data gathered from current ads and classified section of the newspaper.
Did not expect your own personal values to have changed so much.	Uncertainty, confusion	This often does come as a surprise to many after returning home. The extent of change can only truly be measured against the standard of being back in one's own culture. Attempt to define the changes which have taken place.
Did not expect so much change of pace; difficulty readjusting to schedules.	Confusion, tiredness	Physically, you may not be up to a faster pace for a while. Mentally, it may take a while to readjust to a different style of scheduling.
Did not expect to feel so uncertain in interpersonal relationships.	Insecurity, withdrawal	You will need to relearn certain cultural bases for relationships-- different levels of commitment, etc.
Did not expect to have to readjust to verbal/ non-verbal mannerisms of home country.	Uncertainty, embarrassment	Relearn social cues--eye contact, gestures, proper etiquette, etc. This takes some time but deliberate observation speeds the process.
Did not expect others to see or understand things in a different way than you do.	Frustration, discouragement	Remember it is *your* perspective which has changed--not theirs.

Staff Returning Home	Response/Reaction	Suggestions
Did not expect others to show such a lack of interest in hearing about your experiences.	Discouragement, withdrawal, resentment	Take it as fact that others are usually not able to relate to your experiences as you would wish. Some are just *not* interested.
Did not expect people to ask so many superficial questions.	Irritation	Be prepared to face these questions. Work on ways to make *transitions* into what you really want to communicate.
Did not expect to be so appalled at the values of society.	Disappointment, discouragement	Be prepared for the possibility of a greater gap between your moral values and those of your own culture.
Did not expect family to be so possessive after initial return.	Impatience, discouragement	Be sure to reaffirm your parents and family. Assure them that you are not "lost" to them and that you love them. Avoid coming on too heavy about your experience overseas.
Did not expect colleagues back home to seem so insensitive to materialism/ wastefulness.	Irritation, disappointment, contempt	Do not allow yourself to slip into feelings of resentment, anger or other responses which appear judgmental.
Did not expect to see so much apathy and unconcern for the needs of the world.	Anger, discouragement	This may rightly disturb you, but do not become self-righteous or indignant over another's response or lack of response. Lovingly try to inform of world needs.

Staff Returning Home	Response/Reaction	Suggestions
Did not expect to be so troubled over the imbalance of Christian workers at home versus workers abroad.	Impatience, discouragement, disillusionment	Accept this imbalance as fact. Instead of reacting emotionally, *plan* how you can use your life and experience to challenge others back home for missions service.
Did not expect people to be so ethnocentric, so narrow in their perspective.	Rejecting, superiority feelings	Remember that you do not have the right to judge others on the basis of your own "enlightened experience."
Expected more needs would be met by colleagues and the home office.	Dissatisfaction, critical spirit	Make your needs known, but do not be surprised if all your needs cannot be met.
Expected to be treated as someone special (VIP) upon return.	Disillusionment, hurt feeling	Even though you are a "special" person, do not view it as a "right" to have attention focused on you. Realize that others are involved in the routine of daily affairs.
Did not expect to be quite so out of touch organizationally.	Uncertainty, insecurity	While still on the field, endeavor to have a friend update you on organizational changes back home.
Did not expect to find things so much more complex organizationally.	Frustration	Realize that organizational structures tend to be more complex as they expand. Be prepared for the possibility of less informality and more "red tape."

244

Staff Returning Home	Response/Reaction	Suggestions
Did not expect difficulty fitting back into the organizational structure.	Uselessness, unfulfillment	It will be easier for some, depending upon past associations. Realize your old position is likely no longer available. Be patient and look expectantly to what God has for you.
Did not expect so much turnover in staff personnel (so many unfamiliar faces).	Uncertainty, disorientation	Be prepared for personnel changes. Prepare to take initiative in getting to know the "new faces."
Did not expect so many policy and procedural changes.	Impatience, confusion	Expect changes to be magnified when you have been away for a length of time. Obtain and review current policy manuals.
Did not expect staff to appear more concerned with job/goals than with people/ relationships.	Disappointment, contempt, irritation	There will be a certain amount of strain returning to a highly goal-oriented society from one which is "relationally" oriented. Realize that it is *your* perspective which has changed.
Did not expect to feel unneeded back home or to have no definite assignment upon return.	Discouragement, feeling of uselessness	It is highly unlikely that you are not needed. It may seem that way coming from an understaffed situation to one which appears overstaffed.
Did not expect it to be so difficult to communicate or apply knowledge and insight gained abroad.	Discouragement, lost motivation	Just as in trying to share new ideas and innovations overseas, you will find the receptor not always open to change or suggestions. Do not attempt to sell your

245

Staff Returning Home	*Response/Reaction*	*Suggestions*
		ideas immediately upon return. Demonstrating the effectiveness of an idea first is usually more productive.
Did not expect to feel so out of date vocationally/ professionally.	Insecurity	If possible, try to keep abreast of what is going on in your profession.
Did not expect to return feeling so uncertain about the future.	Insecurity, uncertainty	Transition times are sometimes difficult, yet remember that God does have a perfect plan for you. Wait for *His* direction, and do not feel pressured into having to make a quick decision.
Did not expect to find a critical attitude developing toward my own culture or my colleagues.	Guilt, frustration	Keep breathing spiritually. Critical attitudes can easily slip in during the stress of readjustment. Definitely some things will bother you, but do not allow Satan to use these things to defeat you.
Did not expect feelings of superiority due to overseas experience.	Guilt, aloofness	Review Philippians 2:1–11. "Regard others as more important than yourself."
Did not expect to feel so lonely.	Unfulfilled, feeling of rejection	Especially if you have established deep relationships overseas, it is natural that you feel the loss of these friendships. Actively seek out new relationships at home. Get involved with people right away, do not isolate yourself from others.

Staff Returning Home	Response/Reaction	Suggestions
Did not expect to become so emotional over "little things."	Insecurity, unsettled feeling	Sometimes the excitement of returning home--seeing family and friends--causes great emotional release. This is not unusual. However, if this response continues, it would be advisable to talk it out with a friend or advisor.
Did not expect that some redefinition in husband/wife roles would be necessary.	Confusion, insecurity	Realize that while the husband usually maintains pretty much the same role overseas, the wife often finds herself in a "new" role. It is, therefore, natural to expect some readjustments to be made upon return, especially for the wife.
Did not expect children to face emotional, social, educational, lingustic adjustments back home.	Helpless feeling, confusion	Be extra sensitive to the needs of your children during furlough or during the early months of a permanent return. If the children are old enough, begin to talk over areas relating to your return. Assure them that "home" is where your family is and not a particular geographical place.

247

Special Concerns

Parents returning with children
1. Changing environments can lead to stress for a child due to:
   a. Leaving familiar surroundings--friends, possessions, and pets behind.
   b. Reestablishing new friendships and being forced to leave old friends.
   c. Feeling different from other young people because of peculiar mannerisms acquired abroad.

d. Insecurity due to changes in fads, styles, and crazes.
e. Not knowing where their real "home" is located.
f. Making readjustments at school.
g. Adjusting to a less protective and perhaps more permissive society.
h. Contrasting standards of discipline within the respective cultures.
i. Suddenly facing the pressures of a highly complex society.
j. Traveling from place to place during furlough--no set routine.
k. Feeling of loneliness or rejection when parents are so busy preparing to leave--on support trips, during the process of relocation, etc.
l. Feeling of anger or resentment toward parents for "disrupting" their lives, and for not spending quality time with them.

2. Suggestions
   a. Begin to prepare your children for change:
   (1) Display a positive attitude toward returning on furlough or for permanent home assignment.
   (2) Openly discuss and pray with your children about the transition.
   (3) Allow them to know "why" you are returning, what you will be doing, where you will be living and how long you will be away (if on furlough). Let them help plan the return.
   (4) Do not become "too busy" to meet the daily and special needs of your children as you are preparing to leave, travel or get resettled.
   (5) Inform them about life "back home" so they will feel somewhat familiar with names, places, and customs.
   (6) Bring them up-to-date on what youth their own ages are doing in your home country.
   (7) Refer to your "home overseas" and your "national home," but allow the child to see that his *real home* is with you, wherever you may be.
   (8) Plan to take along certain possessions which are part of the child's security, i.e., do not discard certain "favorite" belongings thinking that you will replace them again back home.
   (9) Aid your children in learning social independence and self-respect.
   (10) Love, availability, discipline and instruction are keys to any satisfactory adjustment.
   b. Help your children adjust to a new environment:
   (1) Instruct your children in any basic differences of social custom.
   (2) Help them correct mannerisms learned abroad which are apt to bring peer disapproval or rejection.
   (3) Allow children to adapt, within permissible limits, to new styles and fads if they desire to do so.
   (4) Protect your children from sudden overexposure to negative elements of an overly permissive society, e.g., monitoring television, movies, and reading material.

    c. Aid your children in establishing new friendships:
- (1) Attempt to locate or be in areas where there are other children the same age.
- (2) Take the initiative to invite other children to visit your home.
- (3) Plan to visit families with children during furlough support time.
- (4) If your children will be in school, try to select one which will provide friendships commensurate with your philosophy and ideals, especially if your children are coming out of a conservative, protective environment.
- (5) Do not overlook instruction in boy-girl relationships.

    d. *Avoid:*
- (1) Changes in methods/standards of discipline at home or in public. Become aware of disciplinary methods used at school.
- (2) Making furlough time only a time of "business."
- (3) Allowing your child to isolate himself or withdraw. (Some shyness, at first, is not uncommon).

Children returning home alone for schooling
1. Areas of potential difficulty:
   - a. Suddenly cut off from direct parental guidance and counsel.
   - b. Loneliness--missing family and other close associates and friends.
   - c. Coming out of a protective environment of family and missionary school.
   - d. Adjusting to a society which is more restrictive, more permissive.
   - e. Being misunderstood by others because of a third-culture (different) perspective.
   - f. Realizing and adjusting to differing social customs and patterns--dating, dress, mannerisms, verbal and nonverbal cues.
   - g. Difficulty relating to peers due to differing life experience and goals.
   - h. Feeling of being out of touch with changing events of own society.
   - i. Having to discipline oneself and the use of time.
   - j. Handling situations when in need--during illness or accident.
   - k. Handling logistics--finding a place to live, obtaining transportation, locating a part-time job, having adequate finances and handling finances.
   - l. Making new acquaintances.
   - m. Adjusting to a different school system, curriculum, scholastic requirements.
   - n. Accommodating new values.
   - o. Feelings of superiority, inferiority due to overseas experience.
   - p. Unresolved feelings toward parents, nations--feeling deprived of home country experiences and relationships due to overseas assignment.
   - q. Coming from a tight-knit family into an individualistic and loose-structured society.

249

    r. Coming out of a small school situation where your child is the center of attraction into a situation where your child is just one in a huge crowd of students.

    s. Deciding what to do during summer vacation time--stay and work within own culture or return to be with parents.

    t. Parents' allowing children to make their own choices while away at school (an area of difficulty for the parents).

2. Suggestions

    a. If at all possible, attempt to line up a relative or family friend to take your son or daughter under his wing, at least for the first year during the initial adjustment period.

    b. Inform the one who will be aiding your child about some of his/her unique needs, as well as some of the potential difficulties connected with the reentry process. This will help the "guardian" to understand better and to work with the child during readjustment.

    c. Try to choose a school which is compatible with your family's values and social background, especially if your child is coming out of a highly protective or provincial setting.

    d. It is best to avoid sending a child to a completely unfamiliar area the first year back home. Attempt to choose a location where previous relationships have been developed.

250

    e. As a family, go over reentry materials with your child. Begin to work out difficult or potentially difficult areas. This will help the child realize that you are united behind him/her and foster a feeling of support.

    f. Make sure the child understands that loneliness and stress related to reentry are *not* abnormal. You might view the first semester as a time of likely adjustment.

    g. Encourage your child to view college life as a new "cultural" experience.

    h. Begin to assist your son or daughter to plan long range by discussing career choices, marriage possibilities, a definition of what constitutes "home."

    i. Promote development of independence by allowing your child to get away from home during the summer months--either on a job or through special summer projects, and traveling.

    j. Avoid being over protective--let your child know that you trust him/her and have confidence in their ability to handle themselves while away from home.

    k. Maintain a good and regular communication program via letter, phone and visits when possible.

    l. Think through the advantages/disadvantages of having your child return to live with you each summer, or to remain in the "home" country where deeper roots can be established.

Appendix A

Inventory of
Re-entry Problems

The following inventory was originally developed by a group of foreign graduate students who were within six months of terminating their period of study in the U.S. This inventory demonstrates that students do actually anticipate certain concerns about returning home.

1. Cultural adjustment
   a. Identity problem
   b. Insecurity
   c. Adjustment to changes in life style
   d. Adjustment to a pervasive quality of envy and distrust in interpersonal relations
   e. Adjustment to the localiteness [sic] of kin and friends
   f. Adjustment to a daily work routine
   g. Family or community pressure to conform
   h. No problem
   i. Other

2. Social adjustment
   a. Adjustments from individualism of U.S. life to familism (conformity and submission to the demands of family) in home country
   b. Colonial mentality

From *A program guide for Re-entry/Transition Workshop* by N. C. Asuncion-Lande, 1976, Washington, DC: National Association for Foreign Student Affairs. Reprinted by permission.

     c. Feelings of superiority due to international experience and travel
     d. Lack of amenities which were a part of U.S. existence
     e. Uncertainties in interpersonal relations
     f. Social alienation as a result of foreign sojourn
     g. Dissatisfaction with ritualized patterns of social interaction
     h. Frustration as a result of conflicting attitudes
     i. No problem
     j. Other

3. Linguistic barriers
     a. Adoption of verbal/non-verbal codes which are not familiar to countrymen
     b. Adoption of certain speech mannerisms which may be misinterpreted by countrymen
     c. Absence of colleagues who speak the same code as returnee
     d. Unfamiliarity with new forms of communication or styles of expression
     e. No problem
     f. Other

4. National and political problems
     a. Changes in political conditions
     b. Shifts in national priorities/policies
     c. Shift in political views
     d. Political climate not conducive to professional activity
     e. Political climate not conducive to professional advancement
     f. Dissatisfaction with political situation
     g. Observed lack of national goals
     h. Politicization of office or colleagues
     i. Changes in bureaucratic leadership
     j. No problem
     k. Other

5. Educational problems
     a. Inability to reconcile aspects of U.S. education to education in home country
     b. Relevance of education to home situation
     c. Fulfillment of objectives in coming to U.S.
     d. Aspects of U.S. education which are least helpful to returnee
     e. Lack of facilities and resources for research
     f. Wrong expectations
     g. Failure to improve skills
     h. Absence of professional education programs to keep up with new developments or knowledge
     i. No problem
     j. Other

6. Professional problems

Inventory of Re-entry Problems

a. Inability to work in chosen specialty
b. Placement in inappropriate field
c. Facing a glutted job market
d. Scientific terminology in U.S. studies which are not subject to adequate translation into the native language
e. Inability to communicate what was learned
f. Resistance to change by coworkers
g. Feeling of superiority due to U.S. training
h. Non-recognition of U.S. degree
i. Jealousy of colleagues
j. Low compensation
k. High expectations
l. Isolation from academic and scientific developments in U.S. or in own field
m. Perceived lack of enthusiasm and/or commitment among coworkers
n. Concern with quick material success
o. No problem
p. Other

Appendix B

Practical Relocation Information

The following checklist might be utilized in preparing an information packet for individuals or families who are returning to live in the United States after living abroad. The information should reflect the current availability of services in a particular location.

Departure from foreign location

Travel arrangements
necessary exit visas
travel reservations

Household effects
inventory updated
packing, shipping arrangements for household goods, car insurance

From *Re-entry: An overlooked dimension in cultural adaptation* by F. Silberstein and B. Hoganson, 1982, Workshop Proceedings, 8th Annual Congress of International SIETAR. Long Beach, CA. Reprinted by permission of the Overseas Briefing Center, Foreign Service Institute, Department of State, Washington, DC

Appendix B

Medical/health
records from local physician/clinic
inoculations current for travel, re-entry

Schools
obtain grade reports, test scores, teacher evaluations
request college recommendations for junior/senior year students
notify U.S. schools if possible

Pets
travel arrangements
health records
inoculations

Change of address
insurance companies
credit card companies
magazines, etc.

Finances
settle outstanding local accounts
plan for expenses upon return

Arrival in _____

Initial information
company contacts
newspapers and magazines
helpful publications

Transportation
car rental
taxicabs
buses and other public transportation
driver's license information

Health concerns
hospitals
emergency rooms
pharmacies open 24 hours
special services and clinics

Practical Relocation Information

Housing
temporary lodging
apartments
houses
real estate companies

Recreation
swimming pools
fitness clubs
country clubs
restaurants
concerts
parks programs
YMCA/YWCA
community centers
sports activities
museums
trips/tours
free events

Child care facilities
day care
camps
nursery schools

Schools
sources of information
testing
choosing a school
public schools
private schools
religious schools
colleges

Continuing education
adult education programs
fellowships, grants, loans, scholarships

Handicapped programs
special education
recreation programs
counseling/support groups
transportation

Appendix B

Consumer information
discount stores
specialty stores
grocery stores
specialty food stores

Maintenance services
cleaners
painters
rental equipment
electricians
contractors
landscapers
pest control
plumbers
chimney sweeps
delivery services
car repair

Career investigation
career counseling
women's action groups
volunteer opportunities

Personal services
doctors
lawyers
baby sitters
hairdressers
dentists

Banking
checking accounts
safe deposit boxes
savings accounts
credit cards
check cashing

Religious information
churches
synagogues
other

Practical Relocation Information

Miscellaneous information
library cards
utility rates
voter registration
newspapers
foreign language aid
senior citizen services

Appendix C

Designing Your Own
Re-Entry Program

Some steps to be considered in designing a re-entry program for any particular client group are:

Needs Assessment
Selection of Topics to Meet Those Needs
Determination of Appropriate Setting
Selection of, or Writing Appropriate Sessions
Selection and Training of Staff
Program Promotion
Program Implementation and Evaluation
(see chart page 262)

Needs Assessment
A. What are the needs your clients have?
 1.
 2.
 3., etc.
B. How do you find out what your client's needs are?
 1.
 2.
 3., etc.

From *Re-entry: An overlooked dimension in cultural adaptation* by F. Silberstein and B. Hoganson, 1982, Workshop Proceedings, 8th Annual Congress of International SIETAR. Long Beach, CA. Reprinted by permission of the Overseas Briefing Center, Foreign Service Institute, Department of State, Washington, DC

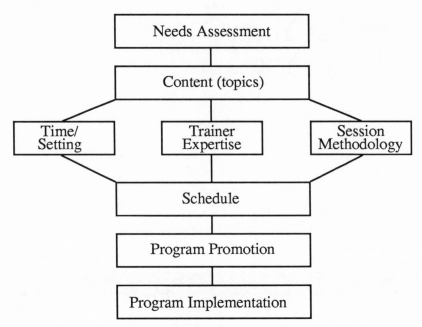

Selection of Topics to Meet Those Needs
A. Which sessions of the simulation would meet those needs?
   1.
   2.
   3., etc.
B. What other topics are needed?
   1.
   2.
   3., etc.

Determination of Appropriate Setting
A. Considerations
   1.
   2.
   3., etc.
B. Possibilities
   1.
   2.
   3., etc.

Designing Your Own Re-entry Program

Selection of or Writing Appropriate Sessions
A. Review all available materials to find session designs to meet your needs.
B. Write session to meet specific needs.

Selection and Training of Staff
A. Considerations
    1.
    2.
    3., etc.
B. Possibilities
    1.
    2.
    3., etc.

Program Promotion
A. Who should attend your re-entry program?
    1.
    2.
    3., etc.
B. How do you get people to attend?
    1.
    2.
    3., etc.

263

Program Implementation and Evaluation--a sample checklist

Discuss Orientation with Other Area Representatives,
Support Services Coordinator in Regional Office
A. Determine Number of Participants ☐
B. Negotiate Budget per Student ☐

Make Plan for the Orientation
A. Choose Sessions to be Presented ☐
B. Determine Schedule
C. Identify Staff and/or Helpers and Determine
    Responsibilities of Each ☐
D. Arrange for Location for Orientation ☐
E. Determine Method of Inviting Participants ☐
F. Request Advance Funding, if Necessary ☐

Start
These
Activities
Six Weeks
Before

Plan Details of the Orientation

A. Arrange for Meals or Refreshments ☐

B. Send Invitations or Call Participants ☐

C. Request Posters, Name Tags from Regional Office ☐

D. Gather Supplies, Materials, Visual Aids ☐

E. Duplicate Handouts ☐

F. Make Posters, Flip Charts ☐

G. Assign Sessions to Staff/Helpers Who Will Help Teach ☐

Start These Activities Four Weeks Before

Meet Staff/Helpers

A. Review Schedule and Sessions ☐

B. Assign Responsibilities ☐

C. Review Sessions with Those Who Will Teach ☐

D. Review Timing and All Logistical Arrangements ☐

Do These One Week Before

Conduct the Orientation

A. Follow Schedule and Session Plans ☐

B. Supervise/Guide Staff ☐

C. Conduct Oral or Written Evaluation with Participants, Helpers ☐

Day of Orientation

Follow-up the Orientation

A. Review Evaluations ☐

B. Write Thank You Letters ☐

C. Complete Orientation Plan and Expense Form (for Reimbursement) (and Send to Regional Office) ☐

D. Follow-up on Any Specific Student Requests, Problems ☐

Do These One Week After

Appendix D

Suggestions of Some Issues To Consider in Discussion Group Sessions

Clifford Clarke

The following questions represent four specified areas of concern for foreign students returning home after a period of study in the United States. These issues for discussion were presented to the students prior to their participation in the Seminar-Workshop for Returning Foreign Students. Their responses were used as valuable resource materials for the workshop.

Area I

1. Motives for coming here to study . . . personal advancement; purely professional interests; desire to initiate and participate in social change at home?

2. Extremes of initial reactions and subsequent feelings about U.S. experience:

a) total rejection--have unfavorable impressions caused individual to retreat within self or among other foreign students? become more nationalistic and defend all aspects of own culture and government? has dislike for American society and institutions limited one's exposure to, and assimilation of, new ideas and people?

b) total acceptance--has admiration for one aspect of America, like

From *The re-entry experience: Foreign students return home* (pp. 7–9) by C. H. Clarke. Paper presented at the Summer Conference on Intercultural Communication at the International Christian University, Tokyo, Japan, July 16, 1972. Reprinted by permission.

economic power and efficiency, clouded one's perspective in evaluating the society as a whole?

3. Here as a representative or just an individual . . . personally involved (like in debates about student power and Vietnam), or just concerned about gaining knowledge in one field, and being a spokesman for one's government or sponsoring agency?

4. Temptation to flaunt one's experiences in front of acquaintances upon arriving home . . . remaining aloof because of new-found worldliness and wisdom. Or will he use this new knowledge and experience with America to discover possible ways of improving his own society, and for bridging the communication gap between his country and the U.S.?

Area II

1. What will be your reactions upon returning home? Will there be a need to put one's new experiences and ideas into perspective with his own culture, recognizing changes in home country, and evaluating how one's living habits and goals will have to be modified to fit in with (or to oppose) these changing conditions?

2. What will be expected of you when you get home . . . socially, professionally, politically? Will people resent you or mistrust you because of your experience?

3. Will you be able to accept the political conditions at home? How has your own political thinking changed as a result of your U.S. experience? Are you now more of an ideologue? more politically passive? is it more of a social consciousness than before? how have the Black Revolution and U.S. urban and rural poverty influenced your feelings about government and politics?

4. How do you feel now about U.S. activities in your country? Will your increased understanding of the American system help you to work with Americans at home, or are you more concerned about changing this influence in degree or kind?

5. Will life be easier, more enjoyable than your stay in this country? Are interpersonal relationships more meaningful and durable in your culture than here? How do you feel your absence will have affected your relationships in the family, community, or job?

Area III

1. Experience in your chosen field . . . Do you feel that your studies here have been worthwhile in terms of applying your newly acquired knowledge and technical skills to real needs on the home front? Or will you find that your courses and/or research in the U.S. system have been irrelevant in regard to the problems that exist in your country? Has your education here been more useful in terms of attitudes and relationships formed than in hard knowledge gained?

2. What to do about professional isolation . . . probably will not have benefits of trade journals, conferences, and equipment you had in the U.S.

3. What to do about slowness in getting approval or equipment? Will you have the patience to wait out the things that move along slowly? Will you have essential facilities?

4. Probable need to overcome petty inter- and intra-professional rivalries. May be necessary to just listen to people at first . . . sound them out. Also, friction between those trained nationally and those abroad.

5. How can one work through his community or professional institutions to effect needed changes?

Area IV

1. Professional goals vs. social commitment to the community . . . how complementary, how in opposition?

2. Beware of believing that a prestigious education and worldliness mean instant success in one's projects at home.

3. Involvement--how far should one go? Passive readjustment . . . tolerance and utilization of existing institutions . . . active total commitment . . . revolution . . . or capitalize on one's American ties and work with U.S. vested interests for personal gain?

4. What happens when one's newly-acquired skills are not needed in the home country? Can the need be created by spending some time laying basic groundwork and cutting through the red tape? Or would it be wiser to go elsewhere?

5. What seems to be the role of your country, in light of things you have learned in another part of the world?

267

Moving On

E

269

The purpose of this sentence completion exercise is to allow participants to focus their thoughts about leaving and reentry. Grouped in pairs, participants take turns reading the sentences aloud while their partners employ free association, completing each sentence with whatever immediately comes to mind. Discussion of the responses forms the basis for problem identification and resolution.

1. When I think of leaving, I feel . . . . .
2. My experience here has been . . . . .
3. For me (host country) means . . . .
4. The things that I'll miss are . . . . .
5. The things I'll be happy to leave behind are . . . .
6. When I talk to other volunteers about leaving, they . . . .
7. When I talk to my (host country) friends about leaving they . . . .
8. (If applicable)
   A. When I talk to my spouse, he/she . . . .
   B. I think that for my spouse leaving will be . . . .
9. When I talk with Peace Corps staff about leaving, they . . . .

STOP: *LISTENER, SHOW YOUR PARTNER HOW WELL YOU'VE BEEN*

From *Peace Corps close of service workshop: Trainer guidelines and workshop materials* (pp. 163–165) by B. Razak, 1981, Washington, DC: Peace Corps Office of Programming and Training Coordination.

LISTENING BY SUMMARIZING IN A FEW SENTENCES WHAT YOU'VE HEARD SO FAR, THEN CONTINUE.

10. When leaving a place I usually . . . . .
11. The easiest point of leaving for me will be . . . . .
12. Before I leave I really want to . . . . .
13. The most stressful part of leaving will be . . . . . .

STOP: *BEFORE GOING ANY FURTHER, SWITCH ROLES. LET THE LISTENER BECOME THE SPEAKER AND THE SPEAKER, THE LISTENER, AND REPEAT 1–13.*

14. When I think of returning to the States I feel . . . .
15. I'll be going back to . . . . . .
16. I expect that for me the process of returning will be . . . . . .
17. (If applicable)
    I think that for my spouse, returning will be . . . .
18. When I think of seeing my family again, I . . . .
19. I think my family will expect me to . . . . .

STOP: *LISTENER, SHARE WITH YOUR PARTNER WHAT YOU'VE HEARD SO FAR.*

20. A. In terms of a career I hope to . . . . .
    B. If this doesn't work out, I'll . . . . .
21. I expect that my friends there will . . . . . .

22. Regarding money I'm going to be . . . .
23. Going back will enable me to . . . . . .
24. I think that the hardest part of going back for me will be . . . .
25. I think the easiest thing for me to handle will be . . . . .
26. I'm really looking forward to . . . . .

Doing Yourself In--A Look at Denial and Re-Entry

This sampling of statements can help individuals to identify their expectations and assumptions about reentry. It is important to realize how these assumptions may affect reentry.

Positive Denial:
Myths We Tell Ourselves:

1. I should be able to cope easily because it's my own culture. No adjustment problems.
2. I can pick up on relationships where I left off.
3. Everything is great back home.
4. Everything will be the same as it was when I left.
5. I won't experience culture shock.
6. The adjustment process should last no more than three months.
7. People will be interested in hearing about my "exotic" experiences in (country).
8. Things work better back home.

Negative Denial:
Setting yourself up to be more miserable than you need to be.

1. I know I'm not going to like it back there.

2. This change is going to be so overwhelming, I'm not going to be able to cope.

3. I shouldn't be feeling so _____. (upset, depressed, disorganized)

4. I know I'm going to be so lonely.

5. No one can understand what I'm going through.

6. Everyone is ahead of me now.

Appendix F

What Have I Gained From My Experience?

Directions:
Listed below are statements describing many of the changes that have been felt by AFS Returnees during the past three decades. Some of these may be changes that you, too, have felt. If you haven't thought very carefully about how you have changed, this list may be especially helpful in making you more fully aware of what has happened to you. Read through the list and place a check (✓) by each change that you believe has occurred in you.

___ I have improved my ability to speak a foreign language.

___ I am more knowledgeable about another culture and lifestyle.

___ I have a greater ability to empathize with others, that is, to put myself in their place when making judgements.

___ I can accept failures and shortcomings in myself more easily.

___ I understand more fully my own strengths and weaknesses.

___ I am more confident and positive when meeting new people.

___ I am more confident and assertive when facing new situations.

___ I have a greater capacity to accept differences in others.

___ I am more able to share my thoughts and feelings with others, and to be open when others wish to share theirs with me.

___ I have more curiosity about and respect for new ideas.

___ I have a clearer notion of what I will do with my life.

___ I am more flexible and able to adjust to changes in others.

___ I am more tolerant of ambiguous situations, that is, of situations that are confusing and open to differing interpretations.

___ I have more ability to see myself objectively, that is, to see my own day-to-day problems in a broader, more realistic context.

274   ___ I am more deeply committed to an idea, cause, or goal.

___ I have increased my perseverance and self-discipline.

___ I am more willing to strive and sacrifice in order to do well in my studies at school or in independent learning projects.

___ I have a greater sense of responsibility for other people.

___ I am more able to express deep emotions freely.

___ I am more able to ask for and receive help from others.

___ I have greater willingness to take on roles and tasks to which I am unaccustomed.

___ I have increased my capacity to experiment and take risks.

___ I am more able to accept as valid other values and lifestyles.

___ I have a deeper understanding of (if not necessarily commitment to) the values and lifestyle of my native community.

What Have I Gained from My Experience?

__ I am more aware of the opportunities in life that are open to me.

__ I feel greater respect and appreciation for my natural family.

__ I am more independent in my relations with family and friends.

__ I feel that I need fewer friends but deeper (more intimate and more trusting) friendships.

__ I am more aware of the way I use and structure time.

__ I have a greater capacity to profit from my mistakes.

__ I am more interested in and capable of laying long-range plans.

__ I am more determined to fully develop my skills and talents.

__ I feel a greater need to have diverse experiences and friends.

__ I am more balanced in my judgements, that is, less likely to judge things as "good" or "bad," "right" or "wrong."

__ I am more likely to do things spontaneously, that is, to do things without undue concern about possible consequences.

__ I am more capable of solving life's day-to-day problems.

__ I think more critically; I am more discriminating and skeptical.

__ I have improved observation skills.

__ I need more time to be alone.

__ I am more confident about the decisions I make.

__ I feel more surely that common bonds unite all human beings.

__ I have a deeper understanding of the problems and issues that confront all human beings on this planet.

__ I have greater awareness of political, economic, and social events occurring around the world.

___ Other: _____

_____

___ Other: _____

_____

Go back now and place an extra check mark (✔) by those *two* or *three* changes that seem the strongest or most significant.

What effects do you think these two or three biggest changes will have on you and your relations with others within the next three to five years? Explain below for each double-checked change.

Appendix G

Suggestions by MKs for MKs

1. Be yourself--this was mentioned numerous times.
2. Be friendly, sociable--don't isolate yourself.
3. Make new friends of the right kind. You must take the initiative.
4. Stick close to your parents.
5. Accept the situation as God's will.
6. Attend social functions.
7. Do not act special because you are an MK.
8. Get involved in sports, if athletic.
9. Visit parents on the field when possible.
10. Accept others for what they are. "Learn to love them as you have learned to love the people on the field."
11. Correspond with your parents often.
12. Save money to alleviate financial problems.
13. Be aware of the differences in the way American kids think.
14. Put Christ first in your life.
15. Maintain a proper devotional life.
16. "Look into the future and don't get caught up in the trivial. Keep your plans in mind and don't think something new is better."

From *Cultural adjustments MKs face* by R. W. Wright, n.d. Paper presented to the Association of Baptists for World Evangelism, 1720 Springdale Road, Cherry Hill, NJ 08034. Reprinted by permission.

17. Get involved in a local church.
18. Don't feel sorry for yourself because you are an MK.
19. Realize that the education you received on the field is as good, if not better, than the U.S.
20. Do not constantly compare the U.S. with your "home" country.
21. Be thankful you are an MK, but do not always be broadcasting it.
22. Work part-time.
23. Be aware that there will not be a community spirit at college as you have experienced on the field.
24. Compare notes with other MKs about their adjustments.
25. Don't put any Christian on too high a plane or you will be disappointed.
26. Don't live in the past.
27. Take college prep courses, develop good study habits, and be prepared to be "on the go" all the time.
28. Don't get "panicky" if you are having a problem.
29. Maintain high values (morals) and do not apologize for them, remembering that those who matter most will respect you for it.
30. Be aware that there may be conflicts regarding moral standards in dating, even amongst Christian kids.
31. Make friends of upperclassmen who are solid Christians.

32. Have the right attitude and be willing to make changes.
33. Let others know that in "your" country, things are done differently, and be honest in telling them that you are not used to doing things their way.
34. Have a willingness to learn.
35. Don't present yourself as a national from the country of your origin.
36. Don't be critical of luxurious living and what you believe to be hypocritical practices. Look for contributions you can make instead.
37. Feel free to discuss those matters openly which you really can't understand.
38. Be almost over-prepared for "culture shock."
39. Be firmly grounded in the Word and develop your own values based upon it.
40. Don't expect everyone to be excited about your life and experiences as an MK. They won't be.
41. In the first few months at school, do more observing than talking.
42. Learn to be flexible, good humored, selfless in attitude toward others.

Suggestions by MKs for Parents
(to help prepare their children)

1. Be available.
2. Train the children with a desire to serve God uncompromisingly, to stand up for what they believe.
3. Let them know that you love and care for them.
4. Write often, especially Dad. Share all the "little things." It makes the child feel he's still a real part of the family.
5. Accept the family situation as the will of God and do not be bitter about the separation.
6. Let the children come home (to the field) on vacation.
7. Save through the years for the child's education.
8. Emphasize to the children that if God led, He will keep.
9. Don't expect your children to be missionaries.
10. Get the children involved in the work on the field.
11. Emphasize to them that other missionaries are special people.
12. Spend much time with them while you have them.
13. Teach a strong appreciation for the fact that parents are missionaries.
14. Teach your children regarding clothing styles, language differences, customs, manners and other things when coming to the U.S.
15. Explain to them that there will be cultural adjustments.
16. Teach the children that a Christian college is not heaven, nor a utopia.
17. Inform the teens on the field of current events so they will be aware

when coming to the U.S. Give them the real picture. Have magazines around the home, both secular and Christian.

18. Teach them what to expect when they get out into the world.
19. Encourage them to do their best in everything they do.
20. Go with them to help them get settled in college. Bring them to the U.S. a few months earlier so as to make adjustments easier.
21. Help them find a local church near the college.
22. Let them know that you are really praying for them. Pray for them.
23. Keep a proper balance on the field between "going native" and "being Americanized."
24. If possible, stay with them during their first year in college.
25. Show them how to love others.
26. Recognize that your children will be undergoing stress and be understanding.
27. Send your children off to boarding school during high school, instead of teaching them by correspondence. (A number who had studied via correspondence mentioned this.)
28. Talk English in the home on the field.
29. Let the children know what is happening on the field, after they leave.
30. Be honest by telling them before going to college that it will not always be fun. Tell of the hard times as well as the good.

31. Show confidence in your children's ability to make mature decisions. Give them a lot of prior opportunities to make such decisions.
32. Don't let them feel they are unwanted or "in the way."
33. Educate your children so they will not be naive about sex, society, getting along with others, and even differences in standards amongst Christians regarding dating, etc.
34. Don't force them to go to your alma mater.
35. Let them be themselves.
36. Teach them principles to live by and not just a set of rules.
37. Help your children develop their own values.
38. Don't hide your own cultural adjustments from the family, but together handle them biblically.
39. Teach them that to be different is not necessarily wrong.
40. Communicate to them a positive, happy outlook.
41. When they are leaving home, do not say that you will miss them terribly.
42. Make sure that your children have the proper place in your priorities. They are special gifts to you.

Suggestions by MKs for College Officials

1. Have an MK Fellowship on campus (only six expressed any doubt of the value of such a group). Suggestions included using this for a time of interaction and sharing of the adjustments, cultural problems. It could serve to help get MKs involved in college life and encourage them to avoid being a clique.
2. Have a staff member (preferably a missionary or former missionary) meet with them right away at the beginning of the year. Have this person available for counsel.
3. Pray for the family of an MK each week in chapel.
4. Treat them like other college kids.
5. Be aware of the MKs cultural adjustments and seek to meet them.
6. Get the MKs involved in helping others.
7. Provide financial assistance.
8. Provide Christian service so they can use their abilities.
9. Provide jobs on campus and aid in locating one off-campus.
10. Orientate the MK as to what is going on. Many MKs have never been in an American school system and when they get to college it is a maze.
11. Assign an upperclassman to be a friend and helper, which will help them feel like they belong.
12. Remember that in writing papers the MKs vocabulary may be lim-

ited and his expressions different, due to translating from his foreign thinking.

13. Abolish initiations.
14. Have older MKs help the new ones.
15. It is important for all college students to feel that the faculty and staff are friends that are willing to help them when they have needs, whether academic or social.

Suggestions by MKs for Missions Administrators

1. Missions administrators should seek to visit the MKs when they are on campus.
2. Correspond with the MKs, even when they are on the field.
3. Advise them of homes to visit in during vacation, or when just passing through an area.
4. Be aware of the adjustments of MKs and when visiting on campus, seek to find out how they are doing.
5. Take a personal interest in the MKs as this will help set our parents at ease.
6. Treat the MK with as much care as you would give to their parents.
7. Have a conference, camp, or get-together in the summer for the MKs.
8. Be prompt with financial help, as authorized by the parents.
9. Keep them informed of work on the field and the whereabouts of other MKs. One mission sends out a monthly newsletter to its MKs and they said it was really appreciated.
10. Send birthday cards.
11. Provide a list of other MKs in the U.S. with same mission.
12. Pray for them as well as their parents.
13. Make the MK aware that you are available to help them with matters, such as insurance and other legal details.

14. Prepare a realistic evaluation of what MKs will face in the U.S., so they will know how to intelligently face situations as they arise.
15. Appoint a counselor to the schools from amongst the missionaries to whom the kids can relate and with whom they can discuss cultural changes.

Index

Returnees (reentrants, repatriates, temporary "migrants")

problems of,

addiction to information, 76

affluence, coming home to, 79–81, 96, 185, 198

alien, professional, 77

celebrities, has met, 61, 67–68

choice, breadth and depth of, 90, 122, 150, 152, 198–199

communication of experience, 3, 11–12, 93, 104, 108, 186, 199, 210

competences, 9, 109, 126, 212

continuity, educational, 99, 121, 136–138, 195–196

crime, incidence of, 99, 199

deviant identity, 50–51, 116, 128–129, 198

disengagement, 104

dual existence, 157, 187

entertainment patterns, 134, 211

euphoria/denial, 51, 92, 97, 99

expectations, erroneous, 89, 91, 96, 111, 121, 125–127

fear of rejection, regression, and guilt, 54–55, 91, 93, 96, 110, 181

financial, 74, 91, 98, 113–114, 121, 136, 138, 150, 152, 156, 186, 197–198

foods, 95, 126, 135, 149–151, 182, 185, 187, 211

foreign languages, speaker of, 61, 68

good life, how to produce, 61, 68–71, 121, 151

immobilization/recidivism, 55–56

independence, loss of, 127, 145, 197, 199

intellectually highfalutin, 61, 66–67

intimacy problems, 56, 91, 114, 187, 198

issue, "soft" in military, 100

job shrink, 36, 47, 98, 121, 126, 137–139, 212

life of fantasy, 3, 11, 90, 126

new goals, acquisition of, 105–108

nonlegitimation of violence, 109

nostalgia, 3, 12, 75, 150–153, 179, 184–185

pace of life, 96, 99, 127, 151, 186, 198

preparation, lack of, 94, 96

provincialism, 185, 187–188, 207

return trip, 209 (*see also* Reentry, interventions: decompression period)

rite of passage, lack of, 109

roots, 13, 112, 180–181, 183–184, 187–189, 197

self-concept, 3, 13, 15, 84, 96, 98, 111–113, 116, 121, 123, 127, 199, 232

self-interest, primacy of, 108

separation, loss, and grief, 3, 10, 53, 91, 97, 105–107, 121, 126–127, 136–137, 150, 156, 180–182, 210–211

spiritual, 124–125, 173–177, 181, 193–194, 198, 244, 246

tradition, cultural, 156–157

unpatriotic, fear of being considered, 97

value change, 10, 68, 79, 84–85, 91, 108–109, 121–122, 124–125, 145, 156–157, 181, 198–199 (*see also* Appendix G).

(*see also* Chapter 25, 239–247; Appendix A, 251–253; Appendix D, 265–267; Appendix E, 269–270)